Teenage Hobos

A Memoir

Harry J. Bohr

Library of Congress Catalog Card Number: 97-91151

ISBN: 0-932970-87-7

Dedication

I wish to dedicate this book to my wonderful wife Arlene, and to Ralph Wood, my best friend and traveling companion during our hobo years.

Acknowledgments

Many people were of great help to me in completing of this book. I would like to thank Vickie Cecil, the librarian of the Hartford City Library, who encouraged me to write this story, and to Sinard Costello and Rebecca Musser who also supported and motivated me. The first completed draft of the book would not have been possible without the fine help of Mary Morris, computer teacher at the Blackford County High School. I appreciated her assistance and that of her computer class, especially Brenda Maddox, Heather Wolfe, Yolanda Bailey, Allicia Rockwell, Cindy Poe, Tasha Teats, and Amanda Hicks. Thank you all very much.

About the author:

Harry J. Bohr was born in Hartford City, a small town in Indiana. He attended high school where he had one year of journalism and was active in athletics. He graduated in 1931 in the depth of the most vicious financial crisis of the century. After his hobo travels with his best friend Ralph, he had a four year apprenticeship in the glass cutting trade, a highly skilled occupation. He worked in the glass business until his retirement. During his journeyman travels he met and marred his wife Arlene. After he retired in 1970 they lived in Honolulu, Hawaii. They moved to Corpus Christi, Texas in 1990 for a short time, and then returned to their present home in Hartford City.

Preface

Some of these events, may not be told just exactly the way it all happened. Yet all are based on fact, most from personal experience.

I had a strange, almost fearful feeling, as we watched out the door. Here we were hundreds of miles from home, in the middle of the night, waiting to leap from a moving train into a very dangerous area, with no money and no place to sleep. I was glad I wasn't alone. I had seen thousands of hobos who traveled by themselves. Tough times made tough men. I thought of myself traveling alone in a boxcar and I didn't like the thought. I was glad Ralph was with me.

Two young hobos.

Contents

Chapter One

I was born in 1913 in a small town in Indiana. My parents were great; they fed, sheltered, and loved me. Nobody could ask for more. My first remembrance, except of my mother and father, was of Perry, the man who came around with that wonderful taste sensation: ice cream. Every afternoon in the summer when I was three or so, my mother gave me my bath. Afterwards, in clean clothes and holding the saucer, spoon and nickel she gave me, I sat waiting on the front porch swing for Perry.

The ice cream wagon was a buggy closed in except for a window cut in the right side to dispense the wonderful ice cream. The horse had a felt hat on its head with two holes for his ears to stick out. Small bells attached to the harness made a tinkling sound when the horse walked. On a quiet afternoon, and there were lots of them back then, the ice cream wagon could be heard two blocks away. When I heard the bells, I could hardly wait for him to get to the house. When he arrived, my mother and I would walk out to the wagon. I would lift my saucer to Perry and always had to be prompted by my mother to also hand up the nickel. He put one scoop of ice cream on the saucer and handed it to my mother to carry back to the porch. If he asked me my name my day was made, who could have a better friend than Perry, the ice cream man?

My next memorable experience was my first day in school. My mother took me to the school about six city blocks away, telling me she would return at the end of the day to take me home. It was upsetting being alone with all those strange children, but after a few days I liked being in school. As I grew older, I liked it more and more.

When I was about ten years old, my dad took me fishing several times. Later I, my brother, and neighbor boys spent a lot of summer days fishing in the creeks and gravel pits around the city. When we were a few years older, my mother took my brother and I, along with a neighbor woman and any of the neighborhood kids who wanted to go, to the Wabash River about forty miles away.

A large lunch was prepared for the noon meal. The Dodge touring car was loaded with kids, some riding on the front two fenders and standing on the running boards. When we got to the river, everybody went fishing or exploring along the riverbanks.

After we ate lunch, everybody went swimming. Around three o'clock my mother loaded up the car with all the kids, but my brother, I and sometimes a neighbor boy, were going to stay behind. She counted all the kids to be sure she left no one behind. She said to us, "I'll be back in two weeks to bring you home. Be careful."

After they left, we took a rope and tied it between two trees, threw our piece of canvas over the rope, staked down the edges, and scooped out a trench around our makeshift tent to catch the rain run off so we would not get wet inside it. We walked to the river and carried stones to put in a circle to contain our fire. We had found a natural spring close by so we had plenty of good cool water to drink. This would be our home for the next fourteen days.

We had a twenty-two caliber rifle, fishing poles, and trot lines to set at night to catch channel catfish. We had pie plates, knives, forks, spoons, a large iron skillet, and a pot. We didn't bring much food with us, just two or three loaves of bread that were gone in three or four days, salt, and a few cans of beans, but plenty of bacon so we would have grease to fry.

We had two large gunny sacks about four feet long. Since we fished all the time, we caught more fish than we could eat. We put the surplus in the sack, cut up smaller fish into little pieces and put them in the bags, tied a piece of rope around the opening and the other end to a large rock. When we went home, we had fish for anybody who wanted fresh fish, which was the whole neighborhood.

At night we ran trotlines across the river in the riffles where we caught large two-feet-long channel catfish. We were up to our waists in the water, so wore no clothes. When we ran the line and rebaited the hooks, we would go to the camp and stand around the campfire without bothering to put our clothes on while waiting to run the trotline again. No cars went by the road which was just two tracks along the river. But sometimes a car *would* go by, and we wondered if the people thought we were uncivilized Indians.

In the middle and late 1920s, the country was very prosperous; everybody was working and investing in the stock market. In 1929 on Black Tuesday, the stock market crashed. Within a few weeks, many wealthy people lost fortunes. Even the middle class was in the market, even the legendary shoeshine men borrowed money to get in. Many could not stand to lose everything and committed suicide, some by leaping from high office windows of the buildings where they had made the fortunes they had lost.

The banks failed and people, who had money in them, lost all their assets. This catastrophe was not immediately felt in the small Midwest town we lived in, but in a few months, the largest employer in the city, the American Window Glass Company, closed its doors. Although the people prayed for the factory to reopen, no glass was ever made and years later, the building was torn down.

The country and its inhabitants would experience the harshest financial collapse of this century. As more factories and businesses closed their doors, unemployment grew until, out of a work force of forty million, it peaked at fifteen million workers unemployed. It would be years before some would return to the work force.

Farmers could not sell their crops, so they were left to rot in the fields while a large percentage of the population not only went hungry, but many people who did eat had very poor diets. There were rumors that many poorly paid workers' lunch buckets contained boiled potatoes and bread.

Banks closed and those people who did have some savings lost everything in the banking crisis. There was no deposit insurance or bank examiners as we have now. School teachers in some cities, even large cities like Chicago, went on teaching even though they had not been paid for several months.

Before the recession the Army, Navy and Marines were looked down on as a place of employment; now the recruiting offices had long lines of young single men who thought that a job that fed and clothed you while paying twenty dollars a month was very desirable. The requirements to get in the service went up: you had to be in perfect physical condition. A decayed tooth and you were turned down.

A private first-class walked down the long lines of applicants. If you were wearing glasses or had any other visible disabilities, you were pulled from the line and sent on your way. The service did not want to repair anything after you had passed the physical examination. Furthermore, the services had been cut back by Congress and now the Army had about only 200,000; the other services were also cut back.

The farm land around our town produced hundreds of acres of canning tomatoes for a canning factory east of town. There is a belief now that only Mexican people could do the stoop labor in the fields, but during the depression whites picked tomatoes and were glad to get the work. The pay was seven cents a hamper, about three-fourths of a bushel of tomatoes. My father lost his skilled glass cutting job, but was fortunate to obtain a job at the Overhead Door Corporation. He made about a third of his former wages cutting glass.

The Pennsylvania Railroad running through our town was double tracked from Chicago to Columbus, Ohio. As unemployment increased, I noticed more men riding the freight trains and became accustomed to counting more than fifty hobos on a single train. Food stamps, unemployment insurance, rent subsidies, social security, Medicare and Medicaid didn't exist.

With nowhere to stay, the unemployed took to riding the freight trains all over America, always moving on to another place that might be better. Ones newer to the life of the hobo looked for work. In time, they would learn that jobs were an illusion, a mirage that stayed one town ahead of the hobo.

Chapter Two

The opportunity to travel by freight train was almost unlimited. This great land was veined by over 193,000 miles of mainline railroad track. Steam engines were king, not only in the United States, but all over the civilized world.

Huge engines, some weighing over 600 tons, were able to haul trains of over 150 cars. Other smaller swifter engines with high driver wheels could reach speeds over 100 miles-an-hour and cruised at 70 miles-an-hour hauling passenger cars.

Freight trains carried almost all cargo from coal to cigarettes. The large trucking company's challenge to the railroads had not yet begun. They were confined to local and city hauling.

I can remember as a young boy going to our little railway station and joining a group of adults who had come to see who got off and on the passenger train. I had come to see the engine and to envy the engineer sitting in the cab, the one who drove that panting monster.

This is the story of two teenage boys who joined these luckless men for adventure and a chance to see other parts of this large country.

I was sixteen years old as was my good friend Ralph. One day as we watched a train and the hobos riding on it, he turned to me and said, "Why don't we take a trip on the railroad?"

Most people reading this probably have never ridden a passenger train, even less remote, a freight train. For a few days whenever we were together, we would talk about the trip. Finally, we decided to join the army of aimless wanderers, at least for a few weeks. We went to the library and obtained a map of the United States. We didn't want to plan too long a trip, as it might not be that great. We finally decided on Atlantic City, a good distance in those days, but not too far if we found it wasn't what we expected. Another reason to pick Atlantic City, neither of us had seen an ocean.

Ralph's mother and father were both dead. He lived with his older brother and two sisters. They gave him a hard time for a day, but finally grudgingly gave him permission. It was a different story at our house. My mother and father were both very much against it. My younger brother and sister argued on my behalf and after three days of being buffeted by all three of us, they finally gave in, probably to stop the arguing. My mother said, "I'll give you some stamped postcards, and you must send me one every two days, and you must be back in two weeks."

We started selecting what to take with us, learning later that hobos who carried bags, suitcases, or any container were called "bindle stiffs" and were disdained by true hobos who wore only the clothes on their backs.

We both had small leather bags for our gym shoes, clothes, and equipment. We crammed an extra pair of trousers, shirt, handkerchiefs, underwear, socks, a sharp knife, a spoon, and a quart jar for water in those bags. We had gone out to the coal docks a half-mile west of town where the trains stopped for water and coal. One stopped there near midnight with only one man working at that time. We would take that train.

The next afternoon I lay down to get some sleep but only dozed off for a little while. I ate a large supper; it might be a long time before we would get a home-cooked meal. After we had eaten, my mother and I fixed enough sandwiches for both us with some apples and several candy bars. We had about five dollars between us. We didn't plan on spending any of it until we reached Atlantic City.

Around ten o'clock at night, I picked up my small bag and the sack of food, kissed everybody good-be, and walked over to Ralph's house. He was ready. We started walking down the dark railroad track to the coal docks.

When we reached the coal docks, only one man was working there. We walked around the tower and down the track about a hundred feet. It was so dark the man never saw us. We thought when the engine was under the tower, we would be in a good position to find an empty boxcar. We sat on a pile of railroad ties. The only noises came from the inhabitants of the small swamp behind us. We watched the man getting ready for the train. Because we had no watch we began wondering if the train wasn't coming that night. At last we saw a small pinpoint of light from the west. In a few minutes, the train came thundering in, iron brakes screeching against iron wheels, halting just under the tower. We ran along to the back of the train until we found what we thought was an empty boxcar and threw our bags in, quickly climbing aboard the train. My heart was pounding, we were really on our way to Atlantic City.

We were talking excitedly when from the darkness of the car a voice said, "Will you guys shut up? We're trying to get some sleep."

Finally, the train started. Sitting with our backs to the side of the car, it was not long until we realized riding in a boxcar was rough. The car swayed and bounced and the wheels screeched on the tracks. How the men in the end of the car could sleep was beyond us. We were sure we would never be able to sleep at all, but after an hour or so, my eyes began to close and I slid down on the floor of the car and went to sleep.

When dawn woke us, we found we were with a group of about ten men. One hobo came down and asked us where we had boarded the train. We told him and he asked if we lived there. We told him we did, and he asked how far it was to Columbus, Ohio from there and we told him we thought it was about two hundred miles.

He said we should be in Columbus in a couple of hours. After learning it was our first trip to Atlantic City, he thought a few minutes and added, "You better get off the train when I do. If you ride into the yards, you may get picked up by railroad detectives. We asked him about railroad detectives. "The railroads hire detectives to keep people off railroad property," he told us. "I think they get paid for every arrest. Your best bet is to get off before you get in the yards of any large city, walk through the city, and catch a train on the other side of the yards."

A few hours later, the train began to slow and I could see we were entering a large city. The train slowed further and came to a stop.

"This is where we get off," our friend said. We all jumped off. Ralph and I went with the others out of the railroad yards. When we reached the street, our new friend said, "Walk through the city following the railway."

Columbus was the largest city either of us had ever been in. As we walked along, we could see that we were not going through the downtown part of the city, but could see the tall buildings in the distance. The number of cars on the streets surprised us; everybody seemed to be riding, very few walking.

It was a long walk through the city. We stopped in a small park and ate a sandwich, filled our water bottle at a fountain, and rested awhile. When we resumed our walk, we discussed how we were going to find a train to Philadelphia. This might be a big problem; we should have asked our hobo friend. We saw the passenger station a few blocks away. Ralph thought we could go to the station where there were restrooms to get washed and, maybe, find out where all the trains go.

"They'll never know we're not going on a passenger train, especially since we'll be carrying our small bags," I answered.

It was a large place, but we found the restroom. When we came out the door, we ran into a police officer, but he never gave us a second look, so we walked out and went back up the street to continue walking until we reached the east end of the yards. We were on a small hill, able to see down into the yard. Three or four trains looked ready to be leaving soon, but only one had an engineer in the cab. We decided to run down and ask him where the train was going.

When there, I asked him, "Is this train going to Philadelphia?"

"No, to Harrisburg, Pennsylvania," he said.

We started back to the yard fence when Ralph exclaimed, "I have relatives in Hershey, let's go there. We'll be going in the right direction."

We looked around for any railroad detectives and then walked down along the train until we found a boxcar and climbed in. We looked around the car and saw it was clean. Only some empty cardboard boxes cluttered one end. We heard a noise coming down the train toward us while we were standing. When it reached our car, it jerked so hard we were almost thrown off our feet. We were moving along in our side car pullman. We sat in the door and watched the scenery go by. Once in a while, we would go through a small town. We enjoyed ourselves, no longer bothered by the car's motion or the screeching of the wheel flanges rubbing against the iron rails. Not much farther along we pulled into a siding outside a small town and stopped alongside a large building. A brakeman uncoupled the engine, and it moved off, leaving us on the siding. We didn't know what to make of this. The engineer had said we were going to Harrisburg, but he hadn't mentioned when we would arrive.

We tore up the cardboard boxes and flattened them to lay on. We were not too concerned about detectives out here. The town was so small it probably didn't even have a policeman.

When we woke, it was late in the afternoon and the engine hadn't yet returned. Ralph, said, "I can't believe they would leave all these cars on this siding in this small town. I think he'll be back," and I said, "Yes, after all, we're a long way from Harrisburg."

We looked out the door. Eight or ten hobos were walking toward the small town. We decided they were going to try and find something to eat. We had asked the hobos where they got their food if they didn't have any money. They told us about going down alleys to back doors to ask whoever came to the door if they had any work in exchange for food.

If stores were around, you could ask for cold meat ends and second day bread. Lots of missions in the larger cities fed you, while The Salvation Army had places to sleep. They said they slept out in the open in the summer. We decided to eat a snack before it got dark. We had just finished when we heard a train whistle, and we looked out the door of the car, We saw our engine with seven or eight boxcars. It was backing them into the siding and with a crash, hooked them onto the train. In the moonlight, we could see the hobos, who had gone into the town, running to the train. When they were almost to the train, it began to move; it was moving slowly, but too fast to get into a boxcar so they caught a ladder. All of them got on, but they would have to ride on top until the train stopped again.

We were rolling along very fast now, not even slowing for the small towns. The engineer would hold down the train whistle and go roaring through with crossing lights and bells ringing. Soon we began to get sleepy, and lay down on our cardboard bed. With the swaying of the car, we were rocked to sleep.

When we woke in the morning, we were in the mountains. Living in flat country all our lives, we were delighted with the tree-covered hills. We were sure we were in Pennsylvania. We opened both car doors and sat on the floor so we could look out both sides. Eating the remainder of our food, we watched the scenery go by. When we went around a curve, we looked behind us for the hobos on top of the car, but they were gone. The train may have stopped while we were asleep. From now on, we would try to find work for our food and perhaps a place to sleep.

When we approached Harrisburg, the train slowed, but not enough to get off. Finally, we entered the yards and the train rolled to a stop. Heeding the warning from the hobo about railroad detectives, we jumped down and ran for the fence, climbing over trains to get there. There were several holes in the fence made by hobos and we crawled through one of them.

The train station was a few blocks away. When we got there, we found the telephone. Ralph put in a nickel and called his relatives. They said to stay at the train station and they would come get us. When they arrived, they asked how our trip was. Slowly it dawned on us that they thought we had come by passenger train. When we told them we had come by freight trains, they couldn't believe we had come all the way from Indiana in this manner. We assured them that we had and that we had plans to go to Atlantic City. They shook their heads in amazement and took us home with them. After we had a bath and put on our clean clothes, Ralph's family questioned us for a few hours about our trip and Ralph's relatives.

Then they took us to their neighbors and introduced us, always adding that we had arrived riding freight trains. It was almost like we were celebrities.

That night they took us to a very nice restaurant. In fact, neither Ralph nor I had ever been in this grand a place to eat. When we left the restaurant they asked if we would like to go to the Hershey amusement park. We told them we had never been in an amusement park, and we would like that very much. We rode on several rides, but liked the Roller Coaster best. I remember climbing slowly to the top and then that instant of pause before you were falling, your heart pounding at the bottom and back up again, the car rocking you back and forth.

It was midnight when we left the park. It had been a great day and night for both of us. When we got in bed, I said, "Your relatives sure know how to entertain someone." Ralph's sleepy response, "They sure do."

All three of Ralph's relatives worked at the Hershey factory. We got up when they did. While we were eating breakfast, the lady said it was one of her days off and she was going to take us through Hershey's large candy factory.

We could smell the chocolate for blocks before reaching the factory. It was very interesting how the different candy bars were made. At the end of the tour a large bin of chocolate kisses stood. You could take a double handful as you went by. When we got back to the house, she made us a large sack of sandwiches, fruit, and of course, Hershey bars, then drove us to the train yards. We thanked her and told her how much we had enjoyed our visit. She gave Ralph their address, and we promised to write them a card when we got to Atlantic City. We waved to her as she drove away and she waved back.

Chapter Three

We walked outside the yard fence and looked into the maze of tracks, wondering how we would find a train to Philadelphia. Coming upon a grizzled hobo taking the sun on a grassy bank, Ralph said, "Let's ask him."

The hobo stood up and looked intently at the trains after we asked him. Turning to us, he said, "See that train with the two engines? That's a cattle train and it will get you there in a hurry. He's stocking up coal and water, then he'll be taking off, so hurry down there or you'll miss him."

We yelled our thanks over our shoulders as we ran into the yard, climbing over trains to the cattle cars. We had just got on top of the train when, with a long whistle, the train started to move. By the time we had cleared the yard, we seemed to be going about 70 miles an hour. We didn't know it, but the third train we rode was the fastest train we would ever ride in all our travels.

Cattle lose weight rapidly when they don't have food, and especially water. All other trains were pulled off the mainline so they could reach their destination as quickly as possible. The stacks were really cracking, but suddenly we realized we were facing a barrage of sparks, red hot cinders and clouds of smoke from the two engines. We moved down the top of the train to the last car, but still got a lot of smoke because the train was so short, about sixteen cars. It was a fast ride, but not a very comfortable one. Traveling at that speed, we got a lot of wind.

When we neared Philadelphia, the train stopped and an electric train took over with overhead power lines, so we had to ride between the cars. Riding between the cars was very dangerous. With the electric cable furnishing the power only three feet above the train, we couldn't ride on top the cars. First we just hung onto the iron ladder at the end of the car, but after a short time, our feet cramped from standing on the bar. Then we sat on the end of the car and put our feet out on the couplings. We got a good grip with both hands and were well aware that a misstep or careless grip could send us beneath the wheels to almost certain death.

Philadelphia had a very large yard, and we were well into it when the train stopped. We ran across the yard, climbing over strings of cars and watching for detectives. We reached the fence and found a hole in it and we were safe. I looked at Ralph and his face was black from the smoke. I knew mine was the same.

"You look like you've been mining coal," I told him.

"You don't look any better," he replied.

We walked to the passenger train station, but when we entered the door and looked around for the restroom to get cleaned up, an officer grabbed us and escorted us out the door, telling us not to come back. As we walked up the street, we came to two filling stations. Neither let us use their restrooms.

As we left, a man who had been watching us as we talked to the attendant came over and said, "Are you boys looking for a place to clean up and sleep tonight? The church I belong to runs a mission for homeless people about a mile away down this street, but you better hurry. It only holds about one hundred people, and it fills very fast."

We thanked him and hurried down the street. When we found it, there were a lot of hobos there, but they were still taking people. We fell in line and when we got inside, we were handed a towel and a piece of soap and told that everybody had to take a shower. This was the best news we had all day. When we entered the shower, we saw some of the men washing their clothes.

We were told everybody had to leave the mission at seven o'clock in the morning. I asked one of them how he was going to get his clothes dry by morning. He pointed out a door and told me they had a steam clothes dryer in there. He said clothes would be dry by morning if hung in there. We put our dirty clothes down on the floor and gave them a good washing, then hung them in the dryer and put our other set of clothes on. We also found out they were going to feed us. This was good news. We could save the rest of our food for tomorrow on the way to Atlantic City.

After everybody had showered, we were taken to a large room and seated. I asked if we were going to eat here. He said, "No you're going to get your soul saved first, then eat."

A young man came in carrying a Bible and began addressing us. He talked about three quarters of an hour, then announced that we were to line up at the kitchen for our food.

The food was surprisingly good. We received a bowl of soup, a meat loaf sandwich, and a cup of coffee. They pulled out five or six men and asked them to help clean the kitchen. The rest of us walked to the big room where we would sleep. We found two cots together, and sat around talking until the lights went out at nine o'clock.

We were awakened in the morning by the lights coming on. I asked the fellow next to us what the time was. "Six o'clock," he said.

"I thought we were supposed to be out at seven," I replied.

"You can get a cup of coffee and a donut, if you want."

We saw the long line and decided to pass it up. We still had the food and we wanted to get an early start to Atlantic City. We started to walk, asking the first man we came to how to get to Atlantic City. He told us to go through Philadelphia and across the Delaware River to Camden, then to take the highway to Atlantic City. We had already decided we were going to hitchhike the rest of the way.

Philadelphia was a big city. We kept walking, stopping to look in store windows and up at the tall buildings. We had walked for about two hours and still hadn't come to the river. We thought we had missed our way but a few minutes later we saw this huge iron bridge in the distance.

We had never seen a bridge so large. When we got on it we were even more impressed by its height over the water. Halfway across, we saw a commemorative plaque that had the names of all the men who were killed building the bridge. There were about sixty names on the plaque.

We came off the bridge into Camden, New Jersey, and asked at a filling station what road we should take. The fellow pointed down the street and said we were on it now. We walked through Camden and when we got on the highway we found a ride all the way to Atlantic City. He let us out about three blocks from the famous boardwalk so we decided to walk there and take a look at the ocean. We walked along looking in the shop windows and at the beautiful hotels.

Late in the afternoon, we left the boardwalk and walked four or five blocks back into the residential area. We saw a man standing in front of a men's clothing store and Ralph thought we should ask him where we could rent a room.

He told us there were plenty of places, but one he knew of was just down the street, a big clean room. We asked what we could expect to pay for a room there. He answered it would be easy to get one for two dollars a week.

We found the place. It had a *Rooms for Rent* sign in the window. A woman came to the door and we told her we were looking for a room. She told us to come in and look.

We had decided to stay for a week if we could get a good room for less than two dollars. The room was large, high-ceilinged, clean, and cool, the bathroom just a few feet away. She asked how long we would want the room, and Ralph said, "We'd like to stay for a week *if* we could afford it." She said she usually got two dollars for the room, but Ralph answered we could only pay a dollar and a half. Then she wanted to know where we would eat and we admitted we didn't know yet. "I'll make you a deal," she said. "I'll give you breakfast and supper at night for three dollars for both of you, nothing fancy but filling."

After we had a conference, we decided it was a good deal, even if the food wasn't so hot. We told her we would accept the offer.

She said, "Don't discuss the terms with the other roomers," adding that supper would be at five-thirty and breakfast at seven o'clock.

We moved in. I wrote my mother and father one of the cards and mailed it. It was almost five-thirty, and we talked about what we thought we would get for supper. When we went to the dining room, we found two other men were staying there. She introduced them to us and we sat down with them. We would eat first and then she and her family, a husband and two children, would eat after us. The food was brought in: meat loaf, mashed potatoes, gravy, creamed corn, and beets. It was very good and as much as you could eat. She served very good meals all the time we were there.

After dinner Ralph and I walked to the boardwalk and strolled along watching the people go by. Some rode in rubber-tired carts with upholstered seats able to accommodate two or three people and pushed by a man up and down the boardwalk. We watched them making the salt water taffy and chocolate fudge.

We looked in jewelry stores housing the riches of a sultan and wondered who could buy them in these hard times. It had been a long day so we went back to our room to bed. We asked the lady to call us since we had no watch. She said she would call us at six-thirty in time for breakfast.

Breakfast turned out to be all you could eat hot cakes, toast, jam and coffee.

Ralph wished we could figure out a way to go swimming so we could tell people back home we had swam in the ocean. I pointed out that there was nobody on the south part of the boardwalk, and why not walk down there and look around?

After we left the stores and hotels, we walked a quarter mile until we came to a sea wall about six feet high. No one was nearer than a quarter mile, so we decided to slide down the sea wall and go swimming bare ass like we did in the river.

There was a small beach about five feet wide between the water and the sea wall. We laid our clothes on the little strip of sand, and ran and dove into the ocean. We swam around and floated in the water, talking about what our friends would say if they could see us swimming at the great resort city. About an hour later, I happened to look at the sea wall, it looked different. The water was up on the sea wall and our little beach where we had left our clothes had disappeared. The tide had come in. We rushed back where our clothes were floating around in the water. We found everything except a couple of socks. We laid our wet clothes out on the sea wall and wondered what we would have done if they had been washed out to sea.

I could imagine the scene: two teenagers walking back up the boardwalk with not a stitch of clothes, on the famous boardwalk of Atlantic City. This was the city where men had to wear full bathing suits. No shorts allowed. I'm sure we would have become the most famous hobos in America on our first trip.

We laughed, but it we had lost our clothes, we would not have been very happy. Our clothes soon dried, but we had to rub them to get the salt out.

Next day we decided to visit the lobbies of the great hotels. We thought we might be stopped and escorted out, but we were not bothered. We walked around marveling at the luxury and wealth in those beautiful hotels. They had postcards laying on the tables of the Marlaboro Blenheim hotel which I thought the most luxurious of all. I sent one to my family. Many years later while looking through some old boxes in the attic I found this card with a two cent stamp on it.

In the 1970s when Atlantic City no longer attracted the wealthy, my wife and I met her sister and husband for three days at the Marlaboro Blenheim. It was beginning to age, but still had wonderful food and service. We would sit out in a second story area of the hotel at night. When it began to get cool an elderly Negro came with blankets, just like they did for the famous and wealthy when Ralph and I were first there.

We went swimming every day, and one night we paid fifty cents to go out on the famous steel pier which was a huge amusement park. The fifty cents covered everything except food. We had a wonderful time.

Chapter Four

We borrowed a map and planned a hitchhiking route to new York City. We got an early start the next day and after three or four rides, we got in with a man who was going to New York. He asked where we were going and we told him New York City. Which part he asked. We told him we had never been there and had come up from Atlantic City to see it. He said he would go a little out of his way and would let us out a short distance from Times Square.

When he let us out we thanked him and walked, amazed at the huge tall buildings. Scores of unemployed people in various parts of the city were selling apples for a nickel apiece. As we watched these apple sellers, we noticed about half of the people buying the apples gave them back to the seller.

We went into some big stores and looked at the merchandise being sold. One store was a large department store. We watched a style show where beautiful women modeled the latest in dresses and furs. We walked through the jewelry section looking at diamonds, pearls, rubies, precious gems, gold rings, bracelets, and necklaces. The perfume department alone was larger than the entire jewelry store in our city.

It was late afternoon when we left the store and started back to Atlantic City. We made plans to come back to New York. We could spend a week here, with a little money, maybe even see the Yankees baseball team, even get an autograph from Babe Ruth.

The man who had let us out in New York told us that we would have a very long walk getting back on the highway to Atlantic City. He told us what subway train to take and to ride it to the end of the line, then to ask someone where the highway to Atlantic City was. It was supposed to be close by after we left the subway.

The five cent fare was a bargain and we enjoyed the ride very much. We asked the operator to tell us when he came to the end of the line. He said, "When you see everybody getting off, that will be the end of the line."

We got off and asked a policeman where the highway was and he directed us to it. It took us longer than we thought to get back to Atlantic City.

After dark, progress was slow and we thought we might have to spend the night on the road. We stopped at a filling station to get a drink of water about nine o'clock. While we were there a large truck drove up for gas. Ralph went over and told the driver we were trying to get to Atlantic City and asked if he was going in that direction. He said he was indeed going to Atlantic City and would take us if we would talk to him and keep him from falling asleep.

On the ride we told him about our trip and then asked him to tell us about himself. He had been a World War I veteran so we asked him about his time in the Army, which was very interesting. When we drove into Atlantic City about two o'clock in the morning, we shook hands and told each other how much we had enjoyed each of our tales. Our week was almost over.

We took a trip to Wild Wood which also had a boardwalk, but much smaller. The next day we were to start home. We ate breakfast and the lady made us some meat loaf sandwiches. We hitchhiked to Philadelphia without much trouble, asking the last driver how to get to the train yards. When he found out we would be a long way from them after he dropped us off, he gave us a dime saying, "Catch the bus and it will take you to the passenger station. The yards will be close by." he wrote the name of the bus on a piece of paper and said, "Wait at any marked bus stop and show it to the bus drivers until you get the right one."

Before, when we had walked through the city, it had taken us about two-and-a-half hours, but by bus it was only about forty minutes, and we got to see a lot more of the city.

The yards were big with lots of trains. Railroad detectives seemed to be checking loaded cars ro see if the seals were broken. We were afraid to go down in the yards to ask someone where they were going, and decided to take the first train heading out the west end of the yard. We watched one picking up cars. When that one backed into a siding to pick up the caboose, we ran down the hill and across the tracks, picked out an empty car, and got in it just as he hooked on the caboose.

We didn't know where we were going, but we were on our way home. When dark came we hadn't stopped at any city but we saw by the sun that we were heading northwest.

We ate a sandwich and a donut for supper, found some card-board boxes in one end of the car, and we tore them apart to sleep on. I woke up during the night, and I could see the lights in tall buildings meaning we were stopped in a large city. The train was leaving off cars and picking up others. Finally, it seemed ready to go on.

We heard footsteps crunching the cinders and a flash light swept the car, but didn't touch us. The train started, and we went back to sleep. Maybe tomorrow we would find out where we were.

We went through some beautiful scenery, high mountains with hardly any sizeable cities. By morning the train had picked up a lot more cars. Two pusher engines had been added to the rear and we had two in front because we were in the mountains with some steeper grades. The train looked a half-mile long or more. In the afternoon, we came to a curve so great that in going around it we finally saw part of the train going our way and the rest going in the opposite directions. Ralph said it was the famous horseshoe curve.

The train was going up a steep grade and we could see a tunnel about a mile away. The train slowed almost to a walk and we noticed hobos getting off the train and catching the two pusher trains, hanging all over the two engines. While we were trying to figure this out, the two pusher engines unhooked from the train and stopped. It suddenly dawned on us that without the pushers, we were going to go through this tunnel very slowly, exposing us to a lot of smoke and gas. It was too late to jump off. We shut the door of the car, blocking it with a piece of wood so it would not lock us in. We hadn't gone very far in the tunnel before the gas and smoke got very bad. We were in a refrigerator car and there was some water from the ice melt. We soaked our handkerchiefs in the water and held them over our noses. We were badly frightened and we talked to each other to let each know we were all right. We thought we would be asphyxiated. This was a long tunnel and we were going very slowly. After what seemed like hours, we finally emerged from the tunnel. We opened the doors and breathed the sweet mountain air.

We continued to creep along for about half-an-hour. We saw the two pusher engines catching up and hooking on the rear. They had cut loose and waited until the tunnel cleared of smoke and gas, then came through and hooked on the back. The hobos who got off the train onto the pusher engines had been there before and knew how to avoid the smoke and gas. If we came back this way again, we would know what to do.

We rode, going through very small towns without knowing where we were. The mountains were not as large and kept getting smaller as we rode along. At dusk, the train pulled into a small yard and began shifting cars and picking up others. We didn't see any men around, so didn't get off. Finally, after about an hour, the train without the pusher engines started out. We watched the small towns glide by, but later went to sleep. Sometime in the night, we went through a good sized town and the train stopped, shifted some cars, and left the city. We woke up at daylight and knew we would have to get off the train. We were both hungry. We were in flat country so we figured we were somewhere in Ohio. The train was slowing and we came by a farmer in a field. We hollered at him, "What's the next town?"

He yelled back, "Crestline, Ohio."

We didn't recognize the name, but it was a town so small we wondered it if even had a police department. We decided to ride into town instead of getting off and walking in. The train was going very slowly so we got off at the passenger station. We hadn't walked fifty feet when the Crestline Police grabbed us. They took us down to the jail and locked us up. We were the only ones there.

The jail was a large square room, the big windows boarded so you couldn't see outside. Four iron-barred cells stood in the center of the room. A large light in the ceiling made it as bright as day. We estimated the time at about eight o'clock in the morning.

We studied the graffiti on the walls. Most of them made mention of thirty days and the writer would be heading for Indiana, Chicago, Pittsburgh, and other locations. Ralph and I discussed these remarks. Thirty days in this place would be a long time. If we wrote to our parents, they would probably come to Crestline and pay to get us out, but we didn't want them to spend money they needed to take care of the family. We both lay down in the cell and slept.

I woke up when I heard the door open and the officer said, "All right boys. Let's go, come on." He took us out to the Chief of Police who was the other officer who had nabbed us. He said, "We're going to turn you boys loose, but if we catch you on the railroad property again, you're coming back for thirty days. Now you're free to go."

I asked him what time it was and he said, "Eleven-thirty." We had been in jail for about three hours: too late for breakfast and too early for lunch.

We had a quarter left so we stopped at a grocery store and told the owner what we had, that we were hungry, and we had to go to Indiana. We asked him what he could do for us for a quarter. Maybe he had some boys at home our age, for he really fixed us with enough food to last all the way home. He gave us bread, cold meat, a big piece of cheese, over-ripe bananas, apples, and a dozen second-day donuts. We filled our water jars. After eating we started hitchhiking out the highway.

It was dark by the time we got to Fort Wayne. We thought we could make it home about fifty miles away, but after nine o'clock we knew we weren't going to get a ride all the way home, and we didn't want to get left out in the country. We walked to an all-night filling station and asked the man if we could sleep on a nice grassy lawn behind a big sign. He said, "You don't want to sleep in that grass. Come around back of the station."

Behind the station stood what looked like a large tool bin, about four or five feet wide and about eight feet long. He opened part of it and started pulling out the coveralls worn by the attendants. He pulled out about ten of them and arranged them on the top; then he found a big piece of canvas and put it on top of the coveralls.

"There, that's better than sleeping on grass." He was right. We slept pretty good even with all the bright lights.

Next morning we started hitchhiking to our little town about fifty miles away. We got there about noon. As I was walking through town, I met a girl from my class in school. She stopped to talk to me and tell me about the week vacation she had at Lake George, a high class community in northern Indiana. When she finished, I said, "Sounds like you had a real nice vacation." She noticed the small bag I was carrying and asked if I'd been on vacation too. I said, "Yes, I just got home from a week in Atlantic City." She stared at me, then said she didn't believe it. I shrugged my shoulders and started walking. I heard her again say, "I just don't believe it."

Atlantic City was a far-off glittering city in those days. When I got home everybody was glad to see me, and I was glad to see them. I was glad to get back to eating my mother's cooking and sleeping in a bed every night. The family asked all kinds of questions about the train riding. I told them everything except being put in the jail in Crestline, Ohio.

Chapter Five

A few weeks before we were to go back to school, I heard a lot of people talking outside on the street. I went out and saw a number of people looking up in the sky. I looked where they seemed to be looking and saw one of the dirigibles I had seen in the Pathe news in the movie theaters. It was wonderful seeing the huge, lighter-than-air craft moving sedately across the blue sky. It soon passes from view, and we stood in groups discussing this great event in our lives.

A couple of days later I saw Ralph uptown and I asked if he had seen the dirigible. He said he had, adding he had also read in the papers about a large one being built in Akron, Ohio. We talked about it for a while, then about going to Akron to see if we could watch them making the dirigible. We decided to go the next day.

The Lake Erie and Western went through our town, but it was so slow, stopping to pick up everything including milk, that we decided to start hitchhiking. In fact, the people called the railroad the "leave early and walk."

We started out north of town and soon got a ride to Fort Wayne, Indiana. We got a train out of Fort Wayne that we thought was going to take us back the way we came home from Atlantic City. We hadn't gone very far when we saw we were going more north than east, and we ended up in Toledo. It was dark when we got there. The yards were big and not very well lit. We rode into in and our train stopped, and we got off. We asked the engineer if he was going on east and he said the train would be switching cars for five or six hours.

We didn't see anybody around who looked like detectives. As we walked along we looked for a train that looked like it was ready. We asked the engineer if he was getting ready to pull out and where he was going. We finally found one who said he was going to Cleveland and we found an empty box car. It wasn't long until we heard him whistle and the train started to move. We went very slowly at first, even going on a siding for about half-an-hour. The passenger train came along for which he was waiting; we pulled out and began to pick up speed.

We had brought some sandwiches, fruit, and some candy bars. Let me tell you about the candy bars in the Depression. Candy bars now are not much more than an ounce or so, and sell three for a dollar. Back then, Baby Ruth and Hershey bars were four ounces. A store in town sold four of them for fifteen cents. Fifteen cents was hard to come by in those days. We ate a sandwich and an apple and a candy bar.

We watched the small towns go by, but we had had such a long day so we lay down and went to sleep. When we woke, we thought we were coming into Cleveland. When the train entered the yards, we got off while it was moving and ran for the fence. After we had walked a few blocks it didn't look like a big city. We asked the first person we met if this was Cleveland, and he said, "No, this is Elyria, but you're not far from Cleveland."

A friend of ours at a filling station had given us a road map of the United States. We looked at it, but Elyria wasn't on there. We walked into town having decided it would be too hard to find a train to Akron and so we hitchhiked. We stopped in a restaurant with a long counter, going to the end to sit. When the counter man came to us, we asked if they had any work for something to eat.

He said, "I'll have to see the boss." We told him we could wash dishes and windows, or sweep and mop. He walked back down the counter and came back and said the boss had plenty of work to do so he would feed us. He brought us a huge stack of hot cakes, a couple of sausages, and a cup of coffee.

When we were through, we waited for them to tell us what to do. After about fifteen minutes, I motioned to the counter man who had served us to come over, then asked him what did they want us to work at. He said the boss told him that we didn't have to work. He had just wanted to see if we would work. When we walked out, we thanked him and he gave us a wave of his hand.

We came to a policeman and asked him if he could tell us what road to take to Akron. He directed us to the highway, and we walked through town, found the highway, and hitched a short ride. The next car stopped and the fellow asked us where we were going. We told him Akron.

He said, "I'm going there and I can take you if you're not in a hurry." He was a salesman and he said he would be stopping along the way to pick up orders. We said we didn't mind and we enjoyed the ride and also the stops in the small towns.

We walked around the small cities where he was getting his orders. We had mentioned coming all the way there to see the huge airship that was being built. He said he was going fairly close to the hanger, but had never been there and didn't know if we could get in the hanger or not. When we got to Akron, we could see this immense hanger for a couple of miles before he let us out. I've been told that this huge hanger stills exists in Akron. There was a wide road off the highway leading to this tremendous building. There were men going to work down this road, so we fell in with them and walked into the hanger that was almost filled by this huge lighter-than-air dirigible called the Akron.

After World War I part of the reparations Germany gave to us were two zeppelins. One was a small ship but the second was built especially for the United States and was christened the Los Angeles. It was one of the most successful ships that the U.S. ever had. It flew for eight years, but was finally brought low by the depression and lack of funds to operate, ending up being broken down for scrap.

The first dirigible to be built in the United States was the Shenandoah. It performed very well for a couple of years and then was broken into three separate parts in a storm over Marietta, Ohio.

The Akron, the ship Ralph and I saw, was a huge ship. It was 785 feet long. To put this in perspective, imagine two football fields laid end to end and then add a third out to the 65 yard line. It would be almost three city blocks long. Standing on its nose, it would tower 78 stories high. It was 145 feet in diameter. It was powered by eight large motors and had an air speed of 83 miles per hour. It could and did carry 207 passengers and crew members. The hanger doors, 22 stories high, were opened and closed by electric motors at a cost of one dollar in electricity.

Nobody asked us if we worked there, so we walked the length of it, then under it. It was so enormous I felt like a Lilliputian. The frame was made of duralumin and there were girders, two feet wide and twenty feet long, coss-hatched every two feet or so. It looked big and heavy, but when I picked one up, I almost threw it over my head, it was so light. We stayed in the hanger for about three hours until our necks were cramping from looking up at the ship.

Seventeen months after is was commissioned, it encountered a storm over the Atlantic Ocean. The fury of the winds drove the Akron into the sea and only three members of the crew of 76 survived the crash. The Akron's sister ship, the Macon, was identical to it and within about 18 months, it would also be lost over the Pacific Ocean, off the city of Los Angeles. No further rigid air ships were ever made in the United States.

We decided to hitchhike back home. It was late in the afternoon before we got started and the first ride let us out in a small town. It was dark now, but we still tried to get a ride back, but had no luck. We went into the small town and saw a restaurant with just one person inside who turned out to be the owner. When we walked in, I could see in the kitchen a large sink about five feet long. It was piled two feet high with dirty dishes.

Ralph said to him, "I see you have a lot of dirty dishes. We'd be glad to wash them for you for something to eat."

He said, "All right, I'll feed you."

We started to take off our coats and roll up our sleeves and the man said, "Sit down. I don't work anybody when they're hungry."

And feed us he did. He must have just been ready to close, for the food was still hot. Roast beef, mashed potatoes, gravy, lima beans, apple sauce and a cup of coffee. We ate until we were almost bursting. We finally got up and were ready to start on the dirty dishes.

He said, "You don't need to wash the dishes. I have a man coming in and if you two wash the dishes, he won't have anything to do." Since it was almost nine o'clock, he asked, "Do you have a place to stay tonight?" We said we had no place, but would find something. He said, "Down in the basement is an old mattress that I sometimes use in real bad weather in the winter. If you want to sleep there, you're welcome to. The only thing is, I'm going to lock you in because I don't want you up here in the restaurant."

We all went down the basement and the mattress looked pretty good to us so he said, "I'll lock you in, but I'll be back at five o'clock in the morning to let you out."

Before going to sleep, I thought we'd really be in a bad situation if the restaurant caught fire, but then being a teenager I knew nothing could happen to us.

When he unlocked the door we went up in the restaurant and a fellow stood washing that large sink of dishes. There were no customers in the place so we thanked him for everything and started out the door. He said, "Wait a minute and I'll make you some hot cakes." When he brought them over, we both said we could sweep and mop the place. He said, "No, but don't come back for lunch. I'm not adopting you two."

We laughed and when we left we told him what a nice man he was.

We were getting an early start, but we were not picking up any long rides, most rides were about ten or twenty miles. Then we got lucky and got a ride all the way to Findlay, Ohio. Walking through town, we came to a large grocery store. We decided we would go in and see if we could get something to eat. We figured the middle-aged man was the owner, so we went over and asked him if he had any work for food. He said he didn't, so we asked if he had any cold meats ends and any second-day bread. He gave us a sack of them and also half a bottle of ketchup that, I guess, the help was using.

We stopped at a small park and sliced the meat with our knives that we always carried and made sandwiches with the meat and bread and ketchup. He gave us so much that we had enough to last all the way home.

We got as far as Decatur, Indiana. It was dark and looked like it was going to rain. We walked through the town, and when we got in the main part it began to rain. Seeing a policeman standing out of the rain in a store entrance, we decided to ask him to put us in jail until morning. He said he guessed we could since there were no prisoners in the jail. "When the rain slacks up," he said, "I'll take you to it." The jail was just around the corner. He asked where we lived and we told him we had been to Akron to see the big dirigible, and told him all about it.

He looked at his watch and said, "I guess you two have had a long day, so we'll run down to the jail." When we got there, he said, "There's a shower but only cold water at this time." He went back on his beat, and we took a cold shower and picked out a bed and were soon fast asleep. When another policeman woke us up, he said, "We got some donuts and coffee if you're interested." We accepted the offer and when through, thanked them for breakfast and our night's lodging. This was the first time we had ever asked to be locked in a jail, but we'd been told by hobos that you could do this if you picked a small city. We did this several times while hoboing around the country.

We made it home in a couple of hours. Like always, we were glad to get home to our families and friends. We told our neighbors we had seen a dirigible in Akron that would soon be flying and would make the one they saw over our town look like a baby.

School was starting in a week and our traveling days were over until the next summer when we would be free to go again with the hobos.

It was great to be back in school with our friends and teachers. I had a few weeks before basketball practice started and Ralph and I had a few dates with the girls in our class. Ralph was such a handsome fellow that if you ran around with him all the time as I did, there was no problem getting dates. He even got away with things with his teacher.

Some of the girls called him C.C. for conceited, but he didn't seem conceited to me. That time of year was great: warm days with the leaves turning all colors. The nights were cool with brilliant stars, and, sometimes, a large harvest moon.

Ralph was expelled from school for three days. It was a good thing he was a good student; losing those three days would have hurt most students' grades.

The high school had two large study rooms or assemblies, as they were called. They would each seat 75, or perhaps more, students. The teacher sat in a desk on a raised platform so the large room could be monitored.

One afternoon Ralph and I were in one of the assembly rooms studying. All the seats were full and I was seated about 30 feet from him. The room was completely quiet, not even any whispering. Into this silence a large fart reverberated. For an instant everybody was stunned. Then a roar of laughter rose. Some were laughing and pounding their desks. I looked at Ralph and he was staring indignantly at the fellow across the aisle. Then he reached in his desk and pulled out a tablet, tearing off a sheet of paper and offering it to the student across the aisle. Another roar of laughter from the students.

The teacher came down the aisle and sent the red-faced student to the principle's office. The teacher quieted the room. I looked at Ralph; he had a sly grin on his face.

In about ten minutes, the principal and the student returned and the three had a conference at the desk. The principal went to Ralph's desk where they talked in whispers. Ralph was the picture of innocence, but the principal prevailed and they left together. Ralph didn't return. An hour or more and the rumor was that he had been sent home. Later, I heard he was expelled for three school days.

I went over to his house that night; he was sitting in the living room. I sat down and looked at him and burst out laughing. "What in hell made you do something like that?"

He got a sheepish grin on his face and said, "Well, it was so quiet in there and I just wondered what effect it would have. I was surprised how loud it was."

"Yeah, but how about when you handed that guy the piece of paper?"

"Well, that wasn't planned. I just did what came in my mind."

"What did the principal say to you?"

"He asked me if I did it and I admitted that I did. Then he really read the riot act to me, even called me uncouth. I looked it up in the dictionary; it means I'm not a gentleman."

I laughed, "You proved him right on that count."

"What's everybody saying at school?"

"I see the girls in groups giggling. The fellows are getting a big kick out of it. I heard one fellow say, 'Did you see that teacher's eyes;? They were as big as saucers.' I'll tell you one thing, nobody is going to forget this for a long time."

When he came back to school, he was more popular than before. One thing I did notice when he walked into a classroom, you could see a wary look in the teacher's eyes.

Chapter Six

We learned a lot about hoboing talking on long train rides with the hobos. We listened to them brag about all the fast trains they rode. Passenger trains, silk trains, fruit and vegetable trains, and cattle and hog trains were all given the right of way on the mainline. We learned to catch the front ladder on a car of a moving train.

If you missed catching the cars' front ladder, you would be thrown against the side of the car and get a painful fall to the cinders and stones along the track, perhaps even a broken bone. Miss the rear ladder of the car, and you would probably be thrown between the cars and, in all probability, lose arms or legs, or another possibility, you could lose your life.

We watched one afternoon as a hobo tried to remove a cinder from another hobo's eye. He was using a small sharpened stick similar to a toothpick. The eye was completely bloodshot and swollen. The man with the stick probed and pushed with it in the hobo's eye until I was sure he was going to blind him. We didn't interfere. We were only teenage boys. The hobo's eye was so irritated he couldn't tell if the cinder was still in his eye or not. He left the train at the next city to try and get some help with his problem.

We saw a lot of hobos with broken fingers that had not been set. Most hobos who had lost an leg or arm usually stayed in hobo jungles. They built a shack out of discarded lumber, cardboard, and corrugated tin sheets, anything to keep out the weather. They would go into the city, take up a position, and remove the peg leg, using their hat to beg from the passers-by. I think they probably did well. Hobo jungles were a concentration of hobos living permanently there or just a month or two. They were usually located on the outskirts of larger cities along the railroad tracks. Some were quite large.

We learned to keep a sharp eye out for the railroad detectives when we were in big city railroad yards sorting out trains to find where we wanted to go. If we saw one or more detectives, as they seldom worked alone, we took off running for the railroad yard's fence. On the other side of the fence, we were safe from them, but not from the local police who might pick you up on a vagrancy charge and put you to work on gangs doing work within the city or county. Most of this was done in the South.

The railroad detectives were hired to see that the goods carried by the trains were not stolen by the people who were riding them. A lot of merchandise carried by trucks today were once carried on freight trains. Detectives were in and around the railroad yards checking the cars to see that the seal was not broken and the car entered. If they were checking a loaded train, you didn't have much chance of getting on the train while it was standing still. Once the train started to pull out of the yard, you had to catch it while it was moving and had no chance of getting into an empty car. You had to ride on top or in between the cars if you wanted to get out of the wind until the train made a stop. Then you could get off and look for an empty boxcar.

We saw two instances of people stealing from a train, both times while the train was moving slower than usual. We saw a man, a few cars from us, tie a rope around the runaway on top of the boxcar. We got a good look at the operation because we were riding with several hobos in a car with four feet sides, but no roof, carrying slabs of building stone. We were out of the wind and riding in the sunshine.

After securing the rope, the man tied the rope around his upper legs and waist like a sling and began lowering himself over the side of the moving car. I asked one hobo if he was going to try to get into the car. He replied that was exactly what he was trying to do. He went on to explain the man was a thief, not a hobo, because he knows what is in the car.

Whoever loaded the car was in on the robbery and had marked it in a place so the thief could find it. After dangling on the side of the car for awhile, the thief finally got the door open a foot or so and pulled himself inside.

The hobo said, "This is more often done at night than in the day time." The man had been in the car about an hour when the hobo said, "He's getting the stuff up to the door that he's going to steal."

Fifteen or twenty minutes later, we started going up a fairly steep grade and the train was slowed. Suddenly two men cane running from the woods toward the train. Boxes were being tossed out the boxcar and the two men on the ground grabbed the boxes and ran with them back into the woods. The man in the car continued to throw out boxes until I estimated he had thrown out about fifteen or twenty of them, covering about a quarter mile along the tracks. The train slowed more as we neared the top of the grade. The man jumped from the train and although he tried to remain upright, he stumbled and rolled like a ball down the side of the hill. Evidently, he wasn't hurt much for he picked himself up and ran back to his companions who were carrying the boxes as quickly as they could into the woods.

The hobo spoke, "They probably have a truck in the woods, and they'll be gone in a very short time."

"What do you think was in the boxes?" Ralph asked.

"They look like the boxes that they ship large amounts of cartons of cigarettes. They're easy to get rid of and even at a big discount when they sell them they'll do real good. The next town we come to where the train slows, even if it doesn't stop, we should get off the train. If we ride it to a city big enough to have a yard, when it came into the yard and stops, railroad detectives will run down the train checking the seals on the doors. When they see the seal broken and the rope dangling alongside, they're going to be very unhappy. They'll grab all the hobos they can lay their hands on and take them to jail. Even though they're innocent, they probably will spend months working at whatever anybody wants to hire prison or jail workers for."

He said he had been put on a gang that was working in a quarry. He said the cotton and corn was planted by hobos, was weeded by hobos, picked by jail and prison inmates. When they were not needed they were turned loose to continue their wandering, probably wiser.

The other time we saw a robbery was similar to the first. We were riding in an open car and could see the robbery take place. The train slowed going up a grade when four men with large scoop shovels came out of the woods along the track. They worked their way back down the train until they came to a full coal car where they started shoveling the coal into a pile at one end of the car. They stopped when the pile was eight or nine feet tall.

I asked a hobo what they were going to do. He said, "Wait a few minutes and you'll see four men working faster than you've ever seen men work."

The train started up a steep incline and began losing speed. When it slowed to a walk the four men suddenly attacked the mound of coal, shoveling it off along the track. Within five minutes they had pushed the huge mound of coal off the car.

"How many tons do you think they unloaded?" I asked the hobo.

He scratched his head and said, "Oh, between twenty-five and thirty tons. They'll be back with a truck and their families will help them pick it all up. Then tomorrow they'll sell it."

We were able to get off at the next town when the train slowed and watched our train disappear in the distance. It might be a long time before a train stopped in this small town so we started hitchhiking.

We were told about missions we could sleep at, get a meal and a shower. These were run by the Salvation Army; many churches organized missions and some cities had their own missions. There were lots of places that charged a small sum for a night's lodging, a meal, and a shower. Because of the charge, if you had the money, you could almost always find that it was not full, while the free ones filled pretty fast in the evening. We even slept in a couple of farmer's barns, and sometimes we slept on the grass in a park if the weather was hot. Sleeping on the grass sometimes meant waking up about four o'clock drenched with dew.

We had asked police to lock us up overnight it if was raining and we could find no place out of the rain. We didn't do this too often, but we were never turned down. We asked restaurants to feed us in exchange for work, and we were very successful, I think, because we were young. We offered to work for food in food markets. We went up alleys to back doors and asked for food for mowing the lawn or any work that needed to be done. We were never asked to work after they had fed us.

We also started a bad habit: smoking. I went to Ralph's house one day, and after a while, he said, "Come on upstairs, I want to show you something."

We went into his older brother's bedroom, and he walked over to the dresser. It had a small chest on the top, and he lifted the lid, and there were about fifteen or twenty packages of Chesterfield cigarettes. He said, "You want to try smoking?" I agreed and he said his brother wouldn't miss one pack.

We went to the garage and choked and coughed through a couple of cigarettes. After that, whenever I went to Ralph's house, we would go in the garage and smoke a couple of cigarettes. Observing how other people who smoked handled and used the cigarette, we became more proficient in the habit. We smoked off and on all winter but not in public. I was on the high school basketball team and anyone using tobacco who got caught would be thrown off the team. By Spring we were smoking the cigarettes that we thought Ralph's brother wouldn't miss, but we also were going together and buying cigarettes.

Everybody, it seemed, was smoking. Ads in magazines showed movie stars, both men and women in advertising the brands of cigarettes. Lucky Strike cigarettes had an ad aimed at overweight people and people who didn't want to gain more. Reach for Lucky instead of a sweet was emblazoned everywhere you looked. So, we thought we were very smart and worldly when we smoked. By the time school was out in the Spring we had a new habit to feed.

When school ended we tried to find work, but the Depression seemed to have worsened. We made a little money washing cars for a quarter or mowing lawns at the same price.

One day, Ralph said, "I was down in that field behind the paper mill where all that old machinery and beaters lay around, and I noticed that the end of each slat on a beater had a one inch square of lead with wire running through it. The wire hold the beaters together. There were dozens of those worn out beaters and about fifty or sixty slats in each beater with two cubes of lead to each piece of wood. With a couple of hammers we could knock those chunks of lead off easy. Tomorrow, we'll go down and look at them." He pointed out that we might be able to sell the lead to the local junk man.

"Suppose the paper mill doesn't approve of us breaking up their beaters?" I asked.

Ralph said, "Wait until you see them tomorrow. They're all rusted and the wooden beaters are worn and splintered. When I saw the beaters I knew that they would never be used again."

We went next day. From the road the weeds were about three feet high and the beaters couldn't be seen. I told Ralph if we sat down while we were working I didn't think anybody from the mill could see us, except if somebody was on the second floor, but they didn't have very many windows because it was the rear of the mill.

We walked back home and found a couple of flour sacks and a hammer. Next morning we got up early and headed for the paper mill. We decided to go in the field at the same time the shift changed. Those on the night shift would not be interested in anything but going home and the upcoming shift would be checking into their job. We walked into the field, Ralph leading the way, until we came to the beaters. The lead was so soft that a few hammer blows knocked it loose from the wire.

We worked rapidly, but after awhile Ralph said, "Hey, let's take it easy. Nobody's going to see us sitting out here in these tall weeds."

In about three hours, we each had a bag that we estimated weighed about 20 to 25 pounds. We didn't like the idea of walking out to the road carrying a heavy sack, so we left the sacks planning to come back after dark and pick them up. We crawled through the weeds toward the road. After a short way we got up and walked to the road. We put a couple of stones along the road where we came out so we would know where to go back in the fields to get the bags. We didn't want to use a light as we feared it might attract a watchman in the factory.

It was fully dark about eight. We walked to the mill. We found the rocks and started out in the field, walking where we thought we left the bags, but couldn't find them. We went to one beater after another but couldn't find the bags. We decided one would walk north and south and the other would walk east and west through the area. After about another half hour or so, I stumbled on the bags inside a beater. I called Ralph and we picked up the bags and walked to the road. We decided to leave them at Ralph's house because he could leave them in the garage and no one would ask what was in them.

Next morning I went over to Ralph's and we picked up the bags and walked down to the junk yard. We had gathered iron before and sold it to this man so he knew us.

"What have you got in the bags?" he asked. We told him we had some pure lead, soft as butter. Opening the bag, he took out a piece and said, "Four cents a pound."

This was cheap but he knew we had no other place to sell it. Also, he hadn't asked us where we got it. We told him to weigh it. It came to over fifty pounds. He paid us and we left. We were uneasy that perhaps he might ask us where we got it, and if we refused to say he might not buy it from us.

As we walked back to town, we were laughing and in good spirits. The junk man perhaps would buy a lot of lead from us. We went out to the mill two or three times a week and the junk man didn't appear to care where the lead came from.

During the fourth or fifth time when we were at the mill, I looked up and saw a man watching us. We got down low in the weeds and watched the man. He was definitely looking in our direction. If he started out to the field we were going to run before he got close. After a few minutes the man started walking in our direction.

"Let's go!" I yelled and we burst out of the weeds like a couple of quail. We didn't look back until we reached the road.

He was not chasing us but he was looking around to see what we had been doing in the field. We moved on down the road but we could still see him. We moved into a woods but still watched to see if he had found our sacks of lead. He finally went back to the mill and we didn't think he had found the bags.

We went home and that night while listening to the radio and talking about losing our lead selling business, Ralph said maybe we should go somewhere for a few weeks. Where to? I wanted to know. We had been listening to the Jan Garber Orchestra and the announcer came on and said, "This is Jan Garber playing at the Roosevelt Hotel in New Orleans."

Ralph said, "Hey, that's it. Let's go to New Orleans, to the French Quarter and look around." I reminded him how the hobos had told us the South was very unfriendly to hobo in, but he answered, "We're both pretty fast runners and we'll be careful."

We talked about whether we should go back in a couple of nights and see if we could get the bags of lead which were almost full. We had a few dollars but a couple more would be a big help. We figured the factory man had just been curious and had not found the bags in the high weeds. A couple nights later we went back and easily found the bags and the next day we sold them.

Chapter Seven

We got our bags ready and the next day we left Hartford City. We took the slow Lake Erie and Western that was east of town. There was only one train and it left early in the morning. We waited at the paper mill, where we got the lead, for the train to stop to pick up locked cars. When it came in we picked up some cardboard boxes laying around and found a boxcar, climbed in, laid the cardboard down, and waited for the train to pull out.

The engineer pulled into the siding and picked up the loaded cars, and then we were on our way, but slowly. The train stopped at every little town and village. It was pleasant riding along watching the countryside and laughing.

"If all the trains go this slow," I said, "it'll be time to go to school before we get to New Orleans."

No hobos were on the train but us; I guess it was too slow to attract anybody. We had fixed some sandwiches, fruit, candy bars, and had our fruit jar of water. There was one brake man on the train. Because the train stopped every few miles he had seen us in the car but he didn't bother us. Near afternoon he came by and I asked him where the train was headed. He said, "Vincennes, Indiana."

I had an older cousin who worked in Vincennes whom I used to hunt and fish with when we were younger. I told Ralph and he said, "He might have a place where could sleep for the night." he was single and working so I figured he probably would have a phone, although many people didn't have phones in those hard times. Ralph's and my family didn't have phones. It was dark when we pulled into Vincennes. We got off and walked toward town. When we came to a filling station, I asked the attendant if he had a phone. He said he had one but wasn't allowed to let anybody use it but himself, saying, "There's a pay phone outside the phone company building down-town."

We found the building and I looked in the phone book. Sure enough my cousin was listed. When he answered the phone, I told him who I was and how we had traveled to Vincennes.

"Where are you calling from?" he said.

"We're at the telephone building," I replied.

"I'll be over and pick you up and bring you to my apartment and we can talk."

In a few minutes he pulled up in his Ford roadster. When he got out, I introduced him to Ralph.

"I'm really glad to see you," he said. "It's been two or three years at least. Come on, get in and we'll go to my place."

His apartment was over a large restaurant. There were four apartments. His was a small one bedroom with a small kitchen. The twin bed and dresser were in one part of the living room, while sofa and chairs were in the other part.

I said, "You must have a pretty good job to have that nice car and this apartment."

"I do pretty good," he said. "I work for a corrugated box company and they treat me very well."

After talking for awhile, he said, "I'll bet you guys would like a shower after riding that train all day."

I said, "We sure would. It might be awhile before we get another." He said he'd show us where it was down the hall. We went with him. The bathroom was used by all four of the apartments. It had two showers.

We got undressed and my cousin said, "I'll make some coffee. Come back to the apartment when you're through."

When we got back to the apartment we had coffee and cookies and he asked where we were staying. We told him we would find a place in an empty boxcar down at the station. He said, "You can see I only have a half-bed, but if you want to sleep on the rug it would be better than a boxcar."

We agreed and he put down two blankets and we went to sleep. He had to go to work so we all got up at seven o'clock and he said he would buy us breakfast at the restaurant downstairs. After eating we thanked him and he insisted that I write to him with a chronicle of our trip, which I did when we returned home. He let us out at the train station and we walked toward the tracks. We saw a train pulling out heading south.

We ran and caught it as it was moving and climbed on top of a car. We got off at Evansville and found a boxcar. Climbing in, we found two other hobos. We asked if they knew where the train was going. They didn't know. Soon we crossed the Ohio River and we were in the South that we had heard so much about.

We were told a lot of stories about riding trains in the South, most probably true. We were told about chain gangs, working in the rock quarries; one who had been there said it was hard work, and getting an eye put out with chips of stone flying everywhere had worried him. This punishment was not just for train riders; he was sent there for being drunk.

Another hobo told of how in Georgia if you were caught riding trains and were released after working out your fine, you couldn't leave on a train.

When you started from a town on the highway, the police would watch which road you took and called ahead to the next town. The police there would pick you up on a vagrancy charge and put you back on a chain gang. He said he knew one fellow who took six months to get out of Georgia. I think this was probably an exaggeration, but maybe it was true. We wouldn't know.

The two hobos with us had been riding trains for about two years after being laid off from factory jobs. They had traveled extensively and found very little work anywhere. We enjoyed listening about the places they had been in their travels.

When lunch time came we got out what was left of the food we had brought. We divided it and offered it to the men but they refused. Because they hadn't eaten today yet, we insisted and they finally took the food. We got out our map. After looking as it, we four decided that the train was going to end up in Nashville, Tennessee. We told them we were going to go west there to Memphis, Tennessee, then turn south.

Late in the afternoon we saw the train slowing. We were coming into a big city which we were sure was Nashville. When the train entered the yard it was going too fast for us to get off.

One of the hobos said, "When it slows enough for us to jump off, run as fast as you can for the yard fence."

As we went further into the yard we began to see other trains on sidings we would have to cross before we could get to the fence. The train slowed there and we all jumped off and started running. We had no trouble. When we got to the fence we ran down it until we found a hole and out to the street.

Our two friends were going to go downtown but we had decided we would keep close by the yard. We walked down the street parallel to the railroad and saw what looked like a large store about three of four blocks on a street that was away from the street we were on. We thought we would walk down and see if we could get something to eat.

We were passing through a poor neighborhood and began to see many Negro people. We noticed that as we met Negroes coming toward us that they would step off the sidewalk and walk around us. We knew that running and waiting out in the hot sun we had perspired, but didn't think we smelled that bad. We found a store and it was fairly large that sold not only groceries but also clothing, utensils, in fact, a general store. They even had a meat counter. We went to it and asked the butcher who the manager was. He said he was. We asked if we could do some work around the place for some cold meat and bread. He asked us where we were from. We told him we were from Indiana and he told us to be careful, that some stores would call the police.

We started to leave when he said, "Wait a minute,": and cut several slices of cold meat and gave us a nickel loaf of bread. Then he went over to a barrel and got a big sack and shoveled it full of unshelled peanuts. We asked again if we could do something for him but he said, "No, but remember what I told you."

We said we would and thanked him and started walking back to the railroad yards. As we walked we kept looking for a place to make our sandwiches. There were several buildings, all of them boarded, so when we came to one that had steps and a platform we sat down and made our sandwiches. After we had eaten, we cracked some of the peanuts. They were very good.

While we were doing this a white man limping along with a cane came over and asked if we would mind if he could sit with us and rest. "I've got about ten more blocks to walk yet to get home," he said.

We talked with him for a while and Ralph said, "Do you think we smell?"

The man was startled and after a minute said, "No, I don't smell anything."

Ralph said, "When we walk down the sidewalks people get off the walk into the street and walk around us."

The man started laughing and pounding his cane on the cement. Finally he wiped his eyes with his handkerchief and said, "Where you fellows from? Up north?"

"We're from Indiana," we both answered.

"First time in the South?" Yes, we told him, explaining how we got here. He said, "Colored people, especially when they are in a white section of town, which this is, must get off the sidewalk when they meet a white person."

He went on to say that there were a lot of things colored people could not do in the South: eat or drink with white people, enter any white store, if sent by a white person to fetch something they must go to the back door and show a note from the white person saying they had sent them and what it was they wanted brought back. There were no blacks in our home town. We had seen some blacks in our travels but they seemed to go along like the white people. He was a very nice man but he seemed to think this was all right.

He got up to leave and said, "Good luck on your travels," and hobbled down the sidewalk.

It was getting dark and there were very few lights on the street so we walked back to the yard. We found four or five boxcars sitting on a siding that looked like they had been sitting there for a long time. We found one with the door open and climbed in. As we walked toward the end of the car, I heard Ralph stumble and head a crash and a voice, "Watch where you're going."

We retreated to the door and as our eyes became accustomed to the darkness, we could see the car was packed both ends with hobos. We jumped down and checked the next car, also crowded. The next door was shut. I put my weight on the bar but it wouldn't budge.

Ralph came and we both pulled and finally the rusty lock squeaked and grated, but slowly came open. We knew there wouldn't be anybody in this one. Using our bags for a pillow, we went to sleep. It had been a long day. A noise woke me up. It was still dark and I could see two or three persons climbing into the car. They went to the other end and I guessed that our company was more hobos looking for a place to sleep.

When we woke in the morning our hobos in the other end of the car were gone. We ate a sandwich and some peanuts. We still had enough meat and some bread for lunch. The problem now was to find a train to Memphis. We looked out at the yard and saw two trains that looked like they were about to roll. After looking in all directions for detectives we ran across, Ralph to one and I to the other. I asked the engineer if he was headed for Memphis; he replied that he was going to Atlanta. I looked over at Ralph and he was waving his arms like a windmill.

I ran over and he said, "This is the one."

The train had not started so we went along it looking for an empty car. They were all sealed and locked. We found a flat car with heavy machinery; this was it or ride on top the cars. We climbed in and lay down under the machinery. We didn't think we could be seen by anyone walking beside the car. Soon the train began moving. After we were out of town we looked around to see if we could improve our riding position. The wind was coming in pretty heavy so we looked for some way to get out of it and spied very heavy cardboard stacked in one corner. We pulled out a couple of big pieces and leaned them against the machinery, then sat down with our backs holding it tight behind us. We were very comfortable, even better than a boxcar. We could look around everywhere at the scenery, but we were very visible and if the train stopped we would have to keep a good watch in every direction. Looking at our map, we decided Memphis was a pretty large city and maybe we would get a look at the famous Mississippi River running through it.

We noticed quite a few hobos riding on top the cars; they had probably been riding between the cars until we got out of town.

Ralph had brought part of a pack of cigarettes and we had brought a nickel bag of Bull Durham tobacco with cigarette papers included. As we had smoked the "tailor mades" we decided this might be a good time to try to roll a cigarette from the Bull Durham flakes of tobacco. We had seen cowboys in the movies roll their own and almost all the hobos we saw smoking were rolling their own using Bull Durham or Duke's Mixture. It wasn't as easy as it looked. We spilled a lot of tobacco before we got something that looked like a cigarette. When we lit up and inhaled the smoke, it felt like a hand grabbing me by the throat. I choked and coughed and Ralph was doing the same. After we quit coughing we started laughing and Ralph said, "If I have to smoke this Bull Durham, I may quit smoking."

We tried the tobacco three or four times but it was so strong we couldn't smoke it. Later on a hobo would solve this problem for us. We were riding in a boxcar with several hobos when I noticed one pull out a paper bag and reach inside, bring out a handful of cigarettes, already smoked to about an inch's length. We watched as he tore the paper off about six of them and had a small mound of shredded tobacco from the cigarette butts. He then rolled them in a cigarette paper and lit up. He saw us watching him so he leaned over and offered us the paper bag saying, "You want to roll one?"

We took the bag and looked in. It was three-fourths full of cigarette butts. He said, "If you smoke a certain brand you can sort out Lucky Strikes, Chesterfields or whatever brand you like to smoke. I mix them up and get a pretty good smoke."

We laughed with him. Ralph got some out and was tearing the

paper off. I did the same and we started rolling the tobacco in the Bull Durham papers that we had.

The hobo smiled when we tried to roll a decent cigarette. He said, "How long you boys been smoking?"

We told him not very long and that we had never rolled a cigarette out of the Bull Durham that was much good. We lit up. The cigarette was much milder than the Bull Durham and much easier to roll. We asked him where he got the cigarette butts and he said anytime he was walking in the city and saw a good size butt, or "snipe" he called them, he would pick it up and put it in the bag. After that, every time we had to walk through town we hunted snipes and soon we could roll a fairly good cigarette.

We didn't go through any large towns on the way to Memphis. The train stopped outside a small town but only to take on some coal and water. We didn't need to get off. We ate the last of our food at noon and we still had some peanuts left.

The country we rode through was different than Indiana. We enjoyed watching the numerous small towns we went through. The train was going at a good speed. We thought we might get into Memphis before dark and we did. The train slowed and we began to get into multiple tracks. We watched the hobos on top of the cars; we would get off when they did. Some of them had retreated between cars and in a short time they all were there. We couldn't see them so Ralph looked down one side and I the other. The train slowed until we knew we could get off, but the hobos still were not leaving, even though we seemed to be entering a large rail yard. Then I saw one come around on the side ladder, come down, and drop to the ground. I yelled to Ralph, "This side, they're getting off!"

We climbed down the ladder and hopped off, looking around to see where the hobos were going. We kept an eye out for detectives as we followed the hobos, going over tracks and trains until finally we saw they were going for a fence. When we got there we looked for a hole and came out in a street with only a few houses on it. The other hobos had disappeared going down a street away from the yards.

We started walking west, suspecting we would have to walk to the other end of the very big and busy yard. We seemed to be coming into a small town or a part of Memphis.

We were coming to more houses and places of business. Finally we came to a large store and we decided to see if we could get some food. We went in and asked one of the clerks to point out the manager. He pointed to a man several aisles over who seemed to be watching us. We started to go to him, but before we got there he moved behind another counter.

We continued walking after him, but he continued keeping two or three aisles between us until he disappeared into the stock room where we couldn't follow him. We had the idea this man knew what we were and what we wanted from him. We decided to buy some food, but not there.

We continued down the street, but we saw no more food stores and asked a man if there was a grocery store close. He pointed back the way we had come and said there was a big store up the street. We weren't going back to that one. As we walked on we saw eight or ten hobos come through the fence and walked over to the street. Soon they overtook us. We asked one of the laggards if there was a mission or Salvation Army around to get something to eat.

He said, "No, I don't, but we're going down to the jungle and you can get some mulligan stew." Later we found it was also called "hobo stew."

We had heard of hobo stew but never tasted it so we walked along with them until we were past the yards. About a quarter mile further we came to the jungle. We had seen a couple of these when riding but this one was huge, filled with all kinds of shacks made of any material that would keep out the weather.

Walking through it, our friend pointed to a fire with a fifty pound lard can on it and said, "There's your supper."

They went on but we walked over to the fire which was tended by a rugged, burly, red-haired man. Ralph said, "We heard that we can have some of your stew."

"Yes, you can," he said, "You know the rules. Got to put something in the pot before you take something out."

I said, "We don't have anything to put in but I've been told that you could eat for a nickel."

"Yes, any money is welcome; we use it to buy meat for the stew."

We handed over two nickels and he handed us two clean cans full of the stew. Retreating a ways from the fire, we got our spoons out and dug in. The stew was delicious. There were some things in it we couldn't identify but we decided that, as with sausage, we really didn't want to know what all was in it.

After we had eaten the stew, we stayed around watching the hobos. Some stopped for stew as we had.

All kinds of stuff went into the pot. We saw potatoes, carrots, turnips, all probably raided from somebody's garden. One hobo came in and showed the redhead a Hershey bar. The redhead took it, tore the paper off, and dropped in it the pot, then handed him a can of stew. We thought from what we saw around us, and what we saw of the jungle the next morning, there were thousands of hobos. The jungle seemed to stretch for at least half-a-mile along the railroad.

We looked on side tracks for cars that had been there for some time. We found a string of cars that were close to the fence but most were empty. We looked in several, but they were really dirty from hobos sleeping in them. We decided to retrace our steps and see what we could find. We asked people if they knew of some place we could sleep. They all suggested the jungle but we didn't see any place in the jungle that wasn't occupied.

We asked one man and he said he had a place fixed up in his garage he slept in when it was a real hot night, leaving the garage door open. He said we could sleep there if we wanted to. While walking with him to his house he asked where we were from and how we had gotten to Memphis. He said his wife had died about a year ago and he was living by himself. When we arrived at his home he took us to the back of the house and opened the big garage doors. Inside a mattress lay on the floor with a blanket covering it. We told him this would be great and thanked him. It was early in the evening and he asked it we would mind sitting on the porch for awhile with him and he would make a pot of coffee.

We told him we would be happy to sit with him awhile. We talked and drank coffee for a couple of hours. He was lonesome and needed someone to talk to but we finally said we would like to go to sleep. He said, "When you get up, come and knock on the back door. We'll have breakfast together."

We told him this sounded like a good deal and we would be glad to have breakfast with him. We found the mattress was the best bed that we had since we left home. We left the garage doors open and a soft breeze cooled the inside. We slept well.

When we woke, the sun was shining brightly and we had slept longer than intended. We knocked on the back door and our friend opened it immediately.

He asked how we had slept and I said, "We slept fine, but we should have rose earlier and got on our way." We saw by the clock that it was nine o'clock.

He started slicing some ham and breaking eggs. He asked, "Do you like grits?"

We replied that we didn't know what grits were. He took the lid off a pot and showed us what looked like cream of wheat. We told him we would be glad to try them. We offered to help several times but he insisted that he was used to doing it. He fixed us fried ham, scrambled eggs, homemade bread, and grits which we ate with black strap molasses. After breakfast we insisted that we wash the dishes. He let us and gave us another cup of coffee. We talked with him until the clock stood at eleven, when we thanked him for everything and left.

We went to the yards. Our plans had been disrupted but we didn't care, having made another friend. We had no food. If we caught a south bound train we would probably miss two meals, lunch and dinner, and, maybe, breakfast the next day. We decided to wait and eat stew at the jungle and go back to the big store and buy something for the evening.

When we went in the store we saw the manager right away, but he didn't move away from us as he had yesterday.

Ralph said, "Let's try this guy again." So we walked over to him and he stayed.

"What can I do for you?" he asked.

We said we wondered if he had any work we could do for some food. He picked up a large sack and began to put in ham slices, bread, cheese, a piece of butter. He went to a barrel and pulled out three or four large pickles and handed us the sack. We thanked him and said we would be glad to do any work he had, but he waved us off.

It was almost midday and we decided to go back to the jungle, saving our sack of food for when we were on the train. We would go back to the big Irishman and his pot of stew. We figured he worked the stew pot twelve hours and someone took over at night. He was there. We gave him our nickel and he gave us a can of stew.

We went about twenty feet away and sat with our backs to a tree, and got our spoon. The stew was as good as it was the night before, but no one knew what went into it since last night. While we were eating, a large black man came walking through the jungle. When he saw the stew he came over and picked up one of the cans the Irishman had washed to keep clean for the next hobo.

The Irishman asked, "Do you have something for the pot?"

The black man replied, "I don't have nothing and I'm going to eat."

The Irishman reached for the can the Negro had taken and the black man hit him a terrific blow in the face. He staggered, his nose bleeding. They started the most vicious fight I ever saw. Both were big muscular men and the fight seemed almost even until the Irishman launched a heavy blow to the Negro's jaw and he went down. The Irishman jumped down on his chest and grabbed him by the hair, then pounded his head on the ground. Nobody interfered and he kept pounding his head until I thought he was going to kill him. Finally he stopped and got up, picked up the tin can, putting it with the others. My first thought was if the Negro was dead, the police may come and investigate. But Ralph said, "Let's wait a few minutes."

We sat there with the other hobos watching. Although the Irishman was the winner he looked like the loser. His nose was still bleeding, his lip was cut and bleeding, he seemed exhausted. After about fifteen minutes the colored man groaned and rolled on his side. A minute or two later, he got up on his hands and knees. When he got to his feet, he swayed and staggered for a minute then gained control. He glared at the Irishman with pure hate in his eyes and the look was returned. He staggered away through the jungle.

I said to Ralph, "Do you think we should try to help the bleeding?" He said, "We can try."

As we approached the Irishman, he looked at us like we were another antagonist. When we offered to help him, he snarled, "Get out of here!" We left. We had seen a part of hoboing that we didn't like.

We walked to the yards and went in. A brakeman was throwing a switch and we asked him if he knew of a train to New Orleans. He said he didn't know of any going there but he pointed to one across the tracks and said, "That one is going to Baton Rouge, the direction you're going."

We thanked him and looking around for any detective before running across the tracks to the train. We looked for an empty boxcar but all seemed to be full. We got in between the cars and decided to ride there until exiting the yard. We wouldn't be easily spotted. If a detective came along checking cars, we could slip off on the opposite side and run out of the yard. We watched both sides of the train until it started moving. It went very slowly even when it left the yard; then what looked like an army of hobos came running from both sides and all of them climbed on the train. The train picked up speed. We climbed on top of the car and it looked like there were about two hundred hobos on the top of the boxcars.

I guess as big as that jungle was a lot of people left it every day. Some cars were really crowded, but gradually the hobos dispersed until the train was covered with them. We had some stop at our car and they asked us if we knew where the train was going. We told them we had been told it was going to Baton Rouge. They didn't seem to care much where we were going. We talked to two sitting close to us who seemed to be in their early twenties. They were traveling together as we were and riding trains for a year and a half, but had never been South either so couldn't supply any information.

It was a nice afternoon and we enjoyed hearing of the different places the two had been. They were from Pennsylvania and they had been all over the East, Midwest, and even to California. We told them this was our third trip and we were planning on going to several places.

When it began to get dark we got our food and offered to share with them, but they pulled sandwiches from their pockets and we all ate supper. They had no water so we gave them some of ours. After dark some of the hobos lay down on the side of the roof with their head pillowed on the runway, but I thought the way I roll around in my sleep that I might fall off the car.

It was about midnight when we saw the lights of Baton Rouge in the distance. The train began to slow. Before entering the yard it stopped, still some way from the city. From the back and front of the train, we saw lights on top of the train. One of our friends said, "This is where we get off."

I said, "We're quite a distance from the yards, why are we getting off here?"

He said those lights are carried by detectives and they are going to kick everybody off the train before it gets into the city. "We might as well get off now before they get to us and everybody is running for the ladder."

We were glad they had told us what was happening as we had never experienced anything like this. We walked about fifty feet away from the train. As the detectives advanced down the train, we were joined by all the hobos cursing and howling epithets about the ancestry of the detectives. After a two-mile walk we began to come into the city and walked down a street parallel to the railroad. We heard a hobo with a watch tell his buddy it was one-thirty. Where to sleep was going to be a problem. We stayed close to the railroad and soon were within eight or nine blocks from what looked to be the center of Baton Rouge.

The night was very hot and humid. When we came to a large building with a well-tended lawn, we decided to sleep on the ground. We went along the side of the building to be hidden from the street and, using our small bag for a pillow, lay down on the grass.

When we awoke we were wet with the heavy dew. When we got up you could see the dry outline of our bodies where we had lain on the grass. Walking away from the center of the town we soon saw the freight yards. We walked to the southern end and then to the fence to look over the situation. Only one train seemed to have an engineer in the cab. We ran over the tracks and climbed over a string of boxcars to the engineer. When we asked if he was headed for New Orleans, he said, "No, this train is headed for Birmingham, Alabama."

We went back to the fence and sat down on the bank, then ate the rest of the peanuts we had. Activity in the yard increased as it became lighter. We saw several engines making up a train. Finally one of them hooked on to the string we had climbed over. We ran down the hill to the engineer and asked if he was making up a train going to New Orleans.

He replied, "Yes, but it won't leave for an hour or so." As all freight trains looked something alike, we asked if this number engine would be hauling it. He said, "No, the engine would be a Southern Railroad engine."

We went back to the fence and watched the engine gather cars and combine them on one track. Within an hour we saw the engineer coming with three of four boxcars and a caboose, so we thought the train was complete. He slammed them onto the end of the string. In a few minutes we saw the engine backing into the siding. After looking around we started running to the train. We had already spotted some empty cars and headed for one before the train moved out, having learned how dangerous it was trying to get into a moving boxcar. We learned this by seeing an inexperienced hobo put his hands on the floor of the car and pull himself in, but his legs were under the car. After a difficult struggle, with the train picking up speed, he managed to push himself away from the car and took a nasty fall.

There was a rod on each side of the car about a foot under its bottom, where some hobos placed a board and ride. This was called "riding the rods." If the train was moving slowly you could put one foot on the rods and at the same time grasp the side of the door and pull yourself in the car. We had seen hobos do this but we would never try it. If the train was moving we caught the front ladder on the boxcar and either rode in between the cars or on top.

After the train picked up speed we decided to get some sleep, not having slept much the night before. When we woke we were on a siding. We looked down the train and the engine was still there so we figured he wasn't switching some of the cars. In a short time we saw what was holding us up: a passenger train went by. After that our train pulled out on the mainline and we continued toward New Orleans.

We enjoyed seeing the Spanish moss in trees and the swamps and bayous with water birds. The pine trees surprised us because we supposed they only grew in a cold climate. We watched the small towns and noticed some were completely occupied by colored people, while even the others seemed to have a lot of colored people in them.

It was late in the afternoon when we began nearing the large city of New Orleans. We were hungry; all we had eaten was peanuts that morning. The train slowed and then stopped, so we got out of the car. The city was visible but we were still out in the country. We didn't want to walk that far so decided to ride in between the cars. The train probably wouldn't stop again until it entered the rail yards. After a while the train started to move and we got in between the cars. We crawled at a slow pace for a few miles, then came into the yard. We jumped off and ran for the street alongside the railroad. We seemed to be in a poor section of mostly black people. We continued to walk toward what we thought was the center of the town. After several city blocks things started looking a little better and we saw many more white persons.

We began to see small shops and finally a small restaurant. We had spent hardly any of our money and decided we would buy a meal. Since it was late in the afternoon we decided we would eat and then try to find somewhere to stay. The restaurant was small with only a counter and three or four tables. We sat at the counter and a colored woman came to wait on us. The menu was chalked on a board behind the counter. We decided on fried chicken dinner. She returned with the food: three large pieces of chicken, mashed potatoes, cream gravy, black eyed peas, and grits, all for fifteen cents. When we were finished, we splurged on a piece of pecan pie for a nickel. The man came and asked if everything was all right. We told him the food was very good and paid him the forty cents.

We asked him how far it was into the main part of the city and he said, "It's about a mile of so but you could catch a bus." We didn't think we were going to spend our money on buses. We asked him if he knew a place where we could rent a room. He replied there were places all along the street and they usually had a sign in the window or somewhere.

We left, deciding to walk and see if we could find a place closer to the main part of town. We passed several houses with rooms to rent; closer to the town, we quit seeing the signs. We turned around and went back until we came to a large house and knocked. A man opened the door. We told him we were looking for a cheap room. He said these rooms were very nice and clean at twenty-five cents a night. We went with him to look at it and were pleased at what we saw. The house at one time seemed to have been the home of a well-to-do family. All the furniture, rugs and drapes looked expensive. The bedroom was large with a high ceiling. The bathroom down the hall was large and clean. He asked how long we would be staying and I said, "We don't know. So if it's all right with you, we'll pay you every night." He said that would be fine and we handed over a quarter.

We took a bath and shaved, although neither of us had much to shave. We sat out on a big verandah, running on two sides of the house, and talked about tomorrow when we would go downtown. The owner told us they also served meals, twenty cents for dinner or supper and fifteen cents for breakfast. After seeing the owner and asking him to have us awakened for breakfast, we went to bed early because we were tired.

The owner told us a colored man would knock on our door and that he stayed awake all night to get other people up who had to go to work or some place at night. It was nice to lay in a bed and we were soon asleep. In the morning we put on clean and better clothes and went down to breakfast. There were two colored women working and they said they would get our breakfast anytime we wanted it.

We told them we were ready and sat down at a large round table. While we were waiting on our breakfast, two other men came in and sat down at the table. They didn't speak to us so we didn't speak to them.

The colored woman came in with our breakfast: two fried eggs, a slice of ham, a portion of grits, a huge plate of hot cakes, and a cup of coffee. It was good and we ate everything because we planned to eat only two meals a day to conserve our money. When we finished Ralph asked, "Who do we pay?" She said, "Lay your money by your plate and the mister will collect it."

Outside we started walking toward the large buildings. We met an old gentleman and we asked him how to get to Canal Street, the main New Orleans street. It was supposed to be the widest street in the United States. He directed us and after walking about half-an-hour we came to the famous street. We saw about three or four hundred man working taking up the oversize bricks, cleaning them and replacing them. We stopped and watched the men for a few minutes when a man walked over to us and said, "Are you boys on the bum?" We looked at him in amazement. We had thought we were pretty clean in our clean shirts and trousers.

Ralph said, "How can you tell we were on the bum?"

The man replied, "I can tell by looking at you." He told us all the men working out in the street were hobos who had been arrested for riding on trains, trespassing on railroad property or picked up on vagrancy charges. If they couldn't pay the fine they were used to repair Canal Street. The city of New Orleans would get their streets fixed by hobo labor at little expense to the city. The man asked if we had any money. If not, we could be arrested for vagrancy.

We decided if this guy could see that we were hobos, then maybe a policeman could also tell. We slipped off Canal Street to talk things over. We didn't know that you couldn't be arrested for vagrancy it you had a place to stay, which we had, or had enough money to buy a ticket to the next town. This made us uneasy and we didn't go back to Canal Street, but walked around the city instead.

We found the Roosevelt Hotel and went into the lobby to walk around. We saw an easel that said that Jan Garbor and his Orchestra were still playing in the ballroom. We had reached our destination. We looked in all the stores, surprised to see all the strange people of different nationalities. We walked to the docks and saw the big ocean-going freighters that were docked and being unloaded. We found a place to sit down and watched the activity.

After awhile, Ralph said, "You know when we get a couple of years older we ought to try and get a job on one of these boats, and really take a trip to see the world."

I agreed and we talked of different places we would like to see when we were part of a crew roaming the world. We decided to go back to our room and eat supper there, as we didn't think we could buy a meal anywhere we knew of at that price. We strolled, really enjoying ourselves. Everything was different from the other large cities we had been in.

Arriving at the house we inquired when supper would be served and were told six o'clock. We went down to the dining room. About ten men sat around this large table. The two colored women were there and several of the men were eating. We took two empty seats and one of the colored woman said, "You have a choice of meat loaf, chicken, and baked ham." We told her our selection and she left to go to the kitchen to get our meal.

None of these men spoke to us; they just ate and laid the money down by their plates, got up, and left. Another man came in and it was the same thing. Nobody spoke to anybody else.

We had a very good meal and when we went out and sat on the verandah, I said to Ralph, "Isn't it strange that nobody speaks to each other?"

He replied, "Where's all this Southern hospitality we've heard about?"

All day long we had picked up cigarette butts as we walked around the town. We got some out and tore the paper off and used the tobacco to roll a cigarette. It was easier with the shredded tobacco than the flakes of Bull Durham. We did a credible job making the cigarettes. We thought we were really hobos now. It was cool on the verandah, but we had walked around the city since early in the morning and we were tired. We wanted to get a good night's sleep, planning to go to the French Quarter the next day, Saturday.

Chapter Eight

We forgot to tell the old Negro to wake us up in the morning and didn't wake up until after eight o'clock. We went to the dining room and it was empty. We asked one of the women if we were too late for breakfast and she said, "No, we'll fix it anytime you want it."

We had inquired about where the French Quarter was and were directed to it. They said it was some distance away but we could catch a streetcar that would take us there. We decided we didn't want to spend the money to ride both ways so chose to walk, enjoying going through this large and interesting city.

When we got to the French Quarter we were delighted with the colorful houses with the wrought-iron fences, most had second-floor and third-floor balconies that had beautiful wrought-iron work with flowers hanging in iron-worked baskets. Everywhere there were small parks with statues and more flowers and trees, and small shops with doors that folded back so the store was open to the sidewalk. When we heard music we would find it and look in the door at the musicians, mostly colored playing for the customers.

We walked down the sidewalks and looked at merchandise we had never seen before. There were places selling food and baking goods. We saw people eating boiled crawfish which back home we used for catfish bait. We found a small shop selling coffee and bakery goods.

We sat at one of the tables on the sidewalk and had a cup of coffee and a roll for our lunch. The coffee was very strong, but the roll was delicious and after we finished we got out our snipes and tore off the paper and rolled a cigarette. We were content just to sit there and watch the different people go by. This was the life. It was worth all the rough rides and missed meals and long walks through towns. The owner asked it we wanted a refill on our coffee.

Ralph said, "We can't afford another cup; we don't have a job." The owner told him there wasn't any charge for the second cup. "In that case, we'll have a second cup." Ralph said.

When he returned with the coffee we asked if he minded us sitting for awhile. He said, "No, you may attract other people to come in."

Down the street an Italian-looking fellow started playing an accordion. We rolled another cigarette to smoke with our coffee and looked at each other and smiled. We were having a great time in this part of the city.

Ralph said, "I wonder what our teachers would think if they could see us taking our ease on Bourbon Street in New Orleans." We laughed.

We saw policemen in this area but we didn't feel uneasy here in the French Quarter. Late in the afternoon we decided to walk back to our room and save the money. Tomorrow we would walk back to the French Quarter and stay all day and eat dinner there, staying late to see what was going on, then riding the streetcar back to our room.

We got lost going back, street and buildings looked different going the opposite direction. We walked a long way out of our road but we finally got in the neighborhood we knew and found our house. The dining room and kitchen was dark. We had to get something to eat so walked around the streets and asked a man if there was a restaurant near. He said there was one a couple of blocks away, but it might be closed. We got directions from him and hurried to the restaurant, relieved when we saw a few customers still inside. When we tried the door it was locked. A man came to the door and said the restaurant was closed.

Ralph said, "We haven't eaten since breakfast and we need something to eat."

The man said, "Come on in. We're not going to send you away hungry, but there isn't much choice on the menu."

I said, "Why don't you fix us whatever you have back in the kitchen? We'll be happy to get it." He said he'd see what they had left.

He came back with two large meat platters and they were filled with chicken, ribs, two sausages, sweet potatoes, and of course, grits. With bread and butter and a cup of coffee, we really got filled up. When we were through, we asked how much we owed him. He said, "This was just stuff that was left over. Do you think ten cents a piece will be all right?"

We thought we were lucky to find this place that late at night. We gladly paid our ten cents, thanked him and walked back to our room.

We saw the old colored fellow and asked him to wake us at nine o'clock. He said he would. We went to bed. We were awakened early and talked about what we were going to do that day, arriving at the dining room late. No one else was there but the two women, who went to the kitchen to get our breakfast. We ate plenty because we weren't going to eat again until our French Quarter supper.

We took a little different route than the day before to see some other parts of this fascinating city. We walked by a large cemetery. In all the cemeteries we had seen the dead were buried in the ground. In this one, the dead were put in mausoleums or cement crypts all above ground. Walking through the city was like being in a foreign country. Lots of people wore colorful clothing, especially the women and children. We lingered awhile watching a man getting a shave in a chair right on the sidewalk, while a colored boy shined his shoes.

It was noon when we got to the French Quarter. We walked to the French Market, a section we missed yesterday. This was a large market and it had a variety of other things for sale besides large piles of vegetables and fruit. We walked down the aisles and looked at strange fruits and vegetables we had never seen anywhere else, piles of watermelons, gourds, beets, turnips, bins of peppers, and strings of garlic. There was also fish, crab, lobster, and crayfish. We decided we would buy something for our dinner before we left as everything was so cheap. It was a noisy place with people bargaining with the vendors and others calling for someone to buy their wares.

When we left we bought six bananas for a nickel which we ate walking down Bourbon Street. There were musicians all over the place playing their instruments with their caps on the ground for any contributions from the listeners. Plays were performed at parks and some right on a street corner.

We went back to the little shop where we sat yesterday and decided we would sit and watch the people for a couple of hours. The owner was glad to see us as he had no other customers. We ordered a cup of coffee and a roll and got out the cigarette butts we had been picking up to roll a cigarette. We decided to dump the Bull Durham tobacco and tear up all the butts and put the tobacco in the Bull Durham sack. People were looking at us strangely when we got the butts out and rolled a cigarette.

Across from the coffee shop was a row of two-storied buildings. On the street level were shops but the second story were living quarters and all had balconies with the graceful iron railings. As we watched the people of the street pass by, I noticed a young girl come out on the balcony directly across from us and lean on the iron railing. She seemed to be looking directly at Ralph. She had coal black hair and blue eyes and her complexion was tan ivory. She was wearing what looked like a gypsy dress, very colorful. She seemed about our age, sixteen or seventeen.

I said to Ralph, "She's looking at you." He said he knew that and thought he would ask her to come down and have coffee with us. Ralph was a very handsome teenager. Some people back home thought he looked like the popular movie actor Franchot Tone.

He got up from his chair and walked over to the apartments and looked up at the girl and she looked down at him. I couldn't hear what was said but in a few minutes Ralph came back and sat down.

"Is she coming over?" I asked.

"No, she isn't allowed to come down and sit with us without one of her parents coming with her, which she says she know they'll not do."

With a wave of her hand she turned and entered the living quarters.

We discussed the strict rules that the girl must obey. Even in our home town lots of girls our age were restricted to certain places and how long they could stay out at night.

We started to look for a place to eat. We wandered around looking at several places until we found a fairly large one with a line waiting to get in. We thought if people were willing to wait to get in, then the food must be good. We checked the large menu chalked on a blackboard and the prices were pretty good.

We fell in at the back of the line. When we reached the door, a woman asked if we would mind sitting at a table with two other people. We said we didn't mind. She seated us with a couple who appeared to be in their forties. The man smiled at us and said he welcomed our company. Ralph asked if he lived in New Orleans.

The man replied, "My wife and I have lived here for about twenty years. We like the city very much."

We told them we lived in Indiana and how we had arrived in the city. We asked them if they would order for us as weren't familiar at all with a lot of dishes on the menu board.

The lady said, "You picked a good restaurant for Southern and Creole food. One dish you should eat is the gumbo."

"We'd like that," we replied because it was one dish we had heard of but never tasted.

She said, "Another Louisiana dish that you should try is boiled crayfish."

We both knew about the crayfish back home and we had heard the Belgian people on the south of town by the glass factory ate them. We caught them in a seine and removed and shelled the tail for bait to catch channel catfish in the Wabash River. But all around us people were eating them so we told her we would try some. When the waitress arrived, the lady ordered the same meal for all four of us.

First we were brought a small dish of spaghetti with a sweet hot sauce that was very good. Then the waitress brought the gumbo; it seemed to be on the same order as hobo stew with lots of different things in it. It was very good and I asked the woman what was in it.

She rolled her eyes and said, "Almost everything can be in it, but I can tell you some of the things in this dish," and rattled off, "shellfish, corn, tomatoes, sausage, chicken, okra, carrots, to name a few."

When it came to shellfish, we were a little hesitant but everybody in there was eating them. They were a reddish color and our new friends showed us how to peel them. The sauce was hot with peppers and barbecue flavor. For dessert we had a dish of custard and strong coffee.

They both smoked and when we got out our Bull Durham sack and started to roll a cigarette, he said, "Wait, here have one of my Chesterfields." We both took one and it was the first manufactured cigarette we smoked since we left home.

We talked to them for some time and had another coffee and another one of his cigarettes. He told us he was in the crushed stone business and they had no children and about their home in New Orleans. The lady asked what we were going to do the rest of the evening, and we told them we were just going to walk around and watch what was going on. She asked if we had been in any of the musical halls. We told her we had looked into them but didn't go in.

The man said, "We have nothing in particular to do, how would you like us to show you around some of the music halls?" We said we would like that very much. It was about nine o'clock so he suggested we start off. Ralph and I were ready so he called the waitress for the bills.

When she brought them he took both of them. We objected but his wife said, "You're our guests tonight. We've enjoyed talking to you about your hobo adventures and trips."

Outside the streets was crowded and noisy. We walked along stopping to listen to a gypsy play a violin. A block further a colored man played jazz on his saxophone. We stopped in front of a fairly large hall, and our friends told us it had one of the best bands. Since there were a few empty tables, they took us in. They ordered drinks but as Ralph and I never drank any liquor we ordered the strong coffee.

It was very warm and only a couple of overhead fans didn't stir up very much of a breeze. The band was mostly colored players and were very good, especially the trumpet and saxophone. When we left, our friends took us to the Absinthe House where absinthe liquor was served. They told us that continual drinking of this would eat away your brain. We didn't go in but looked in the door. Everybody inside was drinking a green liquor that our friends said was flavored with wormwood. It was almost midnight so we thanked our friends for the very enjoyable evening. We told them where we were staying and asked if they knew what streetcar we should take.

He said, "I don't know, but I'll find out for you." He took us to a boarding station for the streetcar and when one came along he got on the car and asked the operator. When he came back he told us which car to get and where to get off and catch another that would take us close to our street.

It was a nice ride and we got off at the right stop and walked to our house.

We spent the next two days at the French Quarter but our money was going fast. When we got down to our last dollar we decided it was time to get started back home. We used most of the dollar to buy food the night before to take with us the next day, asking the old Negro to wake us early. He woke us at six o'clock in the morning. We spent our last thirty cents for breakfast, eating eggs, hot cakes and grits till we were really full.

It took about three hours to walk to the yards. We started picking up snipes as we walked along tearing off the paper until the Bull Durham sack was filled with tobacco. We walked along the outside of the fence until we came to several trains being made up. We would take any train going north. We slipped through a hole in the fence, keeping a sharp look out for detectives. We walked down in the yard. The first engineer we asked said he was going to Houston.

We went on and asked another it he was going north. He said north to Birmingham. We ran along the train looking for an empty boxcar. The first one was so dirty inside we went on looking, although we knew we were in danger of running into detectives. We kept a sharp look out for detectives and after a few minutes the train started. It was always a relief when the train started; then we didn't have to watch for them until it stopped. The train went slowly out of the yard and through the city.

We came to lake Pontchartrain and started across the world's longest bridge, twenty-four miles long. Although the people called it a bridge, it was really a causeway of soil dredged from the lake bottom with the tracks laid on it. The train still moved slowly, perhaps they didn't want a derailment or something. We watched for alligators, but saw none. After we could no longer see land it was like being out on an ocean. We fixed a sandwich from the groceries we had bought and sat in the door watching for alligators or anything unusual. In the distance we saw land and soon we were across the lake. After we had crossed the lake we seemed to be going east rather than north.

Looking at our map we thought we were in Mississippi. After a little while we saw the train was coming around and was going north again. We watched the small towns go by and talked about going back to New Orleans. It was an unusual city. Before dark we made a sandwich and ate a couple of bananas. I wondered how much sleep we would get after sleeping in that soft bed for several nights. Would the bouncing, swaying, the wheels screeching keep us awake after living the soft life? We lay down and both of us went to sleep.

I woke up and everything was quiet. The train had stopped. I woke Ralph and we went to the door and looked out. We were on a siding but we were out in the country. We decided we would not go back to sleep until the train moved. We had no idea how long it had been on the siding. After what seemed like an hour or so we saw a pin point light that quickly grew larger and we could see it was a passenger train we were waiting for. As it sped by, we could see it was the "Rebel," a stream-lined train that ran from New Orleans to Washington, D.C.

Our train moved slowly out on the mainline and began to pick up speed. We fell asleep and awoke to daylight. We ate some of the food we had bought. We were in cotton country and saw the shacks the colored people lived in who worked on the plantation. They were pitiful, set off the ground with no glass in the windows and only a wooden closure hinged at the top of the windows which was opened for ventilation, or closed in cool or rainy weather. Lots of children, mostly colored, roamed around the houses. Ralph and I talked about the children. They probably didn't get any schooling for we saw no schoolhouse. We went through another small town that seemed to consist only of blacks.

We saw our first chain gang. They were working about two

hundred yards away from the railroad by a swamp. They seemed to be shoveling out a ditch that had some water in it. Three white men guarded them, two on horses and one on a mule. The white men were armed with rifles or shotguns; they were too far off for us to be sure. It seemed about two-thirds of the prisoners were black although quite a few white men were in them also. This was the first gang that we had seen although I am sure there were a lot of them. They just were not along the railroad when we were on the train.

The prisoners wore black and white striped prison clothing. As they passed from view I had an uneasy feeling. The train had picked up speed and soon we came into a city and we were going too fast to get off. We rode into quite a large rail yard. We passed the passenger station and saw we were in Hattiesburg, Mississippi. The train kept going through the yard before it pulled into a siding.

We saw a lot of hobos running for the fence. The fence was not very far from the train and we seemed to be almost out of the yard. We decided to stay in the car. We could see both ways for a long distance which gave us plenty of time to get to the fence and off railroad property. We sat there all afternoon getting concerned. The engine had left when we first stopped and had not come back. About dark a switch engine came with eight or nine cars and added them to our train.

We thought that was a good sign and sure enough in twenty or thirty minutes our engine came back and hooked onto the train. We didn't move and when it started to get dark we ate some more of the food and the last of our water.

At last the train started to move. In the moonlight the hobos were running to catch the train. We watched the small towns go by and now the train was going pretty fast. We went to sleep and meant to wake up early.

When we awoke it was daylight and the train had slowed. We ate the last of our food. We were now not only out of money but out of food. We saw a city ahead; we were coming into the yards. The train was too fast to get off and we were in the middle of yards which were large with several trains being made up. We were getting worried. Although the train was slowing, it was still moving too fast to jump from the door of the car. It was too dangerous to go further in the yard so we both jumped, both falling but not getting hurt.

We started for the fence but had to climb over three or four trains. When we climbed down from the second train we were confronted by two railroad detectives. They started running toward us. We ran in the other direction and were easily out distancing them when another climbed out of a car directly in front of us. We were trapped. Ralph yelled, "Over the cars!"

We each grabbed an iron ladder but by this time the two detectives were close enough and dragged us off the car. The three of them marched us down to the police car. One officer said, "Do you boys know you're breaking the law in trespassing on railroad property?"

We didn't answer him; we didn't think it was any use. They took us to the Meridian-Mississippi Jail, took our bags and our names, asked where we were from and locked us up. There were about ten or twelve cells that opened into a larger barred area. There were about five or six other prisoners and they watched us as the gate was opened. We walked in and the gate clanged shut behind us. We had been in jail in Crestline, Ohio, but had a feeling we were not going to get out of this one as easily as we did then.

The other prisoners were in cells sitting on the bunks. There was no place to sit in the central area. One of the men said, "Pick you out a room down at the end."

We walked down and took the two cells at the end. None of the cells were locked and you could mingle with the other prisoners. We sat down in one of the cells and Ralph said, "I think we have got us in a mess." I agreed with him.

We hoped being teenagers would encourage them to let us go like they did in Ohio. All of the prisoners were in their twenties. Later we learned most were charged with assault or intoxication or both. One older man sat alone.

They all laughed when we told them why we were in jail. We didn't think it was funny as they did.

We went back and lay down in our bunks and in a while I heard one of them say, "Here comes the slop."

We walked out and the turnkey was bringing our dinner. We waited and got ours last. A bowl of black eyed peas, a square of cornbread, and a gob of black strap molasses.

Ralph and I sat in his cell and looked at the food. We were not going to get fat in this jail. The black eyed peas had no seasoning and were almost tasteless. We tried to eat everything, but we were really forcing it down. Perhaps the food would be better at the evening meal. A short time later one of the detectives who arrested us came to the barred gate with the turnkey and called our names. We couldn't believe it; they must be going to turn us loose as they did in Ohio. We went with him to the city building and were taken into a Justice of the Peace courtroom.

Here hope was abandoned for any chance of being turned loose. They would not bring us here if they were going to free us. We were pushed in front of the bench of the Justice of the Peace.

He was a short fat man, most of his hair gone. He looked over his eyeglasses and said, "Harry Bohr and Ralph Woods, you have been charged with trespassing on railroad property. How do you plead?"

Ralph said, "We are just trying to get back home. We had not stolen from the railroad."

The J.P. said, "You are not charged with theft, which is much a more serious charge. Now, how do you plead to the charge of trespassing?"

I looked at Ralph and he shrugged his shoulders. "We will plead guilty," I said.

The J.P. got out a large ledger and wrote in it and then said, "Each of you is fined two dollars and costs of two dollars for a total of four dollars which must be paid at this time."

If he had fined us ten cents we still could not have paid it, for we didn't have any money. Ralph said, "We don't have any money. We're just traveling around the country looking for work."

The J.P. spoke to the turnkey, "Take them back." The turnkey said, "Come on boys," and we went back to the Meridian City Jail.

When we got back in the bull pen the fellows asked, "What did you get?"

"We got fined two dollars and costs of two dollars," I said.

One prisoner said, "Hey, he went easy on you guys because of your age. I got five dollars and costs just for getting drunk on Saturday night."

Everybody laughed but Ralph and me. We thought the fine and costs were high. They all told us what they were in for, mostly assault or drunkenness. All except the older man who seemed to keep his distance.

One of the prisoners had a small radio but he wasn't allowed to have it on the inside of the bull pen. It was wired to the bars on the outside. The cord was plugged into the light above it. Everybody was just sitting around and not talking much. I asked one of them, "Does the radio work?"

"Oh yeah, it works but it has a short in it somewhere and when you reach outside to turn it on sometimes you get a hell of a shock."

I guess that all of them had been shocked turning it on and they were waiting to see who would get so bored that they would turn it on again. After awhile one of the prisoners came out of his cell and walked over to the radio. He reached through the bars very carefully and turned the knob. It came on and everybody cheered. You could hardly hear it, the volume was so low. "Turn up the sound," someone yelled. He reached through the bars again and was able to turn it up a little more.

There was no reading material in the jail and so we sat around and talked or went to the cell and slept. I thought we were going to have a lot of time to think this situation over. I went to sleep and was awakened by the turnkey pounding a tin cup on the iron bars. Ralph and I walked to the iron gate to see what we were having for supper. I could hardly believe what I saw: a bowl of black eyed peas, a square of cornbread, and a gob of black strap molasses, the same as dinner.

"This is what we had for dinner," I said to one of the prisoners.

"That's right," he said. "And that's what you're going to have for breakfast in the morning. No matter how long you're in here the menu will be the same." He pointed to the older man and said, "Ask that fellow over there. He's been in here for over four months and he said this is all he's eaten."

Ralph and I got our plates and set them down in my cell to eat. He looked at it and said, "I don't know how long I'll be able to gag this down."

I answered, "I don't either but these guys in here just eat right down to the last crumb of cornbread."

After we had eaten it was quiet. We were able to hear the radio a little better. We talked about sending home for the money. We knew our folks would send the money but we didn't want them to because they needed the money every week. My father was making only about sixteen dollars a week. The four dollars and cost of sending it to us would be close to two days' wages.

Ralph said, "Let's not do anything. Maybe we'll just lay around until they get tired of keeping us and turn us loose."

All lights except one were turned out at nine o'clock. I had slept a couple of hours in the afternoon and lay in the bunk wide awake. After an hour I got up and stood in the cell door. A match flared down at the other end of the cells where the older prisoner bunked down. I decided to roll a cigarette, walk down and talk to him. As I approached his cell he stood up and I stopped about ten feet away.

"I saw you light your cigarette," I said, "and wasn't sleeping either so I rolled one and thought I'd join you."

"Come on in and sit down," he said. I asked how long he had been in jail.

"About four months. I'm waiting for my trial date," he said. "What are you doing riding freight trains. You don't look or act like a hobo."

"We really aren't. We always have a place to stay whenever we get tired of hoboing. We're just looking for a little adventure and to see parts of the country we wouldn't see otherwise."

"This is a dangerous part of the country if you don't have any money," he said. I asked him if he lived in Meridian.

"I live in a small town about fifty miles away," he answered.

"Tell me what's going to happen to us. We have no money to pay the fine. In fact, we don't have a cent."

"I hate to tell you this," he said, "buy they'll only let you stay here for six days from the time of your sentence and then they'll put you on the chain gang."

This was really bad news. After a few more words with him I left to go down to my cell and think this over before I told Ralph in the morning. We had been warned by hobos that the South was a bad place to ride trains or hitchhike, and it looked like we were going to pay for it the hard way. When we woke in the morning, sure enough we had the same bowl of black eyed peas, cornbread, and molasses.

I told Ralph I had some bad news. He said, "I guess that's about all you can expect in this place. I told him I couldn't sleep last night and went down to the end of the block and talked to the older man. Any thoughts we might have of lying around here until they get tired of us and turned us loose was wishful thinking. I told him the older man had informed me if we didn't come up with the money within the next six days, we'd be sent out to the chain gang to work off our fines and costs of four dollars. Fifty cents would be deducted from the four dollars for every day of work. It would mean eight days out on the gang to get us out of this mess. We talked about our situation all morning, and it always came back to neither of us wanting to ask our families for the money.

Late in the morning they came and took two of the prisoners up to the J.P. office to pay their fines. "They'll be back," one prisoner said. "They don't have any money and they'll take them out to the gang this afternoon."

Dinner was, again, peas, cornbread, and molasses. We could

hardly force it down but we were hungry and finally ate it all. That afternoon a new prisoner was brought in and was he loaded. He entertained us all afternoon by loudly calling for the turnkey. When he came he demanded that he be let out of this dirty cruddy jail immediately. When the turnkey told him to go sleep it off, he said, "I'm a good friend of the mayor and the first thing I do when I get out of here is get you fired."

All us prisoners cheered and yelled. The turnkey started away and the drunk shrieked after him, "Come back here you bastard, come back, you're going to be sorry if you don't let me out of here."

Then all the fight seeped out of him and he slumped down the bars and began crying. We were having fun, but we felt sorry for him. He rolled over on his back and passed out. "When he wakes up in the morning he'll also have a hangover to go with his hate of this place," somebody said. When the lights went out, he was still lying against the gate bars.

After awhile, I thought everybody was asleep. I walked slowly down to the other end of the cell block. In the dim light I could see him sitting on his bunk.

"Come on in, Slim," he called.

I went in and sat down with him. He pulled out his Bull Durham and offered it to me. I pulled out our bag and asked, "Would you like to try some cigarette tobacco?"

He took the sack, pinched it, and looked in; then poured some out in his hand. "Where did you get this kind of tobacco?" he asked.

I told him it was tobacco that we had picked up off the streets after peeling the papers off snipes, and putting the tobacco in the bag. He chuckled softly and said, "Yes, I'll try one of your cigarettes." We both rolled and lit up. "Hey, these taste better than Bull Durham," he said.

I asked him if he had heard any more news about his trial and he said, "My lawyer is supposed to see me tomorrow. Maybe I'll hear something from him."

Although other prisoners had asked us what we were charged with and we had asked them, I hesitated to ask this man who had been here so long. After a long silence I asked, "What are you in for?"

After several moments I didn't think he was going to answer, then he said one word: "Murder."

I was stunned. "You're too nice a man to be a murderer."

"I said I was charged with murder. I don't consider myself to be a murderer." As we sat in silence, he finally said, "Do you want to hear the rest of it?" I nodded.

"There isn't much to tell," he said. "I was out on a Saturday night and drinking heavily in a tavern. I got in a crazy argument with a man over a football game that had been played that afternoon. He said, 'Come out back and I'll change your mind about that game.' If I had been sober I would have just ignored him, but I had had several drinks and I followed him outside to the parking lot. We fought and I knocked him down, jumped on his chest and started hitting his head until he was a bloody mess. I got up and went back in the tavern and went to the restroom and cleaned up my own bloody face with wet toilet paper, covering the cuts and returned to my drink at the bar.

"Two men got up and left. His friends, I guess. I ordered another drink and a few minutes later I saw a police car lights flashing through the window and soon an ambulance pulled in beside the police car. A police officer with the two men who had left came in. They pointed to me and the officer came over and said, 'Come out to the car. I want to talk to you.' They were putting the man in the ambulance but it didn't move off. The officer said, 'Were you the other man fighting?' I said, 'You can tell that by looking at my face.' He said, 'The man's dead. We're just waiting for the coroner to confirm it.' So that's how I happen to be here."

For a few minutes I said nothing. Then I said, "I don't think that's murder." He laughed and replied, "I'm not going to sit in the electric chair. My lawyer said the worst I'll get is manslaughter and if we're lucky maybe even bargain down to less than that. My lawyer doesn't think there would be a trial but more likely a plea bargain."

I said, "Well, you really have a problem that makes ours look small in comparison. Could you tell me something about those work gangs, like what you worked at, what they fed you, how long a day you work?"

"I've never been on one of the chain gangs," he said. "But I've talked to men who have, and they're a very tough way to work off your fine. You and your buddy would only be out there for eight days if you kept your noses clean. When you're sentenced to thirty days or more, you could be in bad trouble. The food is the same as you get here and it isn't enough for the work you do. The work around here is mostly digging ditches to drain swamp land. They don't bring you back at night but keep you in large barred wagons and the mosquitoes will eat you alive. You have someone who would send you the money to pay your fine?" he asked.

"Yes, we could have the money sent to us but we hate to ask them. It would be a hardship on them."

"Well," he said, "if you can get the money I would say you should send and get it. You don't know what might happen to you out there."

After a few more words with him, I decided to go back and try to sleep. After breakfast the next day I told Ralph what I had been told about the work gang. We talked about our problem for a couple of hours and both came to the conclusion that we were going to send for the money. Neither of us liked the idea of the whole town finding out we were thrown in jail and had to pay what was a stiff fine to get out.

"You know what we ought to do is call my brother," suggested Ralph. "He works all the time and is also a gambler. He has money all the time. We'll tell him what our problem is and ask him to send us ten dollars, then pay him back when we get home. We'll go back to pounding lead out at the paper mill and in five days we'd have the money to pay him back."

This seemed to be the best solution to our problem. After dinner, the turnkey came back to pick up the plates. We went to talk to him. Ralph told him we wanted to make a phone call to our family and have them send us the money to pay our fine. "Do you have the money to make the phone call?" he asked.

Ralph said, "We'll make a collect call to my brother and he'll send us the money."

The turnkey replied, "You can't make a collect phone call when you're in jail," and walked away.

This was a crushing blow. It seemed we no longer had control over our destiny.

After we went back to our cell, I said, "You know, I've been talking to that older fellow and I like him, and I think he likes me. Maybe he might have some money that he would let us have to make the call. When the money gets here, we would give it back to him."

It was decided we would wait until lights were out and ask if he had any money and would he loan us enough to make the call. This seemed to be one last chance of getting out of there.

During the afternoon, the drunk from yesterday was bailed out by his wife. When he walked through the gate, he said to the turnkey, "I'm still going to get your ass fired, you son of a bitch."

We talked about getting put on different chain gangs and how we would meet up afterwards if we were. We didn't like the possibility of either of us waiting for the other, having to hang around the courthouse, especially since some people working there knew we had just been sent to work on a gang. Ralph said if they saw us hanging around they would probably think we had escaped and arrest us.

We heard many stories about prisoners being arrested again and returned to the chain gang after having finished their term. We decided to meet two blocks north of the jail if released at different times from different gangs.

I relayed to Ralph what the older man had told me. If we had to go on the gang we should obey all orders, no matter what, to avoid antagonizing the guards. He said never to make a smart remark to the guards and to get along with the other prisoners, pointing out that I would have to sleep alongside them so not to make an enemy. He said never try escaping because then, even if I managed to get away they had bloodhounds that would track me down. Then I'd be on the chain gang forever. "You'll think you were born on it," he had said. Besides that, there had been prisoners shot while attempting to escape.

We listened to the radio and we didn't have much to say to each other or to the other prisoners. After the evening meal with our usual black-eyed peas, which I could hardly get down, they brought in two more drunks. They weren't as entertaining as the first. They found a cell and both went to sleep. Time dragged on as we waited for lights out. It finally came and the radio was shut off by the turnkey. I waited for about an hour to be sure everybody was asleep. Ralph said he would be awake when I came back. I walked down to the other end of the cell block until I could see him sitting on his bunk as usual.

I spoke to him, "How about some company?"

He replied, "Come on in, Slim. You're always good company."

I pulled out our cigarette tobacco bag and offered it to him. "No," he said. "I don't want to smoke up all you boy's tobacco."

"Go ahead," I said. "What's one cigarette? I'll have one with you!"

We both rolled and lit up. I thought I might as well get this over with and plunged in. "After talking with you last night about the chain gang and you saying if we could get the money that we should send for it, we decided we would send for it."

"That's the thing to do," he said. "They're a rough bunch out there and I would hate to see you two boys go out there."

I waited for a minute and then said, "We have another problem.

When we told the turnkey we wanted to make a collect call, he told me that we couldn't make a collect call from jail."

"Well, that's true. They don't intend to make it easy for you in this place."

I said, "Do you have any money that you could loan us to make the call and when the money comes we'd give it back to you."

He didn't answer for a minute and I could feel my heart thumping. He was our last hope of getting out of there. Finally he said, "Slim, I have a little tobacco money." He reached in his pocket and laid some coins on the blanket. He counted it and said, "Sixty-seven cents, this is all the money I have to buy tobacco with until the end of the month when my wife brings me some food and gives me money to buy more."

This man had troubles that made ours look like mole hills. What if we didn't get the money from Ralph's brother? We then would be adding to his trouble by depriving him of what little pleasure he had for the next two weeks.

"Are you sure they'll send the money and are you sure you'll bring it back to me when you get it?

"We're sure the money will be sent and we wouldn't think of not returning your money."

He picked the coins off the blanket and handed them to me.

"I don't know how to thank you," I said.

He waved his hand. "Forget it. Go make your call tomorrow morning and get out of here and back to your home."

I thanked him again and went back to tell Ralph we had the money to make the call. When I walked into his cell he looked at me and jumped up and said, "I can tell you have the money by the look on your face."

We sat down and talked about what time we would call his brother. Ralph was going to call him at the restaurant where he worked. "I know he'll be there because he never misses work. I think I'll call at nine o'clock. The breakfast business will be over by then."

If he should be gone from the restaurant, Ralph would leave word for him to call back. We would get the number of the phone. We decided if they would let us we would both go. We went to bed but I was too excited and it was some time before sleep came to me. After we had eaten the same peas, cornbread and molasses, we hoped it was the last of that horrible menu.

When the turnkey came back to pick up the plates, Ralph told him we had the money and wanted to make a phone call.

"Let's see the money," he said. Ralph showed him the money and he said, "What time do you want to call?"

Ralph said, "I can reach the person I want to talk to at about nine o'clock."

"I'll talk to the J.P. and he'll probably send an officer to take you to the phone."

We had two hours to wait and they would not go quickly. At last a police officer came to the barred gate and called our names. We went over and he opened the gate and we walked to the Western Union office.

"The Western Union office at home is only half a block from the restaurant. I'm sure he'll go right over there and send me the money," Ralph said.

When we got in the office the agent pointed to a phone like this happened often. Ralph made the call. He told his brother what had happened quickly and asked him to send him ten dollars and both of us would pay him back. He listened for a few seconds and then told him where to send it by Western Union. He said thanks and hung up. Ralph said, "He told me to stay right here if the officer would let us and he'd send it right away."

The officer said, "We'll wait awhile and while we're waiting I'll give you some advice. If you get out of here, don't go down to the railroad yards. If you're caught again in this town the J.P. will throw the book at you."

After about twenty minutes the agent waved Ralph to come over to the window where he signed his name on some papers and the agent handed him a ten and two ones. The officer took us back to the courthouse and we went in an office. Ralph paid over the ten dollar bill and the man wrote us a receipt, giving him two dollar bills.

"Don't forget what I told you," the officer said.

We walked out on the street. It was great to be able to walk wherever we wanted to. "Let's get this bill changed and we'll go back and give our friend his money back."

We came to the store and went in. We decided to get three packs of cigarettes; they were cheap in the south, only nine cents a pack. We would keep one pack and give two packs and some matches to him for helping us out. We hurried back to the jail. I didn't want him to worry about us not coming back. When we got to the jail we told the officer that we had some money to give to one of the prisoners. He took us down to the cells. When we got there we could see our friend sitting on his bunk in his cell. We walked to the bars and motioned for him to come over. He came over and I gave him the money and the two packs of cigarettes, saying, "We thought you might like a tailor made cigarette once in a while."

He said, "You boys didn't have to do that. I knew you would come back."

We reached through the bars and shook hands with him and we hoped that he would get acquitted or if not that, at least a lenient sentence. We left and when we stopped and looked back, he was still standing at the bars. He waved and we waved back and walked out of the jail.

By this time it was almost noon so we decided to go back to the store and buy some food. We told the manager that we had very little money and would like to buy second day bread and meat ends and anything else he had for ten cents. He told us he didn't have any cold meat ends; bologna was the cheapest thing he had. We took that and asked him to slice it. After he sliced a good quantity of bologna he picked two loaves of round bread. We asked him to slice that too if he could. He took the bread out without tearing the wrapper and sliced the bread.

He got out a large sack and put the bread and meat in it and said, "I got some overripe bananas and apples in the back room you can have."

We said we'd be glad for anything he wanted to give us. He came back with another sack and set it on the counter. We asked if he had a faucet so we could fill our water bottles. He took us in the back room and pointed to a sink and faucet. We filled the jars, went back and Ralph gave him a dollar. He gave him back the ninety cents and we thanked him.

We left and looked for a place to eat our lunch. We found a vacant store which wasn't too hard in these times, sat down on the steps and made some sandwiches and ate some of the fruit. We couldn't believe how good a bologna sandwich and some half-rotten fruit tasted after the meals we had in jail. Ralph said he couldn't believe our friend had had to eat that slop for four months. We hoped his wife brought him food with the tobacco money, and that he got a good deal when his trial came up.

We both agreed that we would always keep one dollar that we wouldn't spend. We wouldn't be without money for a phone call again, on any trips we would make in the future.

Chapter Nine

We had to figure out how we were to get out of the city. Going back to the yard was out. We believed the J.P. would do what the police officer said if we got caught in the city the second time. We had been told about hobos picked up for hitchhiking and we decided we would be safer riding trains until out of the South. We walked until we saw the railroad yards, then down the street parallel to the tracks.

Once outside the city we found an unpaved road that ran about a quarter of a mile from the railroad. We walked a couple miles and the road stayed in sight of the tracks.

There was no use going over to them because the trains would be going so fast we wouldn't be able to catch them. We finally came to a small village. As we walked through it we could see coal docks. Around a dozen hobos sat on a pile of railroad ties waiting for a train to stop for coal and water, but from what direction? We decided to join them. When we got there we asked one if they were waiting for a train going north. He said they'd come from the north and were waiting for one going south. We told him we were heading north. "Sooner of later one will be stopping here for coal and water, so just hang around," he said.

We told him Meridian had a large rail yard and lots of railroad detectives. That they should be careful. We didn't tell them we had been caught there. In about an hour a train from the north stopped and all of them got on. We waited and two more from the north stopped. Finally in the afternoon one came from the south. We ran alongside it looking for a good car and finally found one, but a bunch of hobos were in it. We went on until we found one empty and climbed in. It was clean and fairly new.

Soon the train pulled out and we were on our way out of Meridian, Mississippi. After an hour or so we seemed to be bearing east again. We got our map and decided that the train would be going to Birmingham, Alabama. It was always interesting to watch the small towns we went through; most of the people turned and looked at the train. We would wave at them and some would wave back; all the children waved at us. Before it got dark we ate sandwiches and some fruit. Afterward we took an inventory of our food. The fellow had given us a lot of bologna with two loaves of bread. We decided to eat the fruit for breakfast since it was going fast. We should have food for the next day.

The train didn't go very fast and we thought it would not get to Birmingham until sometime the next day. There was a full moon and it was almost as light as day. We stayed awake and talked about how we were going to get in the paper mill field where we would pound out the lead to pay back Ralph's brother the twelve dollars we owed him.

Finally we went to sleep but I kept waking up because of the noise and the car swaying. I woke up the last time because it was still and the train was stopped. We were on a siding out in the country. We got up and sat in the door and smoked a cigarette, a tailor made. Although we didn't think there would be railroad detectives out here in the country, we decided to stay awake until the train continued on its destination. After awhile we saw a light coming down the side of the train. We decided to get off and not take any chances. We went off about a hundred yards and when the light got to us, we saw by the moonlight it was a brakeman. He would throw the switch when he left. After he passed we went back and got in our car.

We both dozed and were awakened by a passenger train going by. We could see the lighted cars go by through the door of our car. Still our train didn't move. After a time, we decided he was waiting for another train. This proved to be the case and when the freight train swept by we finally moved out of the siding and we went back to sleep.

When we woke, we were still traveling very slowly. All too soon we were on another siding. This train had a lot of empty cars and evidently not much priority on the mainline. We ate some of the fruit for breakfast and threw the rest away because it was rotten. We were stopped along a large cotton field and we watched as the colored people came out of their miserable shacks and started hoeing weeds in the cotton rows. We saw an iron pump about two hundred yards away and agreed that it probably furnished all the water for the people living in the twenty or so shacks.

A supervisor riding a mule rode slowly up and down the huge field checking on the workers. Some looked like they were early teens or maybe younger. As we looked down the train we saw about twenty hobos had got off the train and were sitting on a bank basking in the morning sun.

We were not sure we were out of Mississippi, seeing no signs of being in Alabama. Finally, a freight came through and all the hobos piled back on the train and with a crash of couplers we were moving again. We watched the swamps and the farmland and the people working on them. Most fields grew cotton, but some corn. We saw our second chain gang working on a road, cleaning out the brush alongside of the road. They had four guards, two of them mounted on horses and two on the ground. We estimated about fifty or more prisoners. Ralph said he was glad we didn't have to work on one of the gangs. I heartily agreed with him.

Our train was really a slow poke. It could be dark before we get to Birmingham. At least that was where we thought the train was going.

Late in the afternoon we saw houses closer together and cars on the road and soon we could see tall buildings. We would know soon what city we were arriving in. As the train approached the yards we watched for detectives and as it slowed to a crawl, we saw the hobos on the back of the train getting off. Picking up our bags, we jumped from the moving train and ran for the fence, scrambling through and walking about a hundred yards to a street.

We fell in with the hobos who had been on the train to see if we could pick up some information about finding food and a place to sleep. It seemed two of the men had been there before and knew where a Salvation Army Mission was located. We decided to tag along with them. After a half-a-mile walking we came to the mission. They had food left but all the sleeping spaces were filled. We fell in line for the food and were surprised to receive a bowl of stew, two slices of bread, a donut and a cup of coffee.

While we were eating, one of the hobos said they would allow us to shower if we wanted to. Most of our bunch walked off after eating, but Ralph and I went to find the shower room. When we found it a man who was in charge of the shower gave us a small piece of soap and a towel. There were only a few men in the shower, so we took our time and really enjoyed it.

When we left we felt good; we had a full stomach and we were clean again. We had watched when we walked up to the mission, and we retraced our steps to the railroad yards. After a short distance, although we were going in the general direction we wanted to go, we realized this was not the way we had come. The night was very warm and we enjoyed walking and looking into the store windows and at the people along the street. We decided we would ask someone if they knew another mission where we might find a place to sleep.

We came to a pool room where several men were standing around talking, and Ralph asked one if he knew a mission where we could sleep. "There's a large Salvation Army Mission back the way you came," he said.

We told him we had been there and it was full. One of the other men spoke, "There's a church mission about a quarter of a mile from here. It might be full too, but you might try it." We said we would and he gave us directions.

We thanked them and started off to the mission. We found if off a small street in a very old building. We rang the bell and a young man opened the door. "We're looking for a place to sleep for the night," Ralph said.

The minister replied, "Come in. We have a few more places to fill." He led us to the shower room and handed us a piece of soap. I told him we had already showered but he said, "This is one of our rules. If you don't shower, you can't sleep here."

Ralph and I looked at each other; then we took the towel and soap and went to the shower room. As we soaped again, Ralph said, "We're going to be so clean and smell so good, we could probably sleep in the train station tonight."

When we turned in our towels to the minister he said, "Supper is over, but I could get you some cornbread we have leftover, some jelly and some coffee."

We never turned down food, even though we had eaten about three hours previously. If they didn't serve breakfast, and if they did it would probably be coffee and donuts, we might as well accept what was offered. He brought a large plate of cornbread, half a jar of grape jelly and a cup of coffee. We weren't hungry but we ate a large portion until we were really full. He kept urging us to eat more. We finally thanked him and assured him we were no longer hungry.

He showed us our cots and we undressed and laid down using our clothes for a pillow. We'd been warned by hobos that the people sleeping in these rooms may steal your clothes.

Ralph groaned, "I'm so full I don't think I can go to sleep."

We were awakened by a bell and everybody got up and started for the room where we had eaten the cornbread. A line formed and when we got to the server, we saw they were giving two donuts and a cup of coffee. This was very good for us. We could walk on down to the yards without having to find something to eat.

When we left the building, two hobos came out with us. We asked one of them if he knew how to get to the train yards. "Come on," he said, "that's where we're going and we've been here before."

One was from Chicago, although he had no home now. The other was from Virginia and had been on the road for almost two years. These men had been all over the United States looking for work, and had found only day jobs and according to them, not very many of them. They were going east and we had to have a train going to the north.

When we got to the yards, one hobo said, "If you have to have a particular train, you'll have to ask a brakeman or an engineer. While you're searching for a train, keep an eye out for the detective. If you see only one run for the yard fence and get on the other side. They only have authority on railroad property and they probably won't chase you. If he follows you to the fence, take off anywhere running."

They left to find an eastbound train. After looking around carefully we went into the yard, which was large with many trains being made up. We saw a switchman and ran to him and asked if he knew a train that was going north. He said the train a couple of tracks over was going north in about an hour.

"They'll check the cars before the train leaves, so I wouldn't get on it now," he said. "Go to where the fence ends and catch it when it comes out of the yard. It won't be going too fast since it's fully loaded and heavy."

We went to the end of the fence and joined about fifty hobos waiting to get on a train. We saw two or three trains come out and most of the hobos caught them and were gone. When we saw our train starting to roll, we were going to catch the first cars back of the engine. If we tried to pick out a car when the train was picking up speed, it might be going to fast to get on if we hesitated.

When the engine passed, Ralph got the first car and I got the second one. When we were on top of the train we started to the back of the train to get away from the sparks, hot cinders, and smoke. It was a nice day and we didn't mind riding on top.

We knew that in two or three hours he would have to stop somewhere for coal and water. We hoped it would be a small town and we could get off to check the cars for a better place to ride. In an hour or so we went on a siding, so we got off and walked down the train but all the cars were sealed. When we started back we saw a switch engine come in with a few cars to add to our train. One of them had a side about four feet high and we couldn't see what was in it or if it was empty. After it was hooked to our train, we quickly climbed the ladder and looked. It was empty. We climbed in, and standing in it we saw the other hobos running to get in this car. When they all piled in there were about twenty or so sitting on the floor and leaning against the sides. Now that we were out of the wind everybody rolled cigarettes and lit up. Then the talk started. Trains were reridden, places revisited, accidents described, jails discussed, where to get food and lodging in different cities.

There was always one who regaled us with a tale of walking up an alley and going to a back door and asking for food. As he told it, the woman asked him in the house and after she prepared him a delicious meal, led him to the bedroom where he had a wild sexual afternoon. We heard this story often when we were in a group of hobos relating their different experiences. If there stories were true, then America was full of sex-starved married women.

I looked closer at the hobo Romeo. He had two or three days growth of beard and dirt in the wrinkles of his face. His clothes were dirty; his pants held up with a piece of rope. When he finished the story, he looked every one of us right in the eye as if to say, "This is the truth. You must believe me."

Ralph and I took it all in; these hobos had really been around a lot of the United States. Some had even been in Mexico and Canada. Most of them thought we were going either to Chattanooga or Nashville. We hoped it would be Nashville; the other city would take us out of our way. The only problem with that was it would be a long trip and we had had only the donuts and coffee that morning. We were glad we had eaten the cornbread. If the train was going to Nashville it was a long way and we may have to get off and get some food.

After all the stories had been told, some lay down and went to sleep. Ralph and I stood and leaned our elbows on top of the side and watched the scenery. Because we had never been very far from home, we never tired of watching people in the fields and in the small towns, or the large bridges we had crossed at rivers and lakes. It was always interesting to us.

In the middle of the afternoon some hobos talked about getting off to look for food when the train stopped for coal and water if there was a town or city close by. We were getting hungry also, but we didn't want to get stuck in some small town. This didn't seem to bother any of the other hobos. A short time later, we stopped at a coal docks and could see a small town not too far away.

Everybody got off but Ralph and me, and two of the hobos and started walking down the railroad tracks to the city. I asked one of the men if he was hungry. He said, "A little, but this train will have to stop again in about four or five hours for coal and we may get off there if it's close to or in a city."

One of the men had a dollar watch which was rare since most hobos didn't seem to care what time it was.

Later on about four o'clock by the dollar watch, the train began to slow and backed into a long siding by a huge paper mill. We seemed to be on the edge of a small city. The brakeman who had thrown the switch walked down the train. When he came to our car, one of the men asked him how long the train would be there.

He stopped and replied, "They're going to unload several cars of Kraft for the mill. They'll have a crew ready and will likely take about two hours."

The four of us decided to walk into the little city and get something to eat. Ralph and I agreed that if we could find a store we would buy some food. Going up alleys, looking for handouts seemed risky in a small town. When we got to the city the men turned off to go to a poorer section of town, and we walked into the business area. We located a store that was part grocery and part restaurant with a counter and couple of tables.

Ralph always did the bargaining for he was much better than I was. He took out a quarter and held it up. "Do you want to spend a quarter?"

"Go ahead and get as much as you can." There were only two people at the counter but we stayed in the grocery section. The man came over and Ralph said, "We've not eaten since morning, and we have a long ways to go."

The man said, "What do you have in mind?"

"We need some sliced meat and bread anything else that's cheap and plentiful."

The man went back of the meat counter and sliced some cold meat. Ralph said, "Your second day bread will do if you have any."

He got out a large paper sack and put the meat in it and two loaves of bread. He got out cheese and cut off a large chunk and wrapped it in butcher paper. He took the sack, went to the restaurant side and back into the kitchen. When he came out he said there was some chicken in there, some baked beans and sweet potatoes. Ralph gave him the quarter and we asked him to fill our water jars.

"You want one filled with coffee?" he asked.

"Yes, we would,": Ralph said and we thanked him.

We were really hungry but we decided to go back to the train and eat in case it left early. When we returned to the train, we sat down on a bank and looked through the sack. We had made out very well. There were six pieces of chicken, a glassine sack of beans, six large sweet potatoes, and ham instead of bologna. If we were lucky, this might last us until we arrived home, at least until we got out of the South. After we ate we rolled a cigarette and had it with our coffee.

The men were unloading the Kraft paper at the paper mill. Quite a few men were working and we didn't think we would be here much longer. We saw our two friends coming down the track. We debated whether, if they hadn't found food, we would share with them. We decided we would give them some but wouldn't let them control the sack.

When they came and sat down with us, I asked, "Did you both find food?"

"Oh yes," one said. "We found a house and the lady said she had been wanting to clean out her ice box. We had some meat loaf, roasted chicken, potato soup that she warmed for us, rice, bread and jelly. We won't feel like eating for a week."

The brakeman was heading toward the switch and we heard the workers slamming the boxcar door shut. The four of us decided it looked like it might rain so we walked down to the empty boxcars and opened the doors and crawled in. In a few minutes the couplings banged and we were moving again. I asked the two men, "Which city do you think we're going to?"

"If we don't get into Chattanooga in a couple of hours, then we're going to Nashville."

"Do you think we'll get in there while it's still dark?"

"I think it'll be daylight when we get in there, and there are officers in the yard at night checking cars and the seals."

We asked them about hobos stealing from the railroad cars. "There's some stealing by hobos, but most of it was people getting on the train and throwing the merchandise off to people waiting along the track. In other words, working as a gang."

"Did you ever get caught by detectives?"

"Yes, I have, but not down here in the South. We were caught at the California border, but they only held us for a few hours then took us back to the border and told us not to come back. California was where all the homeless wanted to go. Even the police would stop you at the border. If you were hitchhiking, they would turn you back."

We told them about being in jail in Mississippi and how we got out.

"You're lucky you had a prisoner who had money and would agree to lend you all the money he had. Otherwise, you'd right now be out on one of them chain gangs you see once in while riding along. Georgia chain gangs are the ones talked about, but Mississippi is worse than Georgia, although none of the southern states will treat you very well. You see how they treat the blacks down here in the South. A white man with no money or place to stay is considered white trash and is treated no better than blacks."

"Have you ever rode the rods on a train?" I had heard about hobos riding the rods, putting a board across the brake rods and riding underneath the cars.

"We've never seen anybody doing that."

I said, "I've never seen that either. I've heard hobos talk about it but it would be very dangerous. Also if the train was going fast it would pick up cinders from the road bed which would be very uncomfortable."

"I would never try it," he said and pulled out his dollar watch to look at. "We're almost certain that we're going to Nashville."

"We hope you're right," I said. "That's the best route for us."

"You're going to have to watch it in Nashville. You'll have to get some information to find a train going north. Coming out of the yards they all go in one direction, but when they go a distance you may find yourself going south or east or west."

"How do you two find out where the trains are going?"

"Well, with us, we don't care," he said. "We have no special place to go."

This made me rather sad. Ralph and I enjoyed riding the trains and seeing large cities and different people and the countryside. If we had to do this for even a couple of months, I would be upset. When I talked to people who had been riding back and forth on these trains for years, everyday trying to find food and clothes just to stay alive, it saddened me to think about the millions of men in this situation. That you could take any train that came along because you had no home to go to, that unless you had a buddy, nobody cared if you were sick or hurt. Years wasted of your life and no end in sight. I decided I would go to sleep and try not to think about it.

When I awoke it was barely light and the train was slowing. I got up and looked out the door. We were coming into a large city. I woke Ralph and asked it he thought I should wake the other two. He thought I should so I shook them and said, "We're coming into a large city. It could be Nashville."

We all stood in the door and looked out. We now had other tracks running along beside us; we must be nearly into the yards. One of our friends said, "I can see the yard fence. We should get off here pretty soon."

The train was going too fast to jump out of the car door. We were inside the fence and still the train didn't slow.

"We're going to have to run for the fence, when he slows a little more. Follow us. Don't waste time going over the trains that will be between you and the fence, just follow us and go underneath the cars."

We had never done that as it seemed dangerous to us, but they evidently had done it before. We were almost in the center of that large railroad yard when the train slowed further.

The hobo shouted, "Let's go" and we all jumped out and ran. When they went under cars, we were right behind them and finally through the last one and running for the fence. When we reached it, we ran along the inside until we found a hole and went through it like rabbits. We trotted down the street until we were a couple of blocks from the railroad. We stopped and talked with them for a few minutes. They said they were going to find some food, and also a pair of shoes. One of them raised his foot and showed us a hole in the sole about the size of a half dollar. We told them we hoped they found food and shoes. We all shook hands and left them walking toward the city and we followed the railroad.

The yard had about fifteen or more tracks and sidings. To find a train going north we would have to go down in the yard among the trains. We walked along the tracks numbered only seven or eight. There were four trains that had steam up and one had an engineer in the cab. Another was on the ground. We looked for detectives but saw only a couple of brakemen. We ran down, climbed over two trains, and over to the engineer on the ground. He looked up as we approached. "Hi," I said. "Is this train going north out of here?"

"No," he said. "We're going to Chattanooga and on to Atlanta."

We climbed over a train and asked the engineer in the cab if he was going north. He said he was taking the train to Evansville, Indiana and we could get off there. The train would continue to St. Louis, Missouri.

"We'll ride it to Evansville," I said.

"This train is going to be checked by detectives. It'd be better for you to catch it as we emerge from the yards," he warned us.

We walked to the end of the fence and joined a crowd of about fifty or sixty hobos. We kept a watch on our train and we didn't think it would be too long. Finally, we saw the detectives looking at the cars and we walked to the track it would be coming on. When the train started it seemed to me it was picking up speed pretty fast. I said, "Do you think we can catch this train? He's coming pretty fast. You try to catch the first car; I'll try the second. If one of us can't get on, then drop off so we'll be together."

About ten or twelve hobos were down there to get on too. When the engine was close, we began running along the track in the same direction. When it passed me, I grabbed at the iron ladder and was jerked off my feet, but I found the bottom rung and looked to see if Ralph had gotten on. He was on and waved to me. I looked toward the back of the train and all the hobos had gotten on. We climbed on top and walked to the rear of the train until out of the smoke and cinders from the engine.

This train was going fast; I guessed about sixty miles an hour. We got our sack of food and ate a ham sandwich and a sweet potato.

After we had eaten we climbed in between the cars to get out of the wind, rolled a cigarette, and drank the cold coffee. It was very pleasant on the cars but we knew it would be hot later on. About an hour later the engineer pulled onto a siding at a town called Springfield. We and the other hobos got off to look for better riding conditions, but all the cars were full and locked. We saw the hobos waving to come on; they had found an empty. We hurried down and climbed in the car. One of them told us it was the only empty in the train. We thanked him and looked around at the men. I counted thirteen, an unlucky number, but if we got to Indiana it would be good luck for us.

Soon a freight train went roaring by and in a few minutes we pulled out on the mainline. I examined our companions a little closer. I saw one of them was a teenager like us. After watching a while, I believed it to be a woman. She stayed close to one person, talking mostly to him. I thought they were traveling together. I couldn't see her hair because of her large cap. Her shapeless pants, shirt, and coat didn't reveal anything identifying. I whispered to Ralph what I thought. After studying the person for several minutes, he nodded yes. We had heard of women hobos but this was the first we had ever seen one. Her features were too delicate to be a boy's, her eyebrows and lips too perfectly shaped. Ralph and I seldom shaved but we did have some facial hairs. This person didn't have any.

Every year in Britt, Iowa, the hobos had a convention or reunion where they elected a king and queen of the hobos. They made lots of hobo stew and everybody told tales about their adventures and their victories. Friends were reunited and everybody had a fine time. The people living in Britt thought the hobo convention was great and encouraged them to come back each year.

We never tired of looking out the doors at the countryside and small towns we passed through, the large cities we walked through, the shops and fine stores unlike any in our small Midwest town.

The people at the other end laughed and I finally walked down to see what was going on. One of the men had a small, grey pet mouse and he was feeding it bread crumbs. It had a tiny thin leather collar on it. He held his hand down by it and it would leap on his hand and run up his arm to his shoulder and look around at the hobos like he was waiting for applause.

I asked him if he wasn't afraid it would run off when he was asleep.

"No," he replied. "This is a hobo mouse and stays where the food is."

Noon came and I asked Ralph if we should eat our food in front of the others. Ralph thought we better wait because we didn't have enough for everybody. I agreed, knowing I couldn't sit there and eat with everybody watching us, especially when they were probably as hungry as we were.

We talked to a man about thirty years old who had gone to California to try and find work. The train had stopped at the border and all were not allowed to enter California. He waited around until dark; then he and some others went out to the fields and walked into California. He made his way down to Los Angeles but there were no jobs.

He said, "Shack towns were all around in the cities there. Not jungles, but shacks full of families from all over the country. Everybody was looking for work. I didn't stay long, too much competition for any jobs that would be there."

The man and the one we thought was a women moved out by themselves and he pulled a sack out of his pocket and handed it to her. She took out a sandwich and broke it in two and gave half to him. He pushed her hand back; she offered again but he refused and she ate the sandwich. I was sure now that she was a woman, very likely his woman.

The train slowed and then stopped at a coal dock to take on water and coal. Everybody got off but Ralph and me, and the pair we thought were together.

Ralph said, "This is a good time to eat a little something." Neither of them looked at us as were eating. If they had we would have offered the man something, but they looked away.

The hobos came straggling back and climbed in the car. A few minutes later the train was moving again. Late in the afternoon, the train pulled into a siding in a small city and the other hobos got off, probably to enter it and look for food. We decided to stay; we had food and we wanted to stay on this train. All were off except the two. He jumped down from the car and she knelt. He reached up under her arms and pulled her out and to her feet. We knew then she was a woman.

Soon we jumped off the train and walked around, figuring we needed a train going in the other direction. After a few hours a couple of trains had passed but we were still sitting. The engine was still there so they we're going to leave the cars there. A short time later an engine came alongside us and stopped. A brakeman separated our engine and it slowly pulled out on the main track and left. The other engine pulled down to the head of the train, backed into the siding, and hitched onto our train. A few minutes and we were moving out on the main track. We had the car to ourselves; none of the others had returned to this train. Maybe they found food and shelter. We hoped so. When we arrived in Evansville, we would have escaped the unfriendly South and if we got caught by the railroad detectives, at least we wouldn't be put on a chain gang. We had no idea when we would get to Evansville, so we decided to stay awake to make sure we didn't get taken to St. Louis, if that's where it was continuing on to.

We saw few people as we went through the small towns or cities until finally we saw no one; we assumed everybody was asleep. It had to be around midnight. We were so sleepy we could hardly keep our eyes open and feel asleep, only to be awakened by lights flashing in the car. Looking out, we saw a railroad yard. The train slowed and we jumped out and ran across the tracks, over cars and out of the yard, down the fence until we found that hole which was always there. We walked in a field alongside the fence until it ended.

We thought we saw a street across the other side of the tracks and crossed over. It looked like the outskirts of the city. We moved down the street to some street lights and the houses were close together. We could see some buildings so we went in that direction, coming into the business part of the city. It was deserted.

Two policemen stood talking to each other about a half-block away. I said to Ralph, "We're back in the North. Do you want to take a chance and ask them to let us sleep in the jail?"

"I hate to take a chance that they might throw us in for vagrancy if they had some work to do. It's a real warm night. Maybe we should just sleep on the grass." I agreed. He said, "The sun will wake us early so we can get an early start and make it home tomorrow."

We avoided the two police officers and walked around for a good place to sleep on the grass. We found it alongside a bank and lay down on the ground. We talked awhile, deciding we would hitchhike from there. Catching a train to our town would almost be impossible.

We woke up wet with dew just before daylight. We asked an early riser what highway would we take to Indianapolis. He told us the number and how to get to it. We sat on a bus bench and ate more of our food, leaving enough to eat at noon.

We came out on the highway at a bad place. There were no stop signs or lights to slow traffic. The traffic was mostly trucks going too fast to stop for us. Finally, a large truck hit his brakes and stopped about a hundred feet away. We ran and asked him where he was going. He said Indianapolis and asked where we were headed. Ralph said we were going in his direction. We climbed in the cab and he started at a good speed.

He said, "I've been driving since ten o'clock last night and I want you two to talk and keep me awake."

"What do you want to talk about?"

"You might start by telling me what you're going to do when you get to Indianapolis."

"We're not going to stay in Indianapolis. We're going on north to our home. We've been to New Orleans," Ralph said. The driver wanted to hear more about New Orleans, so we told him how we got there and how beautiful, strange and exotic a city it was.

After we had traveled about two hours, he said, "We're going to stop for coffee. Keep an eye out for a roadside restaurant."

A few minutes later we saw a roadside diner with room to park the truck. Inside, the driver ordered coffee for all of us. He said he was going to sleep for twenty hours when he got to Indianapolis.

"About what time will we get in there?" Ralph asked.

"I think we can make it by two o'clock."

He would have been driving sixteen hours if he made his schedule. We were out of tobacco so he furnished cigarettes also. When we got back in the truck, he said, "Start up the story." We both continued talking, telling him to say something once in a while so we would know he was awake. Traffic was heavier and we were slowed a little. Suddenly, Ralph was pounding our driver's shoulder, as he told us to do if he closed his eyes. It was almost noon so I suggested we find a place where he could get some more coffee. He told us to look for another roadside diner.

The one we found had two trucks parked at it. "I've heard that a restaurant that has a lot of truck driver business has good food," I said.

"More likely it has a good looking waitress," he replied.

When we sat down at the counter he said, "I'm buying. Order anything you want." We protested, saying that we had money to buy our dinner. He would have none of it, and said, "Forget it, I'm buying."

We ordered quickly for we knew he didn't want to spend too much time off the road. After eating, we had coffee. The truck driver had two cups and asked it we had ever been in Indianapolis. Neither of us had but we didn't think very many of our class in school had been there either. We got back in the truck and got the driver to sing with us to help keep him awake. Traffic became heavier and we began to identify different makes of cars. At that time, there must have been hundreds of car manufacturers. We passed the city limit sign and were in the capital of our state. The truck driver was going to take us out to the highway going north to our town. He said he wouldn't go to sleep now that he was in the city. He stopped and we all got out and shook hands, wishing each other good luck.

When he climbed into the cab, we yelled at him, "Don't go to sleep until you get home!" He grinned and waved.

We had it made, only seventy miles to go. We got a ride all the way to Muncie, only eighteen miles to go. We got a ride all the way to our town. The driver let Ralph out a block from his house. "I'll see you tomorrow and we'll go out and look at the field where the lead is," was Ralph's good-by to me.

When I walked in my house my mother exclaimed, "Well, look who's here!" She gave me a big hug and kiss. It was great to be home. I hoped I never had to be a full time hobo and felt great sympathy for all those without home or family. I couldn't believe how soft the bed was, how delicious the food my mother prepared.

Most of the evening was spent answering questions everyone asked. I told them about the large cities I had seen, the fabulous city of New Orleans and the people who lived there, of different languages I had heard spoken, the musicians and the street plays in the French Quarter, tales we had heard from the hobos we had ridden with.

There were people in town who owned a radio, but we didn't have one at that time. Every night after supper it was question and answer night for about a week. Even some of the neighbors and kids came over to ask questions about everything from railroads to cities.

Chapter Ten

The next day Ralph and I walked to the paper mill. We were afraid that they may have cut the weeds but were elated to see they were higher than before we left. We figured we could crawl through the weeds and not be seen working. Tomorrow we would start.

The next day we gathered our sacks and hammers and walked to the mill. We waited until the change of shift when everybody was either coming out or going into the mill. When they started coming out we bent over and waded into the weeds. In five minutes we were hard at work hammering out the lead. In a couple of hours we had our bags full and retreated through the weeds out to the road. When we took the lead to the junk dealer, he was surprised to see us and asked us what we had in the bags.

"Same stuff," Ralph said. "Can't you do a little better on the price?"

"Well," the man relented, "Lead has went up a little but, how does four and half cents sound to you?"

"How about making it a nickel?" Ralph asked.

"Oh, I couldn't do that!" he said.

"How about splitting the difference and making it four-and-three quarters."

"You boys are pretty good. I guess I could do that." He paid us two dollars and twenty-eight cents.

We discussed how we would pay his brother, whether to wait until we had the full twelve dollars or pay him every time we sold lead. I said I thought it was too big a temptation to spend part of it. I said, "Let's go to the restaurant and pay him two dollars right now."

"You're right. We might spend it. Let's go pay him how. He probably thinks the chance of getting his twelve dollars back is very poor anyway," Ralph said.

His brother was behind the counter. He called to the other counterman, "Hey, you think these hobos have come in to get food?" Everybody laughed.

We sat down at the counter and Ralph got out the two dollars and handed it to his brother. "There's part of what we owe you. We'll get the rest in a few days."

His brother seemed surprised. Here we had been home only three days and we had come up with quite a sum for two unemployed teenagers. He left and came back with two cups of coffee and pulled his cigarettes out of his shirt pocket, laying them between us. I guess Ralph had told him we were smoking. The two men questioned us about our trip while we drank the coffee. When we had finished we went to the pool room to see some of our friends. When we left we made plans to go the next morning to the mill.

It took us a week of work to pay back his brother. When we paid the last two dollars we thanked him and he said, "If you get in trouble again, call me." We went back to the mill one more time to get a little spending money, then decided we wouldn't push our luck any further.

The money was gone in a few days so we planned to go back to the mill. When we got there we were stunned. The weeds were cut down and piled into two large stacks. Probably for cattle feed. Our easy money was over until the weeds grew back, probably next summer.

We started washing cars when we could and mowing lawns. A car wash also included cleaning the inside of the car, sweeping the floor, and wiping the dust off with a damp cloth. We usually got a quarter. For a big lawn, we got thirty-five cents, twenty-five for a small place. This lawn mowing included trimming around the house and walks. The women of the house inspected everything before we were paid.

Labor Day rolled around and we were back in school. I had played basketball for the high school the last two years and was looking forward to playing my last year. I gave up smoking. Most people seeing me smoke would have notified the coach, and I probably would have been dismissed from the team. Everybody on the team had to be home by nine o'clock. This would also be reported if we were seen out after nine.

People in Indiana in those days took their basketball very seriously. How seriously? In those dark financial days, it was proposed that a new field house he built. It would seat 4,600 people. The total population of the city was not much more than that. The cost was over a hundred thousand dollars, a lot of money in those depression times. It would be ready for us to play in my senior year.

Playing basketball took up a lot of my time. I went to school until four o'clock in the afternoon and then practice until six. The walk home was another twenty minutes. The family had all eaten and my mother kept my food warm for me. I was usually in bed by nine o'clock. The season extended through the month of March. In that month, a play-off of all 850 high schools was played — 64 sectionals, 16 regionals, which produced the "Sweet Sixteen," that played before 16,000 or 17,000 fans at the Butler University field house in Indianapolis for the championship.

"Hoosier Madness" was what they called it. Whole cities closed up, stores closed, leaving the deserted city only a skeleton crew of police and firefighters, clustered around a radio listening to the ball game. We won our sectional, but lost in the regional. I was hoping to get a basketball scholarship to college next year if things got a little better.

Chapter Eleven

In September my mother received a telegram from Mayo Brothers Clinic saying her brother Bill was not expected to live. We had visited Uncle Bill when I was about twelve years old. He was a veteran of World War I. There was land in the West that could be homesteaded by anyone staking out 320 acres of government land. A veteran of World War I could stake out 640 or one square mile of land. Certain improvements had to be done on the land in five years to get the title to it.

Bill lived 52 miles from Miles City, Montana. This was primitive country. When we had visited him in 1925, he had shown me the cave he lived in for two years. The cave had a wooden frame with several layers of gunny sacks hanging in it for a door. Some people say that Montana has a summer. It's called July. The rest of the year was winter, 20 to 30 degrees below was common in winter months. He built a barn and a corral first and then a five-room log house with a clay roof. He mined coal from a seam and cut the fence posts, fencing in his land with barbed wire.

He brought his mother and father out and they took up 320 areas. It was a very harsh land and most settlers gave up and went back East. When he had a little cash he bought up this land, some for as little as ten cents an acre, and when we were there he had accumulated about 9,000 acres.

When my mother got the telegram, she went by train to Rochester, Minnesota to the Mayo Clinic. Bill had a goiter operation, a serious operation in those days. He was also operated on for stomach cancer. My mother stayed with him for seven weeks. Bill not only survived but got better. My mother brought him to our house. We went to the train station to meet him.

When they got off the train, I couldn't believe this was the same man I had seen four years ago. His clothes hung on him like they were two sizes too large. We had fixed up a room for him. A few weeks of my mother's cooking and he gained weight and began to look more like his old self. He had to sell the land to pay for medical bills at Mayos. He wouldn't have been able to do the work on the ranch anyway.

Uncle Bill found a small apartment and moved out of our house. We all hated to see him go, but he explained he was going into business and would be coming and going at odd hours. I wondered what kind of business, because he wasn't physically able to do any manual labor and he had very little education for an office job. Before long Ralph told me Uncle Bill was selling whiskey. He was a bootlegger in that Prohibition Era.

He soon bought a new Chevrolet and seemed to be doing very well. Bill was friendly with a very likable personality. He could do very well if he didn't get arrested. It wasn't too long until Bill and his friend T.L. bought a house about three miles out of town. They put sofas and armchairs all through the house and set up a bar in the kitchen. The barn lot was turned into a parking lot. It was very successful. They served free pretzels with the drinks; the customers named it the Pretzel Farm.

I used to go squirrel hunting in that area and go to the back door. They always let me in the kitchen where they gave me a coke. I could hear the crowd talking and laughing in the other rooms, but I was forbidden to leave the kitchen.

On Saturday afternoon the barn lot would be almost full and I imagined it was like that at night. The house was isolated so they could make as much noise as they wished. Even in those hard times the liquor business was very good. The place was raided but no liquor was ever found.

Finally, it was made plain to Bill and his partner that one of them was going to have to serve some time. Bill's partner had a family while Bill was a bachelor so he volunteered to go. He said it would be good for him to get a rest after all those nights working until daylight. He was given a year at the state prison at Michigan City, Indiana. The Pretzel Farm would stay open and Bill's share deposited into his bank account.

I graduated from high school. Ralph and I started looking for a job. It was useless. Who would hire an inexperienced 18 year old when there were plenty of experienced men they could choose from? We went back to the lead mine but soon it was all gone. We then mowed yards and washed cars.

One day Bill's partner, T.L., came to our house and said he was going to the prison, would I like to go and see my Uncle Bill? I said I would and asked when he was going.

"I'll pick you up tomorrow at 7 a.m.," he said.

"I'll be ready," I said.

My mother wanted to send Bill something. I suggested some chocolate fudge, since he always liked that when he had lived with us. She got out the pans and the ingredients and said, "I'll make it right now and you go see if you can find a cardboard box to put it in."

Next morning T.L. was right on time and I saw he was driving Uncle Bill's Chevrolet coupe. When we started he asked me what I had in the cardboard box. I told him Mom had made chocolate fudge for Bill. We rode along for a few minutes and T.L. finally said, "I don't think they'll let you give that to him."

"Why not?" I asked.

"Because you don't get any sugar when you're in prison."

"You mean not any sugar on your oatmeal, in your coffee, or food like that."

"No sugar is allowed to the prisoners."

"Why?" I persisted. "Sugar doesn't cost much."

"Well, it's part of the punishment for breaking the law. But saccharine is smuggled in and you can buy or trade something for it. Then just a pinch will sweeten anything because it's 30 to 40 times sweeter than sugar."

He told me Uncle Bill wasn't up to doing manual work, so he cleaned the dormitory where he and about thirty prisoners were kept. He swept and mopped the floor, washed the windows. "He said he can do all his work in about two hours and has the rest of the time to read, sleep, talk to the guards, or anything he can do in the dormitory."

"Has Uncle Bill got any saccharin?" I asked.

"Last time I asked him he said he had a quarter of a pound. That's enough to last him until he gets out. He has a lot of time so he's running a baseball pool."

The prisoners bet on the games and Bill took a percentage for handling the bets, seeing that the winners get their bets. I wanted to know what they bet if they had no money. T.L. explained that each prisoner was allowed to have a relative or friend bring in a toothbrush and five handkerchiefs every month.

"Some of the prisoners carved the toothbrush handles into intricate statues and traded these for handkerchiefs or saccharin. All three of these things are used to bet on the baseball pool that Bill runs. That's where he got the quarter pound of saccharin. When I was here a month ago, he gave me fifty new handkerchiefs and said he had a hundred left."

I asked how often T.L. visited Uncle Bill and he told me every two weeks. I would find out later why he came so often.

When we got to the prison, T.L. went to the office of the captain of the guard. They shook hands and I could see that they knew each other pretty well. T.L. introduced me to the captain and asked if it was my first time visiting the jail to see my uncle. I told him yes it was and I'd be really glad to see him.

T.L. said, "How about taking Harry for a tour of the prison?"

"I think I can arrange that," the captain of the guards said and picked up the phone to ask for a guard to escort us around. When the guard came, T.L. knew him too. How did he get acquainted with all these people? I began to think maybe he was spending a little of his money or, more likely, some of his stock in the business.

We had left the candy in the car. T.L. said he would see what he could do. We walked along the cells and then went to the machine shop where the prisoners were making license plates for cars. We toured the kitchen and bakery where the guard pointed out the leader of the Ku Klux Klan in Indiana who was serving a life sentence for murdering a woman. He was working as a baker.

The we saw the execution chamber where the guard asked if I would like to sit in the electric chair. "No, I don't think so," I replied.

"Well, you can sit in it and get up out of it and walk away, something most of them who sit in it can't do."

"I know, but I don't think so."

They both laughed. "Well, let's go see your Uncle Bill," one said and we went to the visitors room.

When they brought Uncle Bill out he looked really good. He had gained weight and seemed to be in very good health. He asked about everyone in our family and people he knew. After we talked, T.L. and he talked about the business and soon it was time to leave. T.L. talked to the guard and told him I had brought a box of candy out in the car for my uncle and wondered if he could give it to Bill. The guard walked out to the car and took the box. He said, "I think I can get it to him."

"I'll stop by the house next time I come up," T.L. said.

"Do that," the guard said, "maybe we might have a drink together." Again, I thought T.L. was giving whiskey to the guards.

When we left, we didn't go back the same way we came. I asked about this and T.L. told me we were making a little side trip to Chicago before we started back.

Chicago wasn't far from Michigan City where the penitentiary was located. When we arrived in the city we went through a section with a lot of warehouses. T.L. turned into the yard of a warehouse and stopped the car. Two men came out and T.L. rolled down the window so they could see him. They looked in and called T.L. by name and asked who I was.

T.L. said, "I took him up to see his uncle over at Michigan City. You know, my partner."

"Oh yes," the man replied and turned to the other man. "Go open the door so he can drive in."

Once inside I could see about two-thirds of the warehouse was divided from the part we were in. We drove up where four men were standing. When we got out they all looked at me. T.L. took me over and introduced me to them. I was impressed when they treated me like an equal instead of a teenager. Two of them took T.L. aside and they talked for a few minutes, then T.L. came back where I was.

One of the men called the two who had let us through a door into the other part of the warehouse. In a few minutes the two men returned pushing a cart stacked high with one-gallon cans. T.L. opened the trunk. A portion of the back of the trunk had been cut out, leaving a larger space in the trunk of the car.

One of the men said, "Are you sure you can get 250 gallons in there?"

"I've done it before," T.L. said.

It finally dawned on me that whiskey was in the gallon cans. I found out later it was pure alcohol. I looked at these four men a little differently. Expensive suits, white felt hats, olive complexions, brown eyes, big cigars, just like the gangsters I saw in the movies. The 250 gallons were fitted precisely in the trunk, handshakes went all around, then we got in the car. The door went up and we drove out.

"I didn't see you pay them," I commented.

"Oh yes. I gave him the envelope while you were talking with the other men," he said. Then he added, "Don't tell anybody about any of this. It might get me in trouble."

I promised I wouldn't. I didn't think anybody in our town would believe me, except Ralph, and I was going to tell him anyway. Before we had done far, T.L. reached over and opened the glove compartment and pulled out a large hand gun and laid it on the seat between us. I looked at the gun and then at him. "What's this for?" I asked.

"Bill and I have been dealing with this bunch for a long time and I don't think they'd hijack us, but there are other people in that part of town, who if they saw us come out of that warehouse, might try to take the alcohol from us."

I would be glad when we got away from Chicago.

Chapter Twelve

The Depression continued to deepen, if that were possible. We heard a rumor that an airplane company bought the closed glass factory and would manufacture small planes. We hurried out but were depressed when we found about 300 men already waiting. We waited outside off and on for a couple of days until an official from the glass factory proclaimed in the local paper that there was to be no plane company. We spent a lot of time outside the two paper mills and one glass factory. Many men waiting there were once employed by them. If they were to hire someone it would be one of these. They wouldn't have to train them so inexperienced help didn't have much of a chance of getting hired. Washing cars, mowing lawns and caddying at the golf course made us a little money.

With good time off, Uncle Bill was getting out of prison. T.L. went up and got him. He stayed with us a few days until he found a place. He really looked great and claimed he never felt better. Other businesses were worse and, of course, were closing their doors for good. I think I knew one reason for the success of the Pretzel Farm. Times were so hard that many people went out there to drink and laugh and dance and forget their problems.

A friend down the street had his electricity cut off. Unemployed, he couldn't pay the bill. He ran a line from the pole into his house and marshaled young kids in the neighborhood to watch for the electric company and run to warn him in time to get up the pole and take down the wire. The company men probably knew what he was doing and took their time so he could get the wire down before they got there. They didn't want to catch him.

One of my friends sent in a dollar to a necktie company and they sent him two dozen neckties. The neckties sold for twenty-five cents. After he sold all of them, he was to send the company two dollars and he would have a profit of three dollars. Then they would send him two dozen more neckties.

He carried this box everywhere he went, showing them to anybody who would look at them. People handled them, tried them on, but nobody bought any. After a few weeks I asked how he was doing. He said he was going to quit, for me to come with him and he'd show me what he was going to do.

We went to a drugstore with a soda fountain. We sat down and my friend said to the owner, "I'll trade two ties for two large cherry cokes."

"Let's see the ties," the owner said. He picked out two ties and made the cokes and sat them down in front of us.

"That's how I'm going to get rid of them," my friend said.

"But what about the two dollars you're supposed to send the tie company?"

"The hell with them. Nobody could sell them for a quarter when you can buy a good meal for that."

Just another failed business in the Depression.

Chapter Thirteen

My mother got a phone call. Uncle Bill had been in an auto wreck and was in a hospital about fifty miles away. They said he was badly hurt and Mom went on the interurban car and stayed about a week. When she came home she said he would survive.

There was other news that wasn't so good. The car had a load of alcohol in it. He was driving a Dodge touring car, the alcohol in the back covered with a blanket. He was approaching a railroad crossing in the country and didn't see the train in time to stop. He turned off the road and down into a woods where he tried to go between two trees, but they were too close. The Dodge had a split windshield, an upper and lower glass with a rubber seal between. When the car came to the sudden stop, he was thrown forward and the windshield buckled and hit him in the face.

He lost his right eye, his cheekbone was broken, his nose broken, most of his teeth knocked out, and a piece of glass cut a furrow through his scalp. He had a broken arm and some broken ribs. With all this, he got out of the car and managed to walk a quarter mile to a filling station where he called T.L. to come get the alcohol. Then he collapsed and was taken to the hospital. Now, a deputy sheriff sat by his hospital room twenty-four hours every day.

The doctors took out the eye, pulled the teeth, sewed his scalp, and set the broken arm and ribs. He was going to be there for awhile. When he left he probably was headed back to Michigan City Prison. After the doctors had him on his way to recovery, he began thinking about his problems. The deputy sheriffs were still waiting for him to leave the hospital.

From my mother's side of the family, two distant cousins lived in Indianapolis. Their mother lived in Fort Wayne, Indiana, and whenever they went to see her, they stopped at our house. That's where Uncle Bill had met them when he came from Mayo Clinic.

Robert and Richard were handsome men; they wore expensive clothes and drove large expensive cars. Their wives were beautiful and, likewise, wore expensive clothes and jewelry.

They were bootleggers, different than Bill and T.L. because they were big time bootleggers. None of that pint and quart stuff for them;

they sold by truck loads. The profits were high. They could have about anything they wanted. They also had a lot of fun.

One time after midnight the four of them decided to go see their mother. They were drinking along the way and stopped in a small town to get out of the car and have a drink. Being parked along a cement horse trough full of water, the two men decided it would be fun to throw their wives in the horse trough. They each grabbed their wife and threw them in the water. The two brothers had a big laugh as the women crawled out of the troughs, refusing to go any further until they had dry clothes. They refused to get in the car. Finally, Robert went to a house and pounded on the front door until a man opened it. The man was really upset when Robert asked where the owner of the store lived, but Robert showed a ten dollar bill and the man gave him directions. They got the manager to go open up the store and the women bought complete outfits before they would continue on to Fort Wayne.

Another escapade occurred in Fort Wayne. Robert belonged to a very exclusive club called the Athletic Club. He was making a delivery of 300 gallons of alcohol. When he came through Fort Wayne, he decided to have a couple of drinks at the club. He was driving a large Cole Eight touring car with the alcohol in the back covered with a car blanket.

He parked right in front of the club. When he came out he saw three policemen looking in the car. He went back in the club, out the back door and walked over to the Indiana high-speed-rail system that had cars running at better than 70 miles an hour. He got on a car and in a couple of hours, he was in Indianapolis. He went to the police station and reported his car had been stolen. He described the car. Next day they called and notified him that they had found his car in Fort Wayne. They also asked him about the alcohol. He claimed he had never been in Fort Wayne that day, and had no idea where the alcohol came from.

The cop said, “Probably some bootleggers stealing the car to deliver some booze.” They gave him back his car, but they kept the liquor.

A couple years later when Ralph and I were in Indianapolis to see the 500 mile race, I mentioned to him about the bootlegging cousins. He was all for going to pay them a visit, wanting to know if they knew me. Yes, I told him, and they had said to stop by if I was ever in Indianapolis.

We decided we would go over. It was about three o'clock in the afternoon. I asked at the desk for their apartment number. He said he would call first and asked my name. I thought maybe they were just talking about us stopping by. The man called and said my name over the phone. When he put the phone down, he said, "You're to go right up to this number apartment."

When I rang the bell, Robert opened the door and said, "Come in, come in and join the party. Glad to see you. Go over to the bar and get whatever you wish. Make yourself at home. I'm kinda the host so I have to move around a little bit."

We looked over the bar. This wasn't the rot gut he was selling, this was the real stuff, scotch, bourbon, gin, even champagne. There seemed to be about thirty men and women there in all stages of drinking.

After both of us had mixed a drink, Ralph said, "What's this about the wallpaper?"

When we came in we had noticed the strings of wallpaper hanging from the ceiling; some of the walls also had wallpaper scraped off. It was odd to see this very elegant apartment with walls in this shape. Ralph went on, "Do you think the wallpaper men quit over the holiday and will come back later?"

Before the cousins got in the liquor business they were paper hangers. We mingled with the crowd. People were coming in, others were going out.

Robert came over and asked, "Are you having a good time? Did you find everything you want?" We told him we were okay but wanted to know about the wallpaper.

He started laughing, saying, "When this party started two days ago, my wife told some of the people that she hated the wallpaper and was angry because I wouldn't change it. Everybody was pretty well interested including Richard and me. So someone suggested tearing off the paper, then Richard and I would get some paper and put it on. We still had our tools so we gave everybody a scraper and they started to work on the wall and ceiling.

"Well, you know how these things go. In a short time, most quit and left. Other people came in and asked what was with the wallpaper. We told them the story and gave them a scraper. When the holidays are over, we'll have management get some people over here and put up the paper."

Robert brought in a man from the front door and exclaimed to the entire party, "Look who's here!"

Everybody turned and all started greeting him. "Hi Chico!" the men called and the women made gestures wanting him to come over to them. He seemed very popular. He was not a large man, but compact, with a dark complexion, brown eyes and dazzling smile. Everybody wanted to talk to him or be around him.

It was several minutes before things quieted down and Robert had a chance to introduce Ralph and me to him. "This is my relative, Harry, and this is Chico, a famous painter."

We were really impressed by this handsome man. To have something to say, I asked, "What do you paint?"

Before he could reply, Robert said, "He paints for money. You should see the price he gets for his paintings."

Chico explained that he mostly painted portraits. Robert and Chico moved off as some people who had just come in wanted to talk to him. About an hour later, I heard the drinking crowd around Chico calling for him to paint a picture. He protested that he had no equipment with him, but one man spoke up saying, "Chico, everybody knows you keep equipment in your car."

"But I have no canvas. What can I paint on?" Chico protested.

One woman suggested he paint on the wall, but Robert vetoed that saying, "If he's going to paint a picture, it isn't going to be painted where it would be covered up by the paper hangers."

They all said for Chico to get his brushes and paints and when he got back they would have something for him to paint on. Chico left and I thought he might just go home or some place else. He came back, and the only thing they had found was a bread board of rock maple that had never been used. It was as smooth as silk. Chico examined it very carefully and said he could paint on it. He brought out brushes, paint, and propping the board on one of the kitchen cabinet surfaces by leaning it against the wall, started painting. Everybody gathered around to watch the artist work.

First he painted the board black, then he told them he would have to wait until it dried. After about half an hour he put on another coat of black. The fickle crowd began to leave the kitchen for the other rooms and continued their drinking, laughing and having a good time.

Ralph and I stayed. We thought it was rude to leave after they had badgered him to paint and then walked away before he had finished the picture. Then he started painting. We were seated several feet from the painting and he was using such dark colors that from our position it still looked like a black painted board. Ralph motioned for us to move closer. When we were about three feet from the painting, what did we see? Out of the darkness of the picture, a pirate stared back at us in colors so dark we had to stand close to the picture to see the red of his scarf, gold earrings dangling from his ears, dark skin and the knife clenched between his teeth. A gold necklace encircled the pirate's neck.

Ralph and I said nothing for a minute and Chico remained silent. Finally, I said to him, "This is the most beautiful, unique painting I've ever seen."

Ralph said, "I certainly agree with Harry. It's a fantastic and exceptional painting."

He thanked us and said he was glad we liked it. He was cleaning his brushes when Robert came to the kitchen door. Chico said to him, "It's finished."

I knew that from the doorway, the picture looked like the same black board he had started with. I motioned Robert to come in and he walked to the picture. When he saw the pirate looking out of the night at him, he said, "My god, Chico, what a beautiful picture."

He called to the guests and they came. As they crowded close around the picture, the noisy crowd fell silent for a few moments. Then one women said, "Chico, whenever I see you, I'll remember the dark cruel face of the pirate."

Everybody started talking about the picture and what a marvelous painter Chico was. "It's a gift to Robert and his wife," said Chico. Robert thanked him and all the men shook hands and patted him on the back; the women kissed him and he seemed to enjoy the adulation. He held up his hand to silence them. "I enjoyed the party very much, but I must go back to the real world and make a living tomorrow."

Everyone laughed. He would have no trouble making a good living Ralph and I thought.

When we left late that night, the party was still rolling along.

In a few weeks after Bill was healing and realizing what a desperate situation he was in, he knew only one man could possibly help him. They had taken his clothes and the deputies were sitting outside his door. He was allowed visitors so when Robert came to see him, he told them he was a relative.

Plans were made to get Bill some clothes. Other arrangements were made. What they were I never knew, but five nights later Bill found clothes in his closet and put them on, going out the first floor window of his room.

When he was next heard from, he was somewhere in the state of Ohio. Anyone can imagine the commotion in the city when they found the prisoner they had so carefully guarded for almost a month had disappeared without leaving a trace to follow. It caused a big problem at the hospital because someone there had had to get the clothes and place them in the room. Nurses were suspected of being paid and were in the plot.

A lawyer was procured in the city he had escaped to. He made a deal with the authorities. It was made plain to them that if they insisted he serve his time, Bill would never return to Indiana. Rather than get nothing, the authorities agreed he would stand trial and be fined six hundred dollars. This was a huge fine but Bill agreed, paid the fine, and returned to our town. He could no longer sell whiskey or would serve prison time. He retired with plenty of money and there was talk of prohibition being revoked so he sold out to his partner. He loafed around town for several months and then got married and moved to Arizona. But the soft married life was not for Bill. He was dead in four months.

Chapter Fourteen

The Depression seemed to get even worse as time went on. Ralph and I found no work and fall was coming; days were getting shorter. Unemployed men congregated at the courthouse. If anybody needed men they went there and picked them up. Ralph and I went to the courthouse but nobody chose us. Then one day a farmer drove up to the crowd of men and looked around before heading directly to Ralph and me.

"You boys interested in a few days' work," he asked.

Ralph said, "Sure we are, what kind?"

"I've got a lot of popcorn that needs to be shucked," the farmer said. We could do that, we assured him. How much?

"Twenty-five cents an hour," he said.

"When do we start?" I asked.

"Start right now if you want to. Work as many hours as you want."

We got in the car with him and drove to the farm. He showed us the field of popcorn. Most of it had been blown down by a strong wind.

"There she is, boys," he said, pointing. "The baskets are down at the end of the field. When you get back here, dump the corn in that metal crib."

We walked down and picked up the baskets. Ten hours would make two-fifty a day. This was a bonanza for two very broke teen-agers. We stooped over to get the corn, but soon realized we would have to get down on our hands and knees. At noon we stopped even though we had nothing to eat. The farmer had vanished when we started to work and had not reappeared. We went back to work. It really didn't bother us that we had nothing to eat; we had missed a lot of meals bumming around the country.

The farmer came back and said, "Boys, it's five-thirty. You reckon you done enough today?"

Our knees were sore and our hands were sore. We had enough for today.

"I figured up your hours. Check this paper and see if it's right."

We looked at it. He had nine hours for both of us. We had only figured eight and a half. "It's okay," I said. "Are you going to take us back to town?"

"Sure, I'm going to take you back and I'll pick you up at the courthouse tomorrow at seven. You'll get a longer day tomorrow."

After he had let us out, I told Ralph, "This is harder work than I thought it would be." Ralph agreed and thought it was going to take us four days to get done, calculating our return at about ten or eleven dollars each.

"I know," I replied. "Car washing and lawn mowing are over for this year. I'm going to look around for something like a piece of rug or an old pillow for my knees. See what you can find at your house. And don't forget to bring a lunch for tomorrow."

The next morning the farmer was waiting for us. It was a beautiful fall fay. The farmer said, "Hope this weather holds until we get the popcorn in."

Well, we hoped so too. Our finances would be greatly improved for some months to come. We were sore and stiff when we started, but after a short time we worked it out. I had found a large piece of rag which I cut in two so we each had a pad for our knees.

At noon when we ate our lunch, I said to Ralph, "This guy is never around here after we start to work. How does he know how hard we're working or if we're working at all?"

"He probably looks in the corn crib and figures if we're working from the amount of corn in it," Ralph surmised.

We finished the job. It took us four days to get it all in the crib. We had already figured up what he owed us, forty-one hours or ten dollars and twenty-five cents apiece. We were rich.

The farmed flipped out his notebook and told us what we already knew. "Well, boys, I owe you $10.20 apiece. But right at this time, I don't have the money."

We couldn't believe what he was saying. How could he hire somebody then not have any money to pay them? All the things we had talked about and planned to do with the money, gone like smoke. I looked at Ralph and he was looking at me. I could see in his eyes the same thing I was thinking. We ought to beat the living shit out of this thieving bastard.

As we studied this option, the farmer spoke, "I'm sorry I don't have this money to pay you, but I'm going to give you a better deal where you can make even more money than what I gave you. I got a big crop of potatoes and I'll give each of you a thousand pounds of potatoes that you can sell for three cents a pound. That'll make you thirty dollars instead of the ten and a quarter."

We accepted the potatoes. Ralph had his put in the garage, and I had an uncle who had a garage with a cement floor. I told him to start eating potatoes. I went around trying to sell the potatoes, but most wanted only a sack full. Nobody even bought so much as a bushel. We took all we would use and told everybody to come and get what they wanted.

The things that puzzled me now became clear. Why had we been chosen? Because if he had hired any of the men, he would not have gotten away with a potato deal. He never watched to see if we were working because he didn't care. He knew what he was going to pay us with. It took us a while getting over this disaster.

The first big snow came and I went trying to get a job cleaning porches and sidewalks. But it wasn't much good, people just didn't have any money. Finally, however, Ralph's brother told him a prominent citizen was looking for someone to refinish the hardwood floors in his home.

Ralph said, "You know anything about finishing floors?"

"We could find out how to do it at the hardware store," I said. "Let's go down and talk to him."

We visited the prominent citizen who said his wife was visiting her mother and he would be working, so he wanted a set price for the job. Was this another case of setting us up? We knew nothing about the costs we would incur doing the job. If we asked too little we might end up working for very little. If we asked too much he might get someone else to do the job. We went to the hardware store and told the owner about the job and not knowing what to bid for the job. We told him there were five rooms about average size. He figured supplies and renting a sander from them would cost about fifteen dollars. He advised us to bid sixty-five dollars and see what he says.

"If he balks, then drop to sixty dollars."

We were at the man's house when he came from work. He agreed to the sixty-five dollar price. We started the next day and with the help of the hardware store owner, we thought we were doing a good job. The owner wondered if his wife would approve of the work, but it looked good to him. She came home when we had only one room left to finish and was delighted with the work. The next day when we finished he wrote us a check for sixty-five dollars.

The banks were closed so we would have to wait until the next day to cash the check. "Let's go over to the pool room and see if Fred will cash it for us," I suggested.

When we showed Fred the check he looked at it and said, "Hey, did you know this guy sometimes writes checks when he has no money in the bank?"

Ralph and I exchanged wary glances. Was it going to be another potato deal? Still, Fred didn't give us the check back. "I'll have to go up to the office to get that much money."

When he handed us the money, he reached in the case and gave us each a cigar. "You should have a cigar to smoke while you count all that money," he said.

We laughed, happy we had the money. After paying off our bill at the hardware store we each had a little over twenty-five dollars. With Christmas only three weeks away, we were rich. I gave Dad and Mom ten dollars and bought presents for all of them and still had about ten dollars left.

Chapter Fifteen

The day after Christmas was a cold bitter day with snow piled high along the streets. I met Ralph in the pool room. After commenting about the weather, he said, "How would you like to take a trip down to Florida?" We had never started a trip in cold weather and I still remembered our bad time in Mississippi. When I didn't answer, he continued, "Ott Pethel is going to take a load of shelled corn down to Florida and trade it for oranges to sell up here. He's looking for someone to ride down and back with him."

"That may be all right. Let's go talk to him. He's probably still over at the restaurant."

Walking over we decided we didn't want to come back with him; we wanted to stay in the warm weather. We talked to Ott, who said he had found no one and if we wanted to stay in Florida he didn't blame us. He said he was leaving at midnight on January first. He said he would be in the lobby of the hotel.

I lay down and slept in the afternoon and evening. I had a thought that Ott might want us to do some of the driving. If he did, I didn't want to be sleepy. At eleven o'clock, I got dressed. Everybody was asleep. I had told them goodby earlier in the evening. When I stepped off the porch the cold seemed to grab me by the throat. It was a dark, bitter cold night. I would be glad when we arrived in a warm climate.

When I walked in the lobby of the hotel, Ralph and Ott were waiting. Ott insisted we not start until twelve o'clock. The hotel stayed open twenty-four hours a day. There were two men and the night clerk and the three of us in the lobby. They were all interested in how we were going to get back home. We didn't tell them we had never ridden trains in the winter. The courthouse clock began striking twelve and Ott said, "Let's go boys, we got a long ride ahead of us."

When I got in the truck my heart picked up a beat like it always did when we started a trip. The thermometer outside the hotel read five degrees below zero. I wondered if the truck would even start. I also hoped it had a heater that worked. Luckily, it had a gasoline heater and began throwing out heat immediately. All the windows were frosted over except a small area for the driver to see through.

The truck picked up slowly for it was fully loaded with sacks of shelled corn. This was not the first trip he had made with the corn, and he had a special town to go to dispose of the corn and pick up oranges.

Last year he said that a friend had ridden down and back with him, bringing back a two-foot alligator. In the summer he had put some water and sand in a wash tub, and put the alligator in it and set it in the backyard. He told nobody he had it, fed it raw hamburger and the alligator was content to stay in the tub.

Two houses from this man was a couple, and the woman drank liquor at all times of the day. One time he went to feed the alligator but it was gone. He heard a woman scream and a door slam. He went over and there was his alligator on the woman's porch. He heard the woman screaming to her husband about an alligator on the porch. "Come and see!" she screamed.

The fellow picked up his alligator and ran to his house. When the man came to the back door and looked out, there was no alligator. The man yelled at his wife, "You're going to have to quit your damn drinking!"

"I'll bet that poor woman thought it was about time to quit, too," Ott said. We all had a good laugh at his story.

We were making pretty good time considering the loaded truck, some snow on the highway, but we had the road all to ourselves. We told Ott we would be glad to help him drive; he said we would see how everything went. The sun came up but brought no heat with it. We were approaching Cincinnati but Ott knew a route around it so we didn't get to see much of the city. We stopped for breakfast and Ott insisted on paying for our meals although we told him we had some money. We were hoping we wouldn't have to spend too much so we could stay a while in Miami.

When we finished eating, Ott asked the man if he could get some whiskey. The man didn't seem very anxious to answer. Ott continued, "I'm taking a load of corn down south, go out and look in the truck." The man went out, took one look in the truck and, satisfied we weren't revenuers, disappeared around the restaurant and came in the back door carrying a pint of whiskey. He set it on the counter in front of Ott. "How much," Ott asked.

"Fifty cents," the man answered.

When we got outside, Ott said, "We need a bit of this to warm us up a little."

He handed the bottle to me but I gestured for him to drink first.

He took a big drink and handed it to me. I handed the bottle to Ralph. I had heard about this mountain moonshine and most of it was bad, drinkers going blind, even dying from the stuff. Ralph took a big drink and handed the bottle back to me. I was going to have to take a drink. I took a big swallow and it felt like a hand was choking me. Tears ran down my cheeks, but I finally kept it down.

"Pretty good stuff, don't you think?" Ott exclaimed.

I couldn't answer because I still couldn't talk. Ralph agreed that it tasted pretty good. Ott was right about one thing: it warmed us up. I was on fire from my tonsils to my stomach.

A thermometer on the side of the restaurant showed 35 degrees; it was getting warmer. We pulled onto the highway. Not long after, Ott thought we should have another "shot," as he called it. Ralph and he had one but I refused, afraid I would throw it up in the truck cab.

There wasn't much traffic and we were making good time. About midmorning we stopped for gas and we all had another drink. The bottle was three-fourths gone. I'd be glad when it was all gone.

At noon we stopped to eat and it was warm enough that we took off our outer coats. It was like a beautiful spring day, sunny but cool. The next big city would be Lexington, Kentucky. Ott said there was a lot of horse farms around the city. We hoped to see some race horses. Ralph and Ott finished the bottle and out the window it flew.

We saw our first horse farm. It was beautiful, white fences all around, several large white barns and a very elegant house, but no horses. Ott said they were probably all in the barns. Later on we passed another farm and saw our first race horses.

We had never discussed sleeping arrangements with Ott, but when we arrived in Lexington, he told us to watch out for a motel where we could stop for the night. We were out of the city and hadn't seen any motels; then twenty miles down the road we found one. Ott pulled in and parked. He said he would get two rooms, but Ralph and I both protested.

"Listen," said Ralph, "we're used to sleeping in boxcars and even on the grass. Just get one room and Harry and I will sleep on the floor."

By this time we were in the office and Ott asked the man if he had a family room with two beds. The man told us he had a room with a full bed and a half-bed that was stored under the other bed. Ott was satisfied and paid him, telling him we would be up very early and he might be asleep at that time.

It was a very nice room and we decided that because I was the biggest I would sleep on the half-bed and the other two would have more room in the double bed. Ott asked if there was a restaurant close by. The man had told us there was one run by blacks about a quarter mile down the road. The food was good and also cheap.

After riding all this time we decided a walk would do us good. It was a pleasant night; the stars were bright and the temperature was a lot warmer than when we left home.

When we came to the restaurant it didn't look like much and the inside wasn't much better. There were several colored people eating; the sight of three white men seemed to make them uneasy. We sat at a table and a colored woman came to take our order. We had been looking at the blackboard where the items were chalked up. There were two choices: possum stew or fried chicken. Ralph and Ott discussed the possum stew while I had already made up my mind for the chicken.

Ott said, "Ralph and I think we'll try the opossum stew; we've never eaten it."

I told them I'd heard of people eating possum back home, but had never tasted it. I decided not to share why I would never eat possum. When I was out hunting one time, I had come upon a dead horse in the woods. Each time I came by it, it smelled worse. The last time I went by, I looked at the horse and it was breathing. I could see its side expand and contract. I felt the hair rise on my neck. This couldn't be happening; that horse had been dead for two weeks. I walked up to the animal and all at once three or four opossums bolted out of the inside of the horse and streaked into the underbrush. They had been eating on the inside of the chest of the horse and pushing up in it had made it look like the horse was breathing. After that I knew I would never eat an opossum.

Ralph and Ott declared it was the best stew they had ever eaten. The chicken was good too. I thought maybe tomorrow I would tell them about the dead horse. Then on second thought, I didn't think I would. They might put me out of the truck to hitchhike or maybe ride in the back end.

We walked back to the motel and Ott left a wake up call for five o'cloçk in the morning. We all went to bed; we hadn't slept for a long time. It seemed I had hardly gotten in bed when I was awakened by someone pounding on our door. It was time to get up. We ate a quick breakfast at the colored restaurant and we soon were on our way.

It was still dark but when the sun inched over the horizon, we could see it was going to be a beautiful day. We were going to sleep in the truck that night as we felt we were far enough south and it would be warm.

We crossed into Tennessee and into more mountains. I liked them. The countryside was a lot different than Indiana. Most of the people in this area seemed extremely poor. The houses were very primitive, quite a few were made of logs. At noon we stopped at a log restaurant. Ott said he had stopped there before. We had to cross a deep ditch on a board laid across it to get to the restaurant. Sure enough, the owner greeted Ott by name. Ott introduced us and then we sat down at the counter and ate. When we were finished Ott asked the man if he could get him a pint of whiskey.

The man went out the back door and soon returned and handed Ott the pint bottle. Ott took it and said, "Feel how warm it is. He got that right off the still. It's been aged about five minutes."

When we left I told Ott, "Why don't we move some of the sacks of shelled corn around and make a place to lie down in the back?" He agreed that that was a good idea.

We took the tarp off and moved the bags around until we had a nice place for one person to lay down and sleep or look out the back end of the truck. "Do you want to try it out first?" Ott asked. I agreed because I knew I wouldn't have to drink the moonshine. It made a lot more room in the cab for the other two. We would stop only for gas. One of us would sleep in the truck and we would take turns driving. Ott had been driving all the way.

When we stopped for gas in the afternoon, Ott was a little tipsy. "Hey," I said, "Why don't you go take it easy in the back of the truck and I'll drive for a while?"

He seemed to concentrate a minute, then said, "I think that might be a good idea." He went back and got in the truck and lay down on his back. He pulled the bottle out of his pocket, took a swig of booze and went to sleep.

Ralph was feeling pretty good too, and after singing me a couple of songs he slumped down in the seat and went to sleep. I drove until almost dark, and thought we were probably into Georgia. When it got dark, I found a filling station and drove in and parked. I shook Ralph awake and went to the back of the truck. We woke Ott up and he got out of the truck. "Are we in Georgia yet?" he asked.

I told him I thought so. He said that would be all the booze because we were going to have to drive all night to get into Florida tomorrow.

We got gas and a short distance down the road we stopped at a restaurant. It was really primitive. The table tops were about two inches thick with cuts in them in the shape of plates. They were serving the meals right on the wood and not using a plate.

Ott said, "I don't know. It may be quite a ways down the road before we find another restaurant."

I said, "I don't care if it's two hours further down the road, I don't want to eat here." We all got up and walked out.

When we were outside, I added, "There's a lot of poor people in this country, but this is the first restaurant I ever seen that didn't use dishes." We all laughed and piled into the truck.

We were riding with the windows down; it was definitely getting much warmer. About an hour later we found a place to eat. It was made of logs, but looked much better. We went inside; it was clean and we sat down at the counter.

We ate, then smoked a cigarette with our coffee, and left. When we got outside, we made plans on the driving. Each of us would sleep in the back for four hours. Since Ott had already slept, Ralph said he would go in the back Ott and I got in the cab.

When the moon came up, it looked like a big silver dollar. We could almost drive without the lights. The air coming in the window was warm, like a spring day. The other one in the cab wouldn't sleep so the driver wouldn't get sleepy while driving.

We saw lights ahead in the sky and Ott said we were coming into Atlanta. He knew a shortcut around the city so we wouldn't be going through it. I was a little disappointed since I had read a lot about Atlanta.

We were following a truck route and I saw nothing but shacks, warehouses, and factories. Maybe we would go through the city when we went back north. Ott said we should get into Leesburg, Florida sometime in the afternoon. That was the area where he traded corn for oranges.

Ott told me to go to sleep if I wanted, but I was afraid he might go to sleep while driving. He said if we could find an all night restaurant we would load up on coffee. He said the next large city was Macon, Georgia. That was the city that the big dirigible we saw in Akron was named after. To keep us both awake, I told him about the trip we had made to Akron, Ohio and described the huge ship and how we got there and back.

As we approached Macon, we stopped at a filling station and diner. We woke Ralph and had the truck filled with gas, then went in the restaurant and sat down at the counter. We had coffee and rolled a cigarette. Ott asked if we were hungry and we said, "No, but we'll have a refill on the coffee (which was on the house) and another cigarette."

It was almost midnight when we went out to the truck. Ralph said he had all the sleep he wanted, so I went to the back of the truck. I pulled some of the sacks around so I had a comfortable bed, and with a warm breeze blowing over me I was soon asleep.

I was awakened by the truck stopping. Ralph and Ott were talking beside the rear end of it. I got out and saw a car wreck about a hundred yards down the road. I walked to Ralph and Ott and asked what was going on. There were three cars obstructing the highway and a state policeman was stopping traffic. We weren't close enough to see much of what had happened but it looked like we were going to be held up for some time. There was an ambulance, but no wrecker had arrived to pull the cars off the road.

I asked Ralph what time it was. It was after four o'clock and Ott said we were on the Florida-Georgia line. If we were held up very long, it would be afternoon before we got to Leesburg.

They were putting a couple of people in the ambulance; it seemed if anybody was badly hurt it must have been them. The ambulance left and about twenty minutes later a tow truck arrived. We had a sizable column of cars behind us now.

The tow truck pulled and pushed the cars to one side of the road and the policeman motioned our column to move. The wrecked cars didn't look to be damaged very much, but a lot of broken glass crunched under the truck's wheels. All three of us rode in the cab. Soon we reached a small city, Lake City, Florida, and stopped for more coffee and a cigarette, then were back on the highway. When the sun appeared, we looked around and saw palm trees, palmetto, pine forests and lots of water, lakes every few miles.

We were now down to our short sleeves and enjoying the warm weather. We continued to see very poor living conditions as we had seen in Mississippi and Louisiana, lots of colored people working in the fields.

We stopped near Gainesville and had breakfast. Ott said to eat up, that it would be the last meal the three of would eat together. We had ham, eggs, potatoes, and of course, grits were served even if you didn't want any. After coffee and a cigarette we were back in the truck. Ott said we should get there in the early afternoon.

We had never seen so many lakes; sometimes the road was the

only dry part and we were surrounded by water. We saw lots of water birds, long-legged cranes and others we didn't know the names of. We saw our first orange grove. The trees were a nice green color and the fruit not as orange color as the ones sold in Indiana. Ott said that was because the ones on the tree hadn't been washed.

When we passed through Ocala, Ott told us that there were seven or eight lakes within the city limits. At noon we were in Leesburg and turned off the hard road onto a gravel road to get to the farmer Ott knew. We saw oranges and grapefruit everywhere. Lots of fruit lay on the ground, not a good sign for a seller, but good for the buyer.

We came to a large frame house and Ott turned in the driveway and stopped the truck. A man came out of the house and waved at us. We got out of the truck and Ott called the man by name. They seemed happy to see each other. They asked about each other and we sat down and the two started talking about the trade.

Ott wanted to see some of the oranges and we walked to a large barn-like building while Ott drove the truck down. When we all got there, a Negro joined us and the farmer said he was his foreman. There were many colored help around there and he told the foreman to bring up two or three cases of oranges. When they arrived, Ott looked at several of them and pronounced them satisfactory. The farmer pulled out a knife, cut a corn bag, reached in for a handful of grain, looked at it and even smelled it. I didn't know why but maybe he was looking for mold.

Everything was all right and the farmer called for the foreman to get some help and unload the grain and load the oranges. That didn't take very long and when all the help except the foreman had left, the farmer said, "We ought to have a drink to seal the bargain." Ott said that we had drank all the liquor we had. The farmer turned to the foreman and asked, "Do you have any whiskey?"

The man replied that he had a little and the farmer sent him to get it. When he came back he had about two-thirds of a pint bottle of liquor, which he handed to the farmer. The farmer pulled the cork and handed the bottle to Ott who took a drink and handed it to Ralph. He took a drink and handed it to me. I drank and returned the bottle to the farmer, who took a long drink, corked the bottle and put it in his hip pocket. There was the colored man who had furnished the whiskey for all four of us, but he wasn't permitted to drink his own whiskey in the presence of white men. And it didn't look like he would get the remainder of the whiskey back. We all shook hands and climbed in the truck and rode back to Leesburg.

When we reached the highway, Ott stopped the truck and we all got out. We shook hands and we thanked him for the meals he had bought us, telling him how much fun we had coming down. He said he would miss us going back but would hang around the hotel lobby, making us promise to look him up some night when we got back. We said we would, told him to drive carefully, and said goodby. Ott was a good traveling companion.

Chapter Sixteen

We decided to hitchhike to Tampa because we hadn't seen any railroad tracks for some time. It was rough going until a young fellow picked us up and asked where we were going. We told him Tampa and he said he was going to St. Petersburg and could drop us off at Tampa.

We talked about going with him to St. Petersburg but decided we wanted to see Tampa first. He asked if we had any problems with the police. We told him how we had come down and hadn't been hitchhiking much. "You want to watch for the police. They'll arrest you for vagrancy," he said.

The young man had a nice car and even had a radio in it. We had never heard of a car radio. When he left us off in Tampa, we started for the downtown section of the city. We went past the docks and saw the first big freighters in the harbor. There were lots of black people. Having no black people in our town, we could hardly believe how many blacks there were in the South. As we walked along, the blacks began to thin out and were replaced by Cubans and other Spanish-talking people. The menus in the windows of the restaurants were in Spanish. We looked in the windows of the shops. There were strange fruits and vegetables to us. People wore different clothes than we were accustomed to.

Some of the food prices were very low and we decided to spend some of our money and eat in that section of the city. We picked a place that had very cheap prices. Although some of the dishes sounded familiar, we didn't know what was in them. We sat at a table and a young woman came over and started talking to us in Spanish. We shook our heads and Ralph said, "We don't understand."

"Un momento," she said and left us, coming back with a woman who spoke English with quite an accent. After trying to figure out the menu chalked on a board, we told her to bring us a dinner she thought we would like and that we couldn't pay too much for it.

She came back with a plate and I asked, "Crayfish?"

"No crayfish, shrimp today."

"What parts do you eat?" I asked.

She picked up one, twisted off the tail, took the shell off, and laid it on my plate. She pointed to the sauce she had brought with the shrimp. I dipped the shrimp in the sauce and bit off a big chunk. My mouth was on fire. I almost spit it out.

"Picante?" she asked. "I bring other," and returned with another pot of sauce.

We cleaned the shrimp and dipped them in the new sauce. I talked Ralph into trying the hot sauce and laughed when his face got red and tears came in his eyes, but he swallowed the shrimp. She brought us roasted chicken and sweet potatoes and something called okra cooked in a hot tomato sauce. We had black, black strong coffee that would melt the spoon if you put one in it. The food was very good and after we finished we sat and drank the strong coffee, smoked cigarettes and watched the customers.

Ralph said, "Let's ask the waitress if she knows where we can get a cheap room that has a bath so we can get cleaned up."

"Sounds good to me," I said and motioned for her to come over. We told her what we were looking for and she left, returning with an address.

When I asked how much she shook her head, "Not much, you ask down there." She told us how to get on the street and left.

It didn't take long to find the house and when we knocked on the door a very beautiful girl answered. Soon an older woman came to the door and we told her what we were looking for. She said she would show us the room. It was not large, but was clean and the bed looked clean. I asked where the bathroom was.

She said, "Come with me, it is outside." We went to a small building that had a shower in it; the water came from a tank on the top of the shed. I asked about hot water and she said, "No hot water."

I told Ralph we should look at another before deciding. He agreed and we left to continue walking down the street. We soon saw a sign, *Room for Rent* in a large house. A man answered the door and we told him what we wanted. He showed us a large room, very clean and bathroom with a bathtub. I asked how much. "Twenty-five cents a night for the room," he said.

I looked at Ralph, expecting him to say okay. He didn't answer for a few seconds, then said, "You know, I really like a shower better than I do a bathtub." At this time of night, the water in that tank was going to be cold. Then it hit me: he wanted to see the girl again.

"Okay," I agreed. "I like cold showers at night. Let's go back to the other room."

When we returned the woman seemed glad. The room was thirty cents but included our breakfast. We went out for a shower. The water wasn't as cold as I thought it would be; it was still warm from the hot sun.

The woman's name was Mary Oliveria, a very attractive woman, but the real beauty was her daughter Angelina, who was a senior at a Catholic school and would graduate in the spring. We found breakfast would be any time we wanted it and decided to sleep in a little in the morning. It felt good to be clean again and sleeping in a clean, soft bed.

When I woke Ralph was gone. I dressed and went into the kitchen to see Ralph and Angelina drinking coffee and talking. Mary came in and asked what I would like for breakfast and that Ralph had already eaten.

I said, "Bring me what you brought Ralph." Soon she returned with eggs, potatoes, bread, butter and strong coffee.

It was Friday and Angelina had to go to school. Ralph and I went to our room to decide what to do.

"Do you want to go on down the coast or look around here?" I asked.

"Well, we didn't get to see much of the city. If we stay another night, Mary and Angelina said they would take us down to an Italian section tomorrow."

"I think I know why you want to stay and I'm all for going to the Italian section. It'll be like going to Italy," I said.

We told Mary we were going to stay another night. I asked her if she had a husband. She said he had been washed off a fishing boat and drowned about three years ago.

We decided just to walk around and see what the city had to offer. It was a busy place, especially down around the docks. It was a very colorful city. We saw a lot of foreign people and heard them talk in languages we had never heard. We walked down to the docks and looked at the ships arriving and departing from all parts of the world. We saw a destroyer, the first Navy ship we had ever seen.

We found a seat in a small park near the docks and rolled a cigarette. A small man with the rolling walk of a sailor sat on the bench across from us. He greeted us and we smiled and said hello. He spoke very good English but with a heavy accent, either Spanish or Portuguese. He asked if we were from one of the ships. We told him no, that we were visitors in this beautiful city. I asked if he was a sailor and he said he had been one for many years. I wanted to know what countries he had visited.

"Many," he said and rambled off a string of countries, some pronounced in Spanish I thought. I asked him if he was an American citizen. "I live here but born in Portugal," he said.

"What kind of ship are you on?"

"Small ship, go everywhere, tramp steamer, home in Panama."

"Tell us about some of the adventures you surely must have had."

"Ship almost sink one time," he said, "but we make it into port and get boat fixed. Oh yes, one time we were anchored in Spanish waters, close on shore was military barracks. We watched as columns of soldiers march out of barracks and line up facing stone wall. Two soldiers bring in a man hands tied and lead him in front of the line of soldiers. It comes to me we was going to see an execution. He is given a cigarette and then is blindfolded and pushed against the wall. We can't hear the commands but see the rifles come up and see the smoke from the barrels and see the victim fall to the ground. The column of soldiers march away and the dead man is left lying on the ground. About an hour later two men came with a wheelbarrow and loaded the dead man in it and took him away."

For a few minutes we said nothing, thinking about the tale he had told us. Finally, I asked him what it was like in Panama.

"Very hot in Panama, but good country. Good food, good liquor and pretty women."

"Are you married?" Ralph asked.

"No, no good sailor to be married, always away from home. Women don't like that. Have you been to YBOR city here in Tampa?" he asked.

"Why is YBOR city special?" Ralph asked.

"Mostly Cubans, but other people, Jamaicans, Spanish, Mexicans, all different people," he said.

"This sounds like an interesting place to look around in," I said.

"Lots of fun there, good food, beer, gambling, women, have a good time."

Ralph said to me, "We got to look in on YBOR city."

"It is a city inside a city," our sailor friend said. He pulled out a dollar watch and said, "I have to go back to ship, will leave soon." We wanted to know where he was going on the ship. He shrugged his shoulders. "I don't know, maybe only captain know." We shook hands with him and wished him a safe voyage. He walked away and over his shoulder he said, "Go to YBOR, you will like it."

We walked around and looked in stores and markets. All kinds of exotic fruit and vegetables suffused the outdoors. We passed a cigar factory and looked in the door. There were about thirty or forty men sitting on benches rolling cigars. A man not making cigars motioned us to come in. We walked in and he said, “Like some very good cigars?”

Ralph told him we had never smoked a cigar and we had no money to spend on them. The man went to his desk and came back with two cigars. “These are made from the best Havana leaf and are the best cigars in the world. Take these and smoke them after your evening meal tonight.” We took the cigars and thanked him and asked if we could watch the way the men made the cigars. “Go look anywhere you want to,” he replied.

We watched one man who worked very quickly, his hands flying as he positioned the tobacco in the leaf and then rolled it with the palm of his hand and the top of the bench. When it was the right thickness and length, he wet it with his tongue, then placed it in a groove on a board that would hold about a dozen cigars. They all worked quickly, not talking as I thought they might working so closely together. We went back and thanked the owner for the cigars and also for letting us watch the cigar makers work. “Tell your friends I have the best cigars in the world,” he shouted.

The sun was going down and we were thinking about finding a place to eat. We came to a small building with a big sign on the front that read: *Twenty-five Shrimp — five cents.*

“Did you like the shrimp we had before?” asked Ralph. I said they had tasted pretty good. Ralph answered, “You want to try this place?”

“Well, you can’t beat the price,” I said. “Let’s go in.”

There were a lot of people in the place, especially standing at a long bar. As our eyes became accustomed to the dim light, we could see all the customers were eating shrimp. The smell was something that really stayed with you. When a customer sat down, a man came with a bucket and a large holed spoon. He laid down a piece of newspaper and piled the shrimp on it until he counted twenty-five. These were just the shrimp with the shell and tail on. A saucer of sauce was served with them.

So we started for the tables. When I stepped I felt a crunching sound. A closer examination of the floor showed it was covered with shrimp shells. The people ate the shrimp and dropped or threw the shells on the floor. At the long bar the shells were about three of four inches deep.

One of the men came and put down a piece of newspaper and ladled out twenty-five shrimp for each of us. When we tried to give him the dime, he waved it away. We watched how the people at the next table got the shell off and we found it was easy. The sauce was hot with peppers but tasted good with the shrimp. The place was doing a great business, all they served was shrimp. In the back were two very large iron kettles hanging over a fire tended by two colored men. They had long handled scoops made of wire that they used to scoop the boiled shrimp out of the pot into the buckets for the servers. They raised a large basket and poured the shrimp in the boiling water in the kettles.

We finished the shrimp and Ralph said, "Being that we're only going to have shrimp, do you want to split another twenty-five?"

"Let's do," I said and we called the man over and ordered shrimp.

When he went this time, he left a piece of paper that read *Fifteen cents*. Now that I could see better, I saw a woman near the door taking the money. We paid the woman and walked outside. We breathed the warm sweet air, but it took a couple of minutes to get the shrimp smell out of our noses. Ralph asked if I wanted to go back to the house. Although I would have preferred walking around the town, I knew why he wanted to go back, to see Angelina.

We went to the door and they were sitting at the kitchen table. Mary motioned for us to come in and sit down. After some talk Angie, as she liked to be called, said that she wanted to show something to Ralph so they went into the living room. Mary and I talked for a couple of hours and when Ralph and Angie came back to the kitchen, I told them I was going to bed. Ralph said he would be along shortly. It had been a long day and I was soon asleep. I never knew when Ralph came to bed.

When we got up in the morning, we put on our best clothes and went to eat breakfast. Mary and Angie were waiting for us and we all ate breakfast together. Mary said we would walk to the Italian sections; it would be a nice walk. The two women were dressed in colorful skirts and blouses. They were two very attractive women. When we got to the Italian section, they had a wooden platform with a tent over it and some band instruments. I believed that we would have a concert or a dance or maybe both. People came to speak to Mary and Angie and she introduced them to us. I got the feeling that being with these two guaranteed acceptance by everybody there. We were invited in homes for drinks of wine and food. In the afternoon everybody assembled in the park where the wooden platform was located.

The first piece they played must have been the Italian national song for everybody stood up. Then they started playing and people got on the big platform to dance. Ralph and Angie went to dance and I turned to Mary and said, "Would you like to dance?"

She took my hand and said, "Let's go." The four of us danced all afternoon until the band quit playing.

One of Mary's cousins asked us to share the evening meal with them and we accepted. What a meal it was! The food was delicious and accompanied by large glasses of red wine. I had never drank very much before and I could really feel the effects of the liquor, but I felt great. Mary said it was time to start back. We thanked our hosts and they said to come back next Saturday. I loved those Italian people.

Walking back, we told the women that we were going to YBOR city. Mary said for us to go but to be careful, adding she thought we would like it very much.

We didn't get an early start on our way to YBOR city the next day. We had to ask several people how to get there. YBOR city had no boundaries, but we noticed we were seeing more Cuban shops and eating places. These increased as we walked until we found ourselves in the center of this exotic and colorful city within a city. We browsed among the small shops and everywhere there was gambling: cards, dominoes, dice, even bets were placed on pool games.

It seemed that everyone was selling lottery tickets. The one we noticed selling the most was a crippled hunchback. The customer would rub his back and then buy the tickets. We found out that to rub the hump of a hunchback was supposed to bring good luck.

There were all kinds of smells, fish, cooking fish, and charcoal most of all. We watched the women bargaining with the trades people in Spanish for all kinds of food, vegetables, fruit and meat.

After a couple of hours of walking around observing everything, we decided to try café-leche that everybody seemed to be drinking. We sat down in a place that had a man playing a guitar. We told the waitress we would try café-leche. She put some black thick coffee in a glass, and from a machine she filled it up with some hot milk. We noticed some patrons had the coffee and milk brought separately and mixed the coffee the way they liked it.

We tasted the café and it was all right, but we preferred the regular coffee. We rolled a cigarette and sat back to enjoy the colorful people who passed by and listen to the very talented guitar player. We talked about what we thought it was like back home. Snow crunching under their feet, below zero temperatures, streets covered in snow.

Ralph said, "Here we are looking around in a foreign city, drinking coffee and smoking a cigarette in seventy-five degree weather."

"Don't forget the two women friends we have," I said.

"Hoboing isn't supposed to be like this," said Ralph.

We had located the railroad yards and would leave the next day, although I thought Ralph would be content to stay until our money was exhausted. Ralph and Angie seemed to like each other very much. They made a handsome couple.

We planned to eat where we were. We hadn't seen much pork in our travels, but there was plenty in YBOR city. We were going to eat in a large place where a whole hog roasted over a bed of charcoal. It was very busy and the prices were good. We went in and the waitress led us to a small table for two. The smell of roast pork and the spices was enough to make one hungry even if you weren't. We ordered the pork special. When she brought it to the table it was piled high with slices of pork, black beans, sweet potatoes and okra.

When we finished Ralph pulled out the two cigars that were given to us. "After that gigantic meal I think we need to try out these cigars," Ralph said. We lit up and puffed away. The smoke had a soft and fragrant feel in my mouth, entirely different from cigarettes.

It was dark when we finished the cigars and there were even more people on the streets laughing and talking. The prostitutes had come out with the darkness. They sat in front of small rooms and if anyone looked at them they smiled and slowly pulled up their dress to show a shapely leg.

Ralph asked if I had enough of YBOR city. I knew he wanted to get back to the room so he could talk to Angie awhile, so I said we could leave now. When we arrived the two woman were sitting on their tiny porch fanning themselves. Mary invited us in for a cup of coffee at the kitchen table. We told them how much we were going to miss them, and they said they would miss us.

It was hot in the house so Mary and I went to the front porch and Ralph and Angie stayed in the living room. Mary and I talked for a couple of hours and then I went to bed. I told Mary to call us when she got up so we could eat breakfast with them.

When the knock on the door came, we put on our traveling clothes and packed our small bag. When we went to the kitchen they were waiting for us and we sat down and ate. When we finished we thanked them and kissed them goodby. I heard Ralph tell Angie that he would try to get back to her. We walked down the street and when we looked back, they were still standing on their tiny porch. They waved and we waved back to them. We would never see them again.

When we got to the yards, we walked along the fence looking at the trains. We saw a couple that had steam up and looked like they were going south. We ran across the tracks to a train that had an engineer in the cab and asked if he was going south. He not only wouldn't answer us, but wouldn't even look at us. The train looked as though it was ready to pull out, so we decided to take a chance and get on. We found an open car and climbed in and looked around. It was fairly clean. We hadn't seen any hobos which made us wonder if this might be a dangerous area.

In a few minutes we heard the couplings banging and when it reached our car, it jerked forward almost throwing us off our feet. After the yard it seemed we were crossing a large swamp. The train didn't go very fast and we sat in the car door and watched for alligators. We finally saw one lying on a mud flat. We saw others after that, and hundreds of water birds wading in the swamp and flying over it.

We were a little disturbed. According to the position of the sun, we were going in an easterly direction. Soon we were going almost north. We were on the wrong train to go south. We decided to get off at the first stop and get back south some way. The train pulled into a siding at a large packing plant and stopped. We walked into the small city and Ralph said, "I think we came through this town when we said goodby to Ott."

Ralph asked a man how far we were from Leesburg and he informed us it was about twenty-five miles north. We decided to hitchhike back to Tampa rather than wait for a train. We thought we could make better time. We agreed that to go over to the coast and then turn south would be more interesting.

We got to the coast in one ride and soon had another ride south: an old colored man in a model T Ford that looked new and ran like a sewing machine. He asked where we were going and we told him any place south. He said he lived in Tarpon Springs. He looked very prosperous, had a very nice suit and good shoes. I asked him what business he was in and he said, "Undertaking." He asked if we had ever been in Tarpon Springs. We told him we hadn't. "You should stop and look around town. It's the sponge capital of the world." He added, "Mostly Greek people live there and most dive for the sponge."

That sounded interesting and we decided we would look around Tarpon Springs and see some sea sponges. Tarpon Springs was a small city located along the Gulf of Mexico. When he let us out we saw a basket of sponges in front of a store. We went and looked at them. A man came out and asked it we wanted to buy some sponges. We told him no, that these were the first natural sponges we had seen. He said we should go down to the wharves and see the Greek divers. He told us how to get there.

On our way, we came to a large grocery store and decided to see how much food we could buy for a quarter. Ralph would do the talking as usual. He had developed a tale of woe that was so credible, sometimes I almost believed it. We walked in the door and spotted the owner. Ralph walked over, I followed, and he started his bargaining. He said he only had fifteen cents and needed food to last until we got to Miami where he would meet his father whom he hadn't seen for ten years. The man looked a little sympathetic and went behind the meat counter. He had a large paper bag and began putting things in it we couldn't see. Then he went to the bread counter, then the fruit counter. He picked up a sack of nuts and brought it to us. Ralph gave him the fifteen cents and we left. When we got around a corner, we sat down on some steps to see what we had for our fifteen cents. We had a piece of bologna, a piece of ham with hot peppers in it, two loaves of second day bread, some donuts, the bag of peanuts and several bananas and a lot of oranges, all in good condition. We got our knives, made a sandwich, and ate some of the bananas.

With our stomachs full, we started walking to the wharf. When we got to the water we saw a sign that read: *Rent a boat and diver for a dollar.* The fine print promised a diver would take you out in a boat and dive down and bring you up a real ocean sponge.

We walked around and looked at the diving gear. Soon a sponge boat came in to unload the sponges. They didn't look like the ones we had seen in the basket. We asked a man if these were really sponges as they didn't look like the ones we saw in town. He said that after these were dried and trimmed, they would look like the ones uptown. In the meantime, the tourist boat had enough customers to take them out and find them a real sponge.

They went out only about a hundred yards and we could see the diver go overboard in his helmet and suit. In two or three minutes he was back holding a sponge. I said to the man, "The bottom must be full of sponges to find one that quick."

He started laughing and revealed that the sponges were in a box on the ocean floor; all the sponges there were cleaned out years ago. The diver went down, found the box and grabbed one, coming to the surface and handing it to the tourist. He did very well.

I asked him if there was a railroad in Tarpon Springs. He said there was, but only one train each way and they both had been there that day. We decided to hitchhike to Tampa and try the trains again. We got a short ride toward Tampa and walked to the yards for the second time that day. It was getting close to evening when we looked over the trains. We saw one with an engineer in it, so ran and asked him if he was going south. He pointed to another string of cars with no engine and said that one was going south, but wouldn't be leaving for a couple of hours. It was the only one until tomorrow. He warned us it would be checked so we'd better watch that we didn't get caught. We went back to the fence where we could keep an eye on the train. We saw two detectives checking our train.

It was a dark night with dark clouds that looked like rain coming. Finally we saw an engine coming from the center of the yard. It pulled into the siding and hooked onto the string of cars. When the detectives were almost to the end, we ran down and found an empty car just as a crash of thunder brought on the heavy rain. We didn't worry about the two detectives coming back; they wouldn't stay out in that kind of rain. We heard the couplers banging; we were on our way. The rain didn't come in the door so we sat on the floor and looked out. When the lightning flashed, we could see nothing but swamp land. Most of southern Florida seemed to be swamps.

The heavy rain thudded on the roof of the car, but we were snug and dry in our side-door Pullman. The train moved slowly and the car swayed back and forth, and with the rain drumming on the roof we lay down and went to sleep.

The train stopped and I woke up. Looking out the car door, I saw we were on a siding and a swamp stretched as far as I could see. Not a light of any kind was visible. In this wilderness I didn't think we would be bothered by detectives so I went back to sleep. When daylight came in the car we woke and were still on the siding.

The rain had stopped. Sunlight revealed what a desolate place we were in. Not a house, building, or any man-made object, except the one we were riding on, was in sight. We had no idea how long we had been on the siding. I told Ralph I thought it may have been three or four hours since I woke up when the train stopped. We couldn't reason why a siding existed in the middle of the biggest swamp we had even seen. We sat in the door and looked for alligators and watched long-legged birds hunt for their breakfast. We decided we would eat ours. We ate the rest of the bananas, had an orange, and rolled a cigarette while trying to figure out what was going on.

The swamp was large, as far as we could see a watery wasteland stretched. Trees growing in it were bare and deathly looking. We wondered who owned this sodden wilderness, or perhaps nobody thought it was worth owning. Alligators were probably hunted there; it looked like a good homeland for thousands of them. There may have been a lot of them, but we saw only a few. The swamp seemed to stretch forever.

After we finished eating, we saw a man get out of the caboose and walk toward the front of the train. We opened the other door. If it was a detective we were getting off on the opposite side. As he got closer we saw he wore overalls and was probably a brakeman. When he came to our car, we asked him why we were on the siding so long.

He said, "They had a small problem with the engine and pulled in here to fix it. They had lost time and now they have to wait for a passenger train that's going in the same direction as us."

We saw some hobos get off and walk along the train. We didn't get off because if the train started up suddenly, we wouldn't be able to get back in the car and would have to ride on top in the hot sun. We smoked a cigarette and studied the map trying to figure what cities we would see. According to the map, there were only small cities before we arrived in Miami. We saw the hobos running for the cars and on the mainline a passenger train sped toward us. The hobos made it to their cars and the passenger train flashed by at seventy miles an hour.

We began to move, but very slowly. At noon we made some sandwiches. We saw one small village that was about half mile away, the first sign of human beings. We were leaving the swamp and beginning to see some houses and people working in the fields. The houses were some of the poorest that we had seen in the South. It was really primitive living for blacks and whites with only an occasional crossroads with a small store. We stopped outside of a small town for coal and water. Some of the hobos got off and started walking into town. I hated the idea of being stranded out there for even a day, and the way it looked we would fare poorly in the food department. We did wish we had a little more water. In that hot humid weather we drank more water.

The brakeman walked to the head of the train and we asked him what the next city was. He said it was Punta Gordo. That didn't sound like much of a city.

We were traveling very slowly, sitting in the car door and talking about the things we were going to do in Miami. We crossed a fairly large river and soon were in a small town that must have been Punta Gordo. We pulled onto a siding and stopped. Most of the hobos got off and walked toward the town. They were probably looking for something to eat.

The engine took off and left us, but he unhooked the caboose and took it. Soon it returned with boxcars and hooked everything on the back of the train, then backed out of the siding and went on the main track to the head of the train. The brakeman threw a switch and he backed in and coupled onto the train.

I thought we were ready to go. Within a few minutes, we pulled out on the mainline. We took our usual seat in the open door and watched the town and the people as we rolled through.

We crossed a wide river, or perhaps it was an arm of the ocean, then were back in uninhabited land with only an occasional shack set up on poles above the ground. When we ate at evening we finished our water. We would have to get off tomorrow and get some water some place. A full moon came up and it was almost as light as day. If the train stopped in a town at night, we were still going to get off. We had food, but we had to get some water. We smoked a last cigarette and then lay down and went to sleep.

I always woke when the train stopped, which was good. Being caught by railroad detectives while asleep would be very bad. Ralph never woke up, so I went to the door and looked out, seeing the shadowy outline of buildings in a small city. The engine was getting coal and water. I woke Ralph and we decided to get off. The trains had to stop there for coal and water and we could get back on. When we *could* get back on remained to be seen.

As we walked into the outskirts of the place, dogs barked and we thought we were waking everybody in town. When we reached the business section, we saw it consisted of a very small narrow bank, a general store which was the largest building in town, a few other small stores and a doctor's office. There was a town pump with a large tin cup on the end of a chain to keep anyone from carrying it off. We filled our jars and drank until we could drink no more. We refilled them and looked around for a place to sleep. It was about midnight by Ralph's watch. We stayed away from the bank and store as we didn't want anybody thinking we might rob one of them. We saw a church with a steeple a small distance away and we decided to investigate it.

We were looking for grass, but found none suitable to sleep on. Behind the church we found some rough tables that the church people used for church dinner.

Ralph said, "We've just found our bed for the night."

By not walking through big cities, our tobacco was low, but we had a cigarette, then climbed on the tables and using our bags as pillows, fell asleep.

Sunlight and bird noises woke us early. We needed a place to clean up a little bit. We made sandwiches and ate an orange for breakfast. The meat tasted funny and we suspected it was spoiling. We didn't have much left so decided to throw it away. A dog came to investigate and we fed him the meat. When we left to go back to the town center, he followed us and we couldn't drive him away. We stopped and talked to a group of men in front of the general store. We told them we needed a place to get cleaned up and asked if they knew of one. One man suggested a river but said it was a couple miles away. Another said the owner of the general store had a place in the back he might let us use. We would need more food so we thought we would buy it from him and then ask to use his clean-up place.

We went in and spotted the owner and went to talk to him. Ralph said that we had twenty cents and needed food for two people for two days. We weren't particular what we ate.

He said, "I'll see what I can do." He went to the meat counter and then to the back room, returning to give us a large bag and a smaller bag of peanuts. We still had the bag of peanuts we hadn't finished, so we were loaded with peanuts.

We asked if we might get cleaned up in his place behind the store. He said he guessed so because a lot of town people did just that. We asked if he had soap and he said he didn't, but he went in the back room and handed us a part of a bar of soap. "You have to fill the tank on top from the well," he instructed, "and then pull the chain and the water will come down."

We went out back and looked the place over. It was a small shack with a tin wash tub on top. A ladder leaned against the side. A bucket was inside. The floor was wood laid on the bare ground with a small ditch to carry the water outside. We got the pump started, filled the bucket, climbed the ladder and dumped it into the tub on top. When we had it full, we went inside and took off our clothes. The area was so small we thought we would get them wet. Outside I had noticed a large nail driven in the wall beside the door so we hung our clothes there.

I told Ralph to go first. He pulled on the chain and that opened up the tub on the roof. The water ran into a large can with holes punched in it. When he stepped under the water, he let out a yell because the water was ice cold. He stopped the water, soaped up, and then pulled the chain and got rinsed off.

Then it was my turn. I was prepared for the cold water, but it was a lot colder than I thought it would be. We dressed and filled our water bottles. We decided to find out if anybody knew when a southbound train would be expected. Ralph suggested walking back to the coal docks to see if anyone was around there who knew when a train came through.

When we got there, we saw one man sitting on some steps smoking a pipe. We spoke to him and then asked if he could tell us if a southbound train would stop for coal and water. He said, "Yes, there are two, a freight and a passenger at about four in the afternoon."

We thanked him and decided to go back to town and find some shade. We walked to the store and sat down on the covered porch. We talked to some men about work. One said, "There's nothing here for a job you can depend on. Some fellows hunt alligator for skins, but they don't pay much for them and sometimes won't buy at any price."

As we looked around the town, we could see it had fallen on hard times. The merciless sun had faded the paint on the houses, and on some the paint was gone altogether. "Most of the people who work are working in St. Petersburg or Tampa and as far away as Miami," the man went on.

We decided to go back to the coal docks, not wanting to miss the train which would mean staying another night and part of a day. The man was still working getting the coal and water ready for the train. The train could carry enough coal to go a long way, but the steam engine was a thirsty beast and often stopped for water. This was a coal and water station, the coal coming out by the coal cars.

We could see the smoke in the level country before the train. Freight trains were so heavy that when the power ceased they didn't coast long. We walked to the track, and I was always impressed by the size of those monster engines. The train stopped and we walked, looking for a nice clean car. We passed one full of hobos and one asked, "Where are we?"

"I don't know," I answered.

We found a car, climbed in and looked around; it seemed to be clean. I was surprised that there weren't more hobos on the trains in Florida.

We ate our noon meal, then sat in the car door and shelled and ate peanuts. Ralph and I discussed the lack of people in that part of Florida. It was easy to understand for the land was poor. We looked down the train to the engine and saw we were turning toward the east. Maybe we might make it to the east coast on this train. We saw areas of swamp land and soon we were crossing a large marsh area. As we penetrated it we could see it extending to the horizon. There were no houses or any people in sight. It was very warm and humid and we began to cut down on our water.

We saw a few islands with small trees and weeds growing thick, but everything else was in water. We rolled a cigarette and talked about what we might see in Miami. Suddenly, Ralph yelled, "Look over there!" He pointed to an island and what looked like logs turned out to be two alligators about six feet long. They didn't even move as the train ran noisily by them.

When we crossed those swamps, the train went slowly as if afraid of going off the rails. As the sun sank, we saw we were definitely going east. Perhaps we were going slowly to conserve water for the engine. There was plenty of water there, but none of it for the engine or for us. We ate our evening meal before it got dark and then sat in the door and ate peanuts. We wondered and talked about whether we were crossing the Everglades. Before the moon came up, it was pitch black except for the long finger of light from the engine.

In the moonlight, we could see we were out of the swamp and on higher ground with trees and underbrush growing. On the south side, we saw water so we must have been traveling on the northern edge of the swamp. We were still going very slowly. Soon we lay down and slept.

The train stopped and I woke as usual. I wanted to know what time it was, but didn't want to wake Ralph. I heard coal cascading into the engine, and got up and looked out the door. Although there were no lights, I thought I could see houses and buildings. I didn't think there were any detectives about. I decided to stay awake until the train moved on and I could take a look at the little town. When we moved by the town, I saw the same poor houses and not a light burning in them. I went back to sleep.

At daybreak, we woke and what a change! The swamp was gone and we saw a lot of sand and palm trees. Also, we saw houses and small towns. According to the sun, we were going south again. At that time, the only city in southeastern Florida was Miami. We wondered if we were lucky enough to be going all the way on the train to Miami. The train was going faster and didn't slow going through the small towns. We had yet to see the ocean.

The train slowed and I thought we were coming into Miami. I thought I could see tall buildings far in the distance. We had crossed several paved highways and the houses were getting more numerous. The train kept slowing and we were approaching Miami. We were still moving, but now we were in multiple tracks so it wouldn't be long before we saw the yards. We were out of water and thirsty. We would be glad to find some water. It was a big yard. We saw more passenger trains that we had seen anywhere else.

We seemed to be in the center of the yard, but the train was still going too fast to jump from the boxcar door without risking a bad fall. Suddenly, the engineer applied the brakes and before we could jump the train stopped completely. We ran for the fence, across tracks and going under the cars that obstructed our way. We found a hole and came out on a street in a poor section of the city.

As we walked, we saw a pump in the backyard of a house. We knocked on the door and a woman opened it. Ralph asked, "Could we get a drink of water from your pump in the yard?"

"Of course," the woman replied. "Help yourself."

We filled our jars and drank until we felt water-logged. We continued down the street toward the big buildings in the distance. We liked what we saw: hot climate, palm trees, and flowers. The people seemed a little more prosperous. Far off, we got a glimpse of the Atlantic Ocean.

It was in the middle of the afternoon when we got downtown. Ralph suggested we look for a cheap room before dark. The first person we asked said he didn't know. When we asked a dark complexioned man, he said the cheapest place to live was in the Cuban section of Miami.

I said, "This sounds like what we're looking for." He gave us directions, we thanked him and started off to find a room.

Chapter Seventeen

When we arrived in the area, it was almost like a foreign country. Everybody was speaking Spanish. Occasionally, we heard some Spanish and some English words mixed in. One man in a colorful shirt seemed to be using more English than others, so we approached him and asked if he spoke English. He said he spoke English very well and asked what he could do for us.

We explained that we needed a clean room with access to a bath, and that we wouldn't pay a lot for it.

"I have a friend that has a very nice room," he said, "but only the son who goes to school speaks both English and Spanish. If you can get along with that I think it would be a good place for you." We said we would like to see the place. "I'll go with you and show it to you and will talk for you when we get there," he said.

Ralph said, "When the boy is in school we probably would be gone too, so maybe this might work out pretty good."

The place was an apartment building, the small lobby filled with Cuban men talking. We walked up two flights of stairs and the Cuban man knocked on the door. A pleasant featured, dark-complexioned woman opened the door and greeted our friend in Spanish. They talked for a minute or so and then he turned to us and said the room was two dollars a week. She wanted to know, he said, if we wanted our meals.

"We'd like to look at the room first," Ralph said.

"Of course," he said.

The woman took us through the apartment to the rental room. It wasn't too big, but the bathroom was across the hall and had a bathtub. Everything was very clean. We asked our friend what the room would be with our breakfast and evening meal.

After talking with her, he said, "If you eat with the family and she doesn't have to cook differently or separately for you, it will be three dollars."

We decided we would take it for a week and see how things went. He asked our names and told her them in Spanish. The couple's name was Arturo and Rosa Alvarez and Pepe was their thirteen year old son. Our friend said that Arturo worked as a plumber and that was why they had a private bath. There was a bath at the end of each hall used by everyone on that floor. We handed over the three dollars, telling our friend to tell the woman we wanted to take a bath and clean up. She led us to the bathroom and furnished us with towels and soap.

Ralph went in first, turning on the hot spigot but nothing came out. He turned on the cold and was rewarded with cold water. Another place with no hot water, but if they could take cold baths, then I supposed we could stand it too. When we came out, our friend was still talking to Rosa. He told us breakfast was at seven o'clock and the evening meal at six o'clock. We shook hands with him and he told us Pepe would be home from school and would translate for us. Perhaps we might even learn a few words of Spanish.

Ralph suggested a walk. Rosa handed me a key and we walked out and down the stairs to the lobby. There was a card game going on and we watched it for a short time, but it wasn't a game we were familiar with.

We left and walked down the street until we came to a small park where we sat down on a bench. Ralph stretched out his legs and said, "When I think about how cold it was when we left Indiana and now we're sitting around with palm trees and flowers and 75 degree weather, I could stay here until Spring."

"If we do, we'll have to get a job somewhere because we have about enough money to last ten days at the rate we're spending it," I replied. "With all these colored people working for almost nothing, I don't think washing cars is going to produce much money."

"Well, let's just relax and enjoy it as long as we can," said Ralph.

It was almost time to meet the other two members of the family, Arturo and Pepe, and find out what Cuban cooking was like. When we went in the apartment, Pepe was seated beside his mother on the sofa.

He addressed us in English. "Hello, I am Pepe. Welcome to our home."

We told him our names and asked how things were going at school. He said he was very happy in school and wished to continue if possible and graduate. Arturo entered the room and greeted us in English. His speech was heavily accented, but we had no difficulty understanding him.

Rosa spoke to her husband and he said it was time to eat. We went to the kitchen to a large, round wooden table. As Rosa set the food on the table, I saw we were going to have roast pork, black beans, yams, rice and a fruit salad. At home, rice was cooked in a gluey mess and we ate it with milk and sugar. Here the rice was cooked so each grain seemed to stand alone, topped with a sauce made from the roast pork.

We tried and found it unusual but it tasted good. We would find in the meals to come that rice displaced grits as something that was served every meal. If this meal was a sample of what was to come, then I thought we would eat very well. We were going to walk around the neighborhood that evening.

We walked by the small shops and looked at the merchandise. The smell of cooking and charcoal was everywhere. Although we had just eaten, the smell of cooking meats and spices almost made me want to eat again. Soon we found an open air restaurant and decided to have a cup of coffee. We used our first Spanish, "No leche." We didn't care for the coffee and milk that a lot of people around us were drinking. We rolled a cigarette and leaned back in our chairs and looked around. There seemed about a third of the people were colored. We were getting accustomed to seeing blacks everywhere in the South. After a refill on the coffee we decided to go back to our room and sleep so we could get up early and go into downtown Miami.

It was another strange bed, but it was much better than a boxcar floor. I slept well. A knock on the door got us up. We dressed and went down to a breakfast of scrambled eggs with peppers, toast made in the oven, rolls with icing and strong coffee.

We said goodby to the family and went through the lobby where some old men were already playing cards. It was a beautiful day, blue sky and a warm breeze blowing. It was going to be quite a walk, but we weren't wasting money on bus fares.

When we got to the heart of Miami, we found it wasn't concentrated like most cities, but was spread out over several city blocks. For a southern town, Miami was busy. We looked in the large stores at the different and expensive merchandise shown in the windows.

We stopped in a large hotel lobby and looked around. Ralph said, "Let's go up in the elevator." Neither us of had ever ridden in one higher than three stories, and that building looked at least fifteen stories or maybe more. I looked at the elevators and each was manned by a colored man. By that time I understood that no black man would stop a white person from riding in an elevator, even if he knew we weren't staying in the hotel.

We approached an elevator and the black man opened the door and we walked in. He stood behind us. "What floor, sir?" he asked.

We didn't know what floor to tell him, so finally Ralph said, "18th floor."

The black man said nothing for a few seconds then said, "This elevator only goes to the 16th floor, sir."

I almost burst out laughing when Ralph said, "We'll go to the 16th floor."

"Yes, sir," said the operator and up we went.

We got out on the top floor but there was nothing to see but closed doors, so we pushed the down button. We got the same elevator. When we got on and Ralph said "first floor," the colored man must have thought it was a quick trip, probably guessing what we were doing. We sat down in the lobby but when we noticed a man watching us closely, we decided to leave.

Walking around the city, we replenished our tobacco sack. At noon we hadn't planned on eating but the walking had increased our appetites, so we decided to get a cup of coffee and some kind of roll.

Ralph said, "Things look more expensive here. Let's walk down to the water and see what we can find."

We walked until we got down in the port area and found an outdoor restaurant where we had a good view of the harbor. We had a coffee and two fried rolls that we had never seen before. After we ate the rolls, which were very good, we rolled a cigarette and settled back to see what was going on in the area. After awhile, the owner came over and filled our cups again. We figured he didn't care if we sat there all afternoon. It was probably good business to have some people sitting in your place of business, even if they didn't buy anything but coffee.

It was a very colorful stream of people who went by. It was strange to see so many dark faces. We were accustomed to never seeing a dark face in our little town.

Ralph asked, "How's our money holding out?"

"If we have coffee and rolls every day, including bus money to go out to Miami Beach and back, I think we'll be broke in a week," I said.

"I really hate to leave here and go back to the snow and ice in Indiana," he replied.

"Maybe Arturo knows where we could pick up a day's work or two. Otherwise, we'll be almost broke in a week except for the dollar we said we wouldn't spend until we get out of the South."

"Well, we can ask him tonight," he said.

We planned to go out to the island the next day and look around. We liked the Alverezes very much and I thought they liked us. When we asked Arturo about work, he wasn't optimistic. "If you have a skill, you maybe could get some work but without a skill you are competing with a lot of people," he said.

We were kidding ourselves. We knew from the situation back home that even the unskilled usually had experience which we did not. Oh well, we would stay with them until we ran out of money and then we would leave.

We took the bus to Miami Beach and walked around the big hotels and shops, walking north until we ran out of buildings and there was nothing but sand, beaches and palmetto. As far as we could tell, it probably looked much the same as a hundred years ago. We took off our shoes and rolled up our pant legs and walked in the surf looking for seashells. After an enjoyable morning, we walked back to the southern end of hotels and stores. As we walked by the hotels, I saw almost every hotel including the ones in Miami had the same sentence on the front windows. The sign was always the same: *"Gentile clientele only."*

Ralph said he didn't know what it meant but thought it had something to do with keeping Negroes from entering the hotel. Maybe it was a polite term for the toilets we had seen all over the South where, on their doors, hung one of three signs: *Men, Women, Blacks.*

When we rode the bus back, we couldn't find two seats together so I sat down by an elderly gentleman. We exchanged pleasantries. After awhile I thought I would ask about the sign on the hotel windows. I asked him if he ever saw the words and he said he had. I asked if it meant that Negroes were not allowed to stay there.

"No," he said. "No Negro would attempt to stay there. That sign is for Jews. They don't want them to stay at their hotel."

"But Jews are white people," I said. "We used to sell junk to a Jew where I live."

"Well, he wouldn't be allowed to stay in any of those hotels."

I pondered the answer he had given me.

We found early that blacks were discriminated in the South, poor whites with no money were also discriminated against, and now even a wealthy Jew could be discriminated against. When we got off the bus, I told Ralph what the man had told me. He said he figured it was something like that.

That night while we were eating Arturo said there was a section of town where they had very expensive and beautiful houses; we might want to walk there and look at them. We would do that tomorrow. After we had eaten, we went down to the lobby and wandered around watching the card games, then out into the night. We never tired of walking around the Cuban section; it was like a foreign country with people talking in languages we had never heard.

After wandering around the streets, before going to bed, we devised a plan. Ralph went into a restaurant first and ordered a cup of coffee. I waited, came along later, walked in, and talked to him. Then Ralph invited me to sit down. When the owner came over, I told him I didn't want anything, but was going to talk with my friend. He went back behind the counter and then into the kitchen where I thought he was cooking something. Every few minutes, he looked out the kitchen door to see if he had any customers. When he disappeared into the kitchen, we both drank the coffee. He came out to the counter and brought Ralph a refill and went back to the kitchen.

While we sat there smoking, a couple of young women came near and smiled at us. Ralph waved at them. They abruptly turned and came to our table. "You like good time?"

We had attracted two prostitutes. "We have no money," Ralph explained.

"No money," she exclaimed.

"No dinero," Ralph said using one of the Spanish words he had picked up from the Alvarez family. "Sit down," Ralph said.

"No," she answered, "Not for free. Adios." And they walked out to the street.

We decided we had seen enough for the night and we went back to our room to sleep. We looked at the rich people's homes and were impressed. The houses were not only beautiful, but very large. If you had money, you could buy things you wanted very cheap. Labor was also cheap. Carpenters, bricklayers, electricians could be had for three to five dollars a day. We would have been glad working for a dollar a day, but then so would a lot of other people.

Arturo worked for a plumbing company but when there was no work to be done he was laid off. He wanted Pepe to teach Rosa English and perhaps then Rosa could get a job as a maid in one of the rich family's homes.

We spent our evening sitting in a sidewalk cafe drinking coffee and watching the colorful people go by. Inspecting the various food places, most of the cooking was done out in the open where we could get a good view of it. We bought two mangoes for three cents as we had never seen them before. They were very good.

Ralph had found out there was a railroad running from Miami to Key West. He wanted to go there and I would have liked to make the trip, but was uneasy about it. We were going to the yards the next day to see what we could find out about the railroad. We finished our coffee and walked back to our room to sleep.

When we had finished our breakfast we started out for the railroad yard. We could see that Miami had a large and busy yard. We came upon two middle aged men; they had a bundle of clothes over their shoulders.

We decided to stop and talk to them to see if they had ever been to Key West on the railroad. When they came to us we spoke to them and asked if they were hobos. "You might say that," said one.

"We're thinking about going to Key West and want to know if you two might help us out with information."

"Neither of us has been there and I wouldn't consider it," one said.

"Have you ever heard of anyone going there?"

"No, I've never heard of anyone, but I suppose some hobos probably have," he said.

It was going to be difficult to find that train without going into the yards. We decided we needed more information. We went to the docks and watched the ships load and unload. It was a very busy place. We talked of the different flags on the ships and wondered what part of the world they had sailed from.

Ralph said again, "We should try to get a job on one of these ships and go on a long trip."

But there was the experience again, what would we know about the work on a ship when we had never set foot on one? It was nice to talk about it, but we knew it would never happen.

That night, while having our usual coffee and cigarette at our sidewalk cafe, Ralph brought up Key West again. "That would be a trip that very few hobos had ever made."

"That's probably true and I think I know the reason why," I said. "I was looking at the map and it shows just dots of islands. If we were chased off the train, where would we go? If we were on one of the long bridges, we would have to stay on the train and detectives would soon catch us because we would have no way to get off the train."

"Maybe we could jump in the water," he said. I knew when he said those words that he had given up on the Key West journey.

We had two more days and nights before we had to leave. We would be out of money when we left Miami except for the dollar bill we were determined to keep as long as we were in the South.

We had had a great time on this trip, but I didn't think we could live in Florida without money. Ralph said the cold baths we took every day were getting us toughened for the cold weather up North.

We had a lot of fun with Pepe; he was curious about everything. He wanted to know about the high school, about basketball especially because they didn't have a basketball team at his high school. He wanted to know about our travels and the different places we had seen. As for us, we questioned Arturo about Cuba and Havana the city he came from. He struggled with the English language but with Pepe's help we got a fair picture of Havana and Cuba.

Time passed swiftly and we were to start making our way back to the snow and cold. We were concerned about the trip because we had never hoboed in cold weather. It could be a problem.

We planned to go the next day to see how many detectives were around and if it was possible to get in a car while the train was stopped. Also, we wanted to know the best place to get a train if we had to catch it while it was moving. One problem we didn't have was where the train we caught was going. North, northwest or west, it made no difference—they all were on the way home. If we would catch one going south, well Ralph wanted to go to Key West and we would be committed to go.

I thought a train going west out of Miami would take us back to Tampa the way we came over. If we happened to go this way, I was sure Ralph would want to stop and see Angie one more time. I would have liked to see both of them. They were great people to be around. Ralph had their address and planned to write to Angie.

After our evening meal, we checked out the card game in the lobby and then strolled through the streets of that most interesting section of Miami. We stopped at our sidewalk cafe and the owner knew us. As soon as we were seated, he brought us our cup of strong Cuban coffee.

We tried our Spanish on him. *"Buenos Noches,"* we greeted him.

He gave us a big smile and answered, *"Buenos Noches, Señores. Qué pasa?"*

But that was the end of our Spanish. We didn't know what *"qué pasa"* meant so we gave him a hand wave.

The two girl prostitutes came by every night and we waved to them and they waved back. They didn't come over to our table; they knew there was no money in those pockets.

With a warm breeze, big moon, palm trees rattling in the square, a cup of coffee, cigarette, and a choice place to view the passersby, we had it made. "I really hate to leave," Ralph said. "Just the thought of it is ruining my last two nights."

At midnight things quieted down and we went back to our room and to bed. The next morning when we went to the yards, we found a couple of places with a good view of the yard. We stayed about two hours and looked for detectives and how they were inspecting the trains. It wasn't long before we saw a train made up that seemed ready to go. We saw a pair of detectives, one on each side, checking out every car. In the time we were there, we saw several crews of detectives working the trains. We walked down to the end of the yard and saw a group of hobos waiting outside the fence. We talked to several of them and they all said it was better to stay outside of the yard and catch the moving train. One said if the train was going too fast, just wait and there would be another in a few minutes.

We started back. We would take their advice and catch a moving train. We didn't want to take a chance of getting caught. We walked back to the city and walked again down to the docks to watch the ships.

We headed back to our room for our final evening meal with that friendly family. Rosa had outdone her great cooking. We had a whole roast chicken that was black with peppers, noodles in a sauce, a large mound of rice and baked sweet potatoes.

Arturo produced a bottle of wine and we sat down to one of the best meals I had ever had. We were a happy group. I had never tasted wine except for the time in Tampa, but it was an improvement over Ott's moonshine from Tennessee. We talked to the family until eight o'clock, then went down through the lobby to walk around for the last night.

When we settled into our seats at the sidewalk cafe, the owner, as usual, brought the two cups of coffee. We greeted him in Spanish as we had previously and he replied, *"Buenos noches, Señores. Qué pasa?*

We had learned from Arturo that this phrase was similar to when we said, "What's new?" to a friend. Arturo said we could answer by saying, *"Nada"* which means "nothing."

So we answered, *"Nada."* He smiled and said in English, "You stay here another week and you will be speaking Spanish like a Cuban."

"Well," Ralph said, "This is our last night we'll be in this nice city."

"Why do you leave, you go back home?"

"Yes, we'll leave tomorrow morning."

"I am sorry to see you go," he said. We'll be sorry to leave too, we assured him. He left and soon came back and laid two cigars on the table. "A small present from me to make your last night here more enjoyable," he said. We thanked him warmly and when he left we lit the cigars and settled back, and as he had said, got ready to enjoy our last night.

We had made arrangements with Rosa to make us some sandwiches and paid her. We spent our last dime for two coffees, but it was worth it.

When the two girl prostitutes came walking by, Ralph waved for them to come over. They talked a minute with each other, then walked to our table. We both stood up.

Ralph spoke, "We wanted to tell you how we enjoyed seeing you walk by every night and also to tell you we're leaving tomorrow to go back up North to our home."

"You have home?" one asked.

"Oh, yeah. We both have homes," Ralph said.

"You both married?" she asked.

"No, we're not married."

"You like take us home with you?"

We both burst out laughing, but they looked at each other. They were not laughing. They really meant what they said. We told them we were going back by freight train.

"You mean passenger train?"

"No, we mean freight train."

After studying this for a few minutes, one said, "I think better we stay here."

We told them goodby and one said, "You good boys, come back sometime with money."

We laughed and waved goodby. I could see my mother if I walked in our house with this pretty Cuban girl. I could imagine these girls running to catch a freight train in their high heeled shoes.

At midnight we went over to the counter and shook hands with the owner and told him goodby. He said, "Goodby and come back again." We told him we would and at that time we really meant to come back to Florida.

The next morning we said goodby to the family. They wished us a safe trip home.

When we arrived at the yard, we saw about thirty hobos standing outside the fence. A small train started out of the yard, but by the time it reached us it was going so fast none of us even attempted to catch it. I asked one of them if all the trains came out that fast.

"I've been here about two hours and have seen none I thought I could get on. But there's bound to be a slow one come out sooner or later."

To most hobos, time meant little. If they were there three days before they caught a train, it wouldn't have bothered them.

At noon we retreated from the railroad and sat under a tree and ate lunch. Rosa had made chicken sandwiches, eight deep fried rolls that we had never seen before, and gave us a dozen oranges.

We were disappointed in not catching a train. Four or five caught one train, but they weren't carrying anything. Even they were jerked off their feet when they grabbed the ladders. We smoked a cigarette and then went back and stood with the rest of the hobos.

About three o'clock a cheer went up. I looked down the yard and saw a long train and the engine was having a time getting up speed. This was the one we were all waiting for. I told Ralph to get the car behind the engine and I would get the second one. If one of us couldn't make it, the other was to drop off so we could travel together. When the train came by, we ran alongside and both got on. I looked down the train and every hobo got on. We were going to have plenty of company. We walked down the train until we were out of the smoke and cinders and sat down on a car with three other hobos.

The sun was very hot and I hoped we wouldn't have to ride on top for very long. We were finally on our way back home. After about an hour, we pulled onto a siding in a small town. We saw a brakeman come down from the head of the train and at about a third of the train, he stepped between two cars and uncoupled them, stepped out, waved to the engineer, and grabbed the ladder on the last car. The train pulled out on the mainline and soon disappeared in the distance. We were certainly not making much time on our first day on the road. There were a few hobos on the section who went away, but most of us were left on a train that had no engine and wasn't going anywhere. We decided to get off and look for an empty boxcar but there were none.

That was why the train had come out of the yard slow enough for all of us to catch it. The other hobos had had no success either and were sitting in the shade made by the cars.

We didn't have the patience of a real hobo. They had no place to stay so a stop like this didn't appear to bother them. A passenger train went by and we waved at the passengers but few waved at us.

It was getting dark when the engine returned with the cars he took away. The brakeman got off, threw the switch and backed in and hooked on to us. The brakeman stayed by the switch, so we were going to move out. Everybody climbed back on top with the others and the train slowly moved out on the mainline. When the caboose passed the switch, the brakeman threw it, ran and caught it. The train started to pick up speed. We didn't want to eat anything when they had nothing, so I got out the oranges and gave one to each of us. We talked to them for awhile, and one of them said he was sure the cars the brakeman brought back were not the same ones he left with, that he may have brought back some empties.

At the first stop we planned to look for an empty. It was almost nine o'clock when the train stopped for coal and water. There was a small town in the distance and almost all of the hobos, except the two of us, decided to walk to it. We walked to the new cars and found an empty and climbed in. We looked around as best we could and decided it would do until daylight. We ate a sandwich and an orange. We had two sandwiches left. The oranges we were going to eat for breakfast, the sandwiches at noon. By tomorrow night we would be true hobos, no money, and no food.

The land was different here. We didn't see the swamps, but mostly sandy soil and pine trees. We lay down and slept. When we woke, the sun was shining and we were on a siding. I thought now that we might have been the only ones on the train. We ate the oranges and wondered how long we had been stopped. We were having a hard time getting out of Florida. According to the position of the sun, we were going almost north so, at least, we were going in the right direction.

About an hour later, a long freight train passed us going in the opposite direction, and with a jolt, our train started and pulled out on the mainline.

Ralph said, "You know, we'll have to get off somewhere this afternoon and get some food."

I wished I knew where we were on the map. All the towns we had been through with names on the passenger station were too small to be on our map. And now we seemed to be bearing more to the west.

We ate sandwiches at lunch, folded up the bag and I put it in my back pocket. We were making such poor time we discussed whether to start hitchhiking and see if we could do better. Perhaps, food would be more available.

When the train stopped on a siding, there was a small town. We got off. We would try hitchhiking. As we were walking into the city, we came to an orange grove that had large reddish oranges. We walked into the grove and the fruit lay thick under each tree. They weren't even picking the fruit. We peeled one and it was red in the inside and very sweet. We found out later that they were blood oranges. We picked three or four each and went out to the road to get away from the bees and other insects which were all over the rotting fruit. Those oranges were the best we had eaten since we had been in Florida. After we ate the oranges, Ralph asked, "Have you still got that sack we had?" I pulled the sack out of my pocket. "Let's fill it up with these oranges."

We went back in the orchard and picked the bag full of the largest and ripest oranges we could find. If we didn't find any food, at least we had the oranges to eat.

When we walked into the small town, we looked around and decided this was the poorest town we had been in. There was a store but when we got to it we saw that the windows were broken and it was no longer in business.

The houses were nothing but shacks with no window glass in them. They seemed to be occupied mostly by colored people and the ones we saw looked suspiciously at us. We walked until we came to the road running through the town and turned north and continued walking. We had not seen one car through the place, so we just might do some walking. After a couple of miles we same to a small white church. There were several horse and wagons, and some pulled by mules. We decided we would go in and see what might happen.

When we walked in everybody turned and looked at us. The minister stopped in mid-sentence. We looked back at them. Every face turned to us was black; we were in a colored church. Finally, the minister asked if he could help us in any way.

"We've walked a long way and are tired, and we thought if you didn't mind, we would sit down and rest," Ralph said.

"Yes, sit down and rest," said the minister.

"Please continue your sermon," I said.

The people turned and faced the minister and he continued. A teenage girl stood and sang a hymn with a sweet clear voice that made chills down my spine. No accompaniment, just her pure liquid voice. When she finished the song, the minister asked us to stand for prayer. At its conclusion, everybody started talking and moving to the door where the minister greeted them. Ralph said, "Let's just sit still until everybody leaves, maybe we can find a place to sleep."

When all were gone, the minister came back in the church and walked to where we were sitting. Ralph told him we were looking for a place to sleep. "Would you let us sleep here tonight?" he asked.

"Where would you sleep?" the minister asked. Ralph said we could move some of the benches together and sleep on top of them. "Well, yes, you can sleep here. We don't have a lock on the door. When you leave in the morning, close the door and prop the piece of wood on it so it will stay shut. I'll leave one candle lit for you to see by," he added.

We thanked him and told him we would put the benches back where they were when we left in the morning. We walked with him to the door and I could see a wagon and mule that must belong to him. "How far do you live from church?" I asked him.

"About two miles from here."

"Are you married?" Ralph asked.

"Wife died two years ago. I have four children, all grown up and gone from here. Where are you fellows from? I know you're not from here."

"Our home is in Indiana and we're trying to get back there."

"We'll, I don't think you will sleep very well on those bare boards."

We assured him that we slept in boxcars on the wooden floor and this would be all right.

"I hope you sleep well," he said as he started walking to his wagon. We thanked him again for letting us stay in the church. We watched him drive away and then turned back to the flickering candle and the shadows it made on the walls. The benches had no backs on them so we pulled them together and made a fairly good bed. We ate some more of the blood oranges and then rolled another cigarette and sat in the door and smoked.

"Maybe tomorrow we'll find out where we are," Ralph said. I answered that I hadn't seen a car go by since we had been in the church. "I know," Ralph said. "I didn't like all those wagons here at the church. Not a one came in a car and some left walking down the road."

"Well, let's go to sleep and see what we can do tomorrow," I said.

We put out the candle and went to sleep.

Chapter Eighteen

When we woke in the morning, we put the benches back where they were and sat down to eat more oranges for breakfast. We sat in the front door and smoked a cigarette. Nothing had gone by since we woke up.

"I would rather walk than just sit here, wouldn't you?" Ralph asked.

I agreed and we propped the door shut and started down the road. I looked closer at the road and saw seashells embedded in it. They were held by some kind of white binder. Where, we wondered, would they find seashells in this quantity, enough to pave roads?

We saw something coming behind us. As it drew nearer we saw it to be a pair of mules pulling a wagon. A poorly dressed colored man was driving. When he came up to us we hailed him. He stopped so we asked him if we could ride in the back of his wagon. "Yes, sir," he said. We sat facing the way we had come in case a car came from behind. We'd have enough time to get off and thumb it down.

It was the hardest ride we ever had on that trip. It made a boxcar seem like a feather bed. With no springs and those iron-rimmed wheels, the wagon was really pounding us. After about a mile, Ralph said, "Let's get off. I'd rather walk than ride this wagon." I agreed and we hopped off, yelling, "Thanks!" but the driver never looked back or answered.

At noon we ate some more oranges and the last of our water. After we finished we saw our first car, a young fellow driving a truck. We thumbed him and he stopped, saying, "Hop in. Where are you going?" We said we were going anywhere he was headed. He told us that would be four miles down the road. After we explained we'd like to find a bigger highway, he said to keep walking and we would find one about ten miles further than where he dropped us off. He told us the first towns we'd come to would be Sebring, Lake Wales, Haines City, Kissimmee and the largest, Orlando.

We offered him an orange but he said, "We raise them, but I seldom eat them. We have hundreds of boxes of those we can't sell. We've stopped picking them and they're rotting under the trees." We sympathized with him and told him it was the same up North, that crops weren't harvested because they couldn't be sold at a profit.

He came to his turn and we thanked him and got out of the truck. Ralph suggested we sit and see what came along. We found a tree and sat down in the shade. We studied the shells in the road and wondered again where all those shells came from.

There were very poor houses and not very many of them. We wondered how the people living in them made a living. We saw an occasional black person sitting on the front step, but not very many. This was as desolate place as we had ever seen, except the large swamps. During that hour nobody came by. We didn't say anything about it, but we both knew that we were going to have to walk the ten miles to the highway.

We walked awhile, stopped, rolled and smoked a cigarette. "I don't think we'll make it out to the highway before dark," Ralph said.

"We should have stayed with the railway," I replied.

"But that didn't look too good sitting on that siding. I noticed the brakeman went with the engine."

We started walking again, always hoping when we looked up we would see a highway with lots of traffic. We came to another grove of blood oranges and we filled our sack. As the sun went lower we realized we weren't going to see the highway until tomorrow. We had to think about where we were going to sleep.

We decided to investigate an abandoned small building. When we got closer we saw that it was a school. But now its windows were broken and the door sagged half-off the door frame. When our eyes became accustomed to the dim light, we saw it was similar in furnishings to the church, with several benches pushed over against one wall. This was no church; there was a broken blackboard and several drawings and crayon pictures painted on the walls. Ralph said he thought we could use the benches again for a bed.

The same fellow must have made those benches, for they were identical to the ones in the church. We pulled them out by the door, and then we decided to build a small fire close to the door. We could see what looked like a playground and around in back, a rusty pump. I pulled the handle a dozen times, but all we got was a dry raspy sound.

We drank the last of our water. If not for the juicy oranges, we would have been out before that. We sat watching the fire and smoked a cigarette before we ate more oranges, and then went to sleep. We had lain there only a few minutes when I heard squeaks and rustling. I found a match and flared it. Tiny red eyes stared at us.

The place was alive with mice. We carried the benches outside and surrendered the schoolhouse to them.

The sun shining in our eyes woke us. Then Ralph leapt from the benches and ran, hollering, to the road where a Model T Ford was passing us. The man saw Ralph but he didn't stop. If we had awakened ten minutes earlier we might have gotten a ride to the highway. We sat on the benches and ate some oranges and then rolled and smoked a cigarette. We carried the benches back in the building, looking around for the mice but never saw a one.

It was a blue sky, sunshiny day with the birds singing and our spirits were high as we started down the seashell road. The highway couldn't be far off. By ten o'clock we saw no highway.

"I know we've walked more than ten miles since that man let us out of his car," I said.

"Seems more like twenty to me," Ralph replied.

By noon we couldn't believe we were still not in sight of a highway. We stopped and got out the oranges. We tried to eat some but our mouths were so sore from two days of eating oranges that we couldn't eat any more. I heard Ralph's stomach rumble and mine was doing the same.

I looked down the road and a car was coming. We stood alongside the road and smiled, giving him the thumb. He stopped and we ran and got in the Model T.

"Where you going?" he asked.

"We're trying to get to the highway," I said. "Then we're going north on it."

He was a little round man with a very pleasant smile. He said we were nearing the highway and Ralph and I could go north with him for about ten miles. We reached the highway and were glad to see a few cars on it. We told him we thought we would never get out to the highway. When we told him where we had started from, he said it was seventeen miles instead of ten. We offered him an orange and he stopped and peeled it.

"Aren't you having an orange?" he asked.

"We've only eaten oranges for two days and our mouths and tongues are sore from the acid," I said.

"Where are you from"?

"Indiana, trying to get back there, but we've run out of food and money."

We came to a small town and he said that was his stop. He reached in his pocket and pulled out two dimes. "This is all I have.

Take it and get you some food somewhere." We took the dimes and thanked him and told him to take the sack of oranges with him. He yelled, "Good luck!" and we waved goodby.

Ralph said, "I see a store down there. Let's see what two dimes will buy."

In back of the store was a chicken yard with a couple dozen chickens and a pig pen with three hogs in it. When we walked inside, most of the store was taken up with clothing, farming goods, and canned goods. Over in one corner was a large, black, wood-burning cook stove with a large oven in the center and a large cooking oven on top. There was one table with four small benches. We walked to the dry goods part where a man behind the counter looked like he was the owner. The only other person was a colored woman by the stove.

Ralph started, "We've had nothing to eat for the last two days but oranges and we're really hungry. What can you get us for twenty cents?"

He walked to the woman and said, "How much chicken have we got left?"

The woman said, "We hardly sold any today, we got a lot."

"How about some chicken?" he asked.

"If we get enough of it we'll be all right," Ralph said.

He laid a newspaper on the counter and opened the big oven. It was piled high with fried chicken. He started piling it on the newspaper until I thought we had two or three pounds of chicken. "How does that look to you?" he asked.

Ralph replied, "That's good but could we have some bread to go with it?" The owner picked up a half loaf of bread and a large knife and sliced it for us. "Do you have a place where we could fill our water jars?" Ralph asked.

"There's a well on the side of the store, you can fill up there." We thanked him and went around to the pump, drank and filled our bottles.

We walked down the main street until we came to a store that was out of business but had a porch on it. We sat down and unwrapped the chicken and started to eat. The chicken was still warm. After eating oranges for two days, we thought it was the best fried chicken we had ever eaten. When we got through, there were only three or four pieces left. We were full, almost to bursting.

We rolled a cigarette and while we smoked, a mongrel dog came cautiously over to us, his nose twitching at the fried chicken smell.

"Now what do you want?" Ralph said to the dog. He whined and edged closer to us.

"Are you going to give him a piece?" I asked.

"And what do we eat later on?" he replied. "Remember how hungry we were just an hour ago?"

"Just give him one piece," I said.

He tore the meat off the bone and held it in his hand. The dog still wasn't sure; he came closer, made a wild grab and ran with the chicken about twenty feet and ate it in one gulp. When he edged closer again, Ralph yelled at him and he ran down the street. Ralph sighed and said, "Remember that dentist in town that moved to Kissimmee? One of his boys was in our class, you remember what his name was?"

"Yes I do. His name was Paul Wilson. There was a lot of kids in that family," I replied.

"That fellow said Kissimmee was just up the road. Let's hitchhike up there and see if we can find him."

"Let's go," I said.

We asked the first man we met how far it was to Kissimmee and how to get there. It was only about thirty-five miles away on the highway running through the town where we stood.

We immediately got our first ride of about fifteen miles, got out of that car and in five minutes had another ride to Kissimmee. As we rode along we asked the driver if he knew a dentist there by the name of Wilson. He said he had heard of him but didn't know him.

When we arrived in town, he said, "Ask somebody in town. They can probably tell you where his office is located."

When he let us out, we thought we must be in a Texas cow town. They had wooden sidewalks, and cowboys all over the place. We stopped in a store and asked the owner if he knew a dentist named Wilson. "Sure, come outside and I'll show you his office." We didn't know how we would be received. It had been two or three years since we had seen Paul.

No one was in dentist Wilson's waiting room. When the door shut, Mr. Wilson came from the office. When we told him who we were and where we were from, he shook hands and asked us to sit down. He asked about several people from our city, and then said, "I have no more appointments today. Would you like to go out to the house and see Paul and the rest of the kids?"

We said we would like that and he locked the office and drove out to his home. It was a large house with a large screened in porch.

We went in the house and he called for Paul. Paul was surprised to see us in Florida. They asked us to stay for the evening meal, and whether we would like to take a shower.

"Would we ever," we replied, and they told us they would fix us a bed on the floor of the screened in porch and we could stay all night.

There were a lot of questions from Paul and the other children about friends in school and in our town. After we rose from the table, Paul and a younger brother said there was going to be a party out at the lake starting about nine o'clock. Paul said, "I've fixed you up a date with two real nice girls. We'll have a good time tonight."

When we arrived at the lake, a large fire was burning which lit the party area. Paul introduced us to Carol, my date, and Esther, Ralph's partner.

Paul told us coming out in the car that some of the teenagers would have hard liquor, cautioning us that a lot of bad booze was imbided around there. He said some were drinking denatured alcohol that was poured through a loaf of bread that had the ends cut off it. Some people had been blinded drinking that stuff. We decided we would drink only soft drinks. There was a tub full of them on ice.

We sat around the fire talking and drinking. Carol wanted to know all about our travels and we talked until midnight. By that time, some of the fellows were pretty drunk so Paul said maybe we had better go home. We said goodnight to the girls and told them how much we enjoyed being with them.

It had been a long day and when we got back to the house we went right to bed. In the morning we asked them about the cowboys we had seen in town. They told us this was the center of the cattle business in Florida, that lots of cattle were raised on large ranches in central Florida.

When we got ready to leave, Mrs. Wilson had prepared a large sack of food. We had told them about eating oranges for two days. When she sat the bag on the table, I kidded her, "You didn't put any oranges in there, did you?" She laughed, "I think you've had enough oranges for awhile."

We thanked them for everything. Paul drove us down to the highway. When he let us out, he said, "Come back next year." We were impressed with that family.

We got a good ride to Leesburg and walked through another very poor city. On the other side of town we got a ride with a young man in a new Chrysler roadster. When he asked where we were going,

Ralph said, "Anywhere north." The driver said he was going to Gainesville but had to make a side trip that would only take a few minutes. "We'll go with you," I said. We were enjoying ourselves riding in that new expensive car.

Shortly he turned off on a narrow dirt road. In a few miles we came to a one room shack. He drove up to the front and said he was there to buy a pig. "Can we go with you?" I asked. He said to come along.

An elderly colored man with white hair came out and was greeted by name by our driver. "I came over to see that pig of yours," he said.

The elderly man took us back of his house to a pigpen with the biggest pig I had ever seen. He stood about three feet high at the shoulder and about seven feet long. He was a monster. Our driver walked around looking at the pig and then declared, "I'll give you ten dollars for that pig."

The old man protested, "I can't sell that pig for ten dollars. I just can't do it."

Our driver pulled out his billfold and handed him a ten dollar bill. He took the bill but said again, "This pig is all I got. I can't sell him for ten dollars."

"Come on, boys," the driver said to us and to the old man, "I'll send a truck over tomorrow to get the pig."

That episode shut down the conversation in the car and I was glad when we got out. That poor old fellow living in that shack had just been cheated out of the only thing he had.

We were just outside of town when Ralph yelled, "Police!"

I looked up to see a police car bearing down on us. We left the highway and ran through an orange grove, slipping and sliding on the rotten fruit. The police car stopped but we were two hundred yards into the grove. The car moved on and we decided to go back to the city and try to catch a train. We had seen the tracks in town, but figured that it most likely hauled fruit, and most of the fruit was lying around on the ground.

When we returned to the city, we went where all the sidings and fruit warehouses were. We saw one engine with steam and watched it for several minutes and decided it was making up a train. The engineer was in and out of several sidings, picking a few cars here and there and adding them to a string on a siding. We saw no detectives so we sat and watched the engineer and brakeman work. Finally, we saw the engine pushing a caboose and hooking it on to the long string.

We were already running for the train. When we got there we could find no empties so we climbed on top as the train pulled out on the mainline. We sat on top of a car, but it was clouding up like it was going to rain. The train was going at a good speed and soon a few drops splashed on us and then the heavens opened up. We were getting drowned. The speed of the train increased the amount of rain. We were driven to ride between the cars where we were sheltered from the worst of the rain. I never liked to ride between the cars. I was aware that death rode three feet below me under the iron wheels. One slip or mistake would probably be fatal. Because everything I held onto was wet didn't make me feel any better.

The rain continued to come down in torrents. The sky then began to clear and the rain slowed until we could get back on top of the cars. With the train moving along, the breeze really chilled us. We were soaking wet. If the sun didn't come out soon, we would have to get off when the train stopped. There were lots of clouds with the sun breaking though once in awhile. We were really having a difficult time getting out of the state of Florida.

Riding on top of a car, even in warm weather can be cold at night, and very cold when you are wet. We came out of the cloudy weather and the sun made a big difference, but we were still uncomfortable. We stayed on the train. If the sun stayed out we knew we would dry off during the afternoon. We stopped on a siding and saw by the train station that the town was Lake City.

We got off and started checking the train to see if we could find a better place to ride. There were three cars loaded with logs, one of them, because some logs were shorter than the others, making a cave in one end. We had been cautioned that these timbers could shift and crush an arm or leg so we decided to pass it up. We found a boxcar that wasn't sealed and opened the door. It was about one-third stacked with wooden boxes.

We decided to wait at the fence to see if the train was going to be checked by detectives. It wasn't long until we saw two detectives checking the cars. When they came to the one which we had opened the door, he looked in and shut and locked the door. It looked like we would be back on top of the cars during the afternoon. When the detectives left we crossed the yard and climbed on the car we knew was two-thirds empty. If we made another stop we could get in the car. The train pulled onto the mainline and the sun finally shone on us.

The clouds were disappearing and we should be dry before dark.

After about an hour the train stopped for water but we stayed on top of the car until our clothes were dry. We were traveling through pine wood country and we saw a lot of small lakes and small towns. The small towns were very poor. The sidewalks, when they had them, were made of wood planking and most were twisted by the rain and sunlight.

We saw our first chain gang in the state of Florida, or we could have been in Georgia. That reminded us to be very careful and not spend the one dollar bill we still had. I still thought how close we had come to serving on one of those gangs. After a couple hours the train slowed and we saw the brakeman throw a switch and we rolled onto a siding with several large warehouses. The train stopped and the engine left with several cars and the brakeman. The caboose stayed on so we figured the engine would come back.

At five o'clock by Ralph's watch, we opened the food sack that Mrs. Wilson had given us. We had decided that to conserve our food supply we would not eat at noon time. We had several chicken sandwiches, some bananas, about a dozen rolls and donuts. We had a sandwich, bananas and a roll. We rolled a cigarette and discussed how long the engine would be gone. The town, what we could see of it, looked a little better than the others. The houses were more substantial than in the other towns, and there were some three-story buildings.

Two other hobos were walking along the train, looking for an empty car. When they came to our car, they stopped and looked in.

"Come on in," I said. "I think this is the only empty car at hand."

They stood awhile and we talked about where we thought the train was going and when it would pull out on the mainline. They didn't think it would be back very soon and decided to go into the city and get some food. Ralph and I decided as long as this train was going north we would stay on it. We had plenty of food and water. We talked and even sang some songs until Ralph looked at his watch which read nine o'clock. We saw the two hobos coming back. They stopped at our car.

"There are no empties up ahead, so if you don't mind we'll ride with you," one said. They climbed in. The first thing they asked was what was in the boxes. I told them we never looked. They went to the boxes and began to pull and pry on the wooden top of one of them. I didn't like this and I knew Ralph didn't either. They finally got the lid off and to their disgust it was some kind of chain hoist. They threw the box top on the floor and went to the other end of the car to sleep.

I remembered what that Justice of the Peace in Meridian, Mississippi had said, "You boys are not being charged with theft, which is a much more serious crime." Suppose we got caught tonight with that case open? It would look like we were getting ready to steal something. Ralph looked at me and I whispered, "Let's get out of here." I thought he was thinking the same thing I was for he nodded his head.

We grabbed our bags and slid off to the track bed. We cursed the two for causing us to leave a place to sleep and now we would likely have to sleep on the ground. As we approached the city, we saw it was larger than we thought and the railroad yard was fairly large. The sign on the passenger station read "Valdosta." We were in the state of Georgia.

It was past eleven o'clock and any mission, if there was one here, would be closed. We came by a small park and playground. No grass, but there were four or five wooden tables. We decided to sleep on them.

When we awoke in the morning we ate some fruit and a roll and went to the yard. When we looked into it, we saw detectives everywhere. No chance of getting on a train in the yards. We walked down to the end and there were a least a couple of hundred hobos waiting around. When I asked one why so many were waiting, he said, "The trains came out so fast, nobody could get on them."

The first train we saw came out of the yard like a frightened jackrabbit, so fast nobody tried to catch it. Then a couple more came with the same result. I heard a yell from the hobos and looked toward the yard. A long train was coming and the engine was having a hard time picking up speed. When the train came out of the yards, the hobos looked like a charging army attacking an enemy. When we got on and climbed on top of the car, I looked down the train. It was covered by hobos.

After an hour or two I told Ralph we were going toward the southwest according to the sun. We didn't want to go too far out of our way and decided to get off at the next town or city we came to. Another thing was that all those men on one train might attract detectives.

At the next city we went under a viaduct and I could see a train track that should be going north. When the train slowed for the freight office, we jumped down and ran out of the yard. Now all we had to do was find a train that was going on the northern track. We saw no detectives and kept a good watch as we walked along the fence. None of the trains looked like they were ready to roll. I didn't see anybody but a brakeman and thought we should ask him about a northbound train. We hurried down to him and asked which trains were going north. He turned and pointed to one of the two trains we had been watching.

We walked to the end of the yard and found about fifteen hobos waiting. We watched the train that had been pointed out to us and soon saw it move. It was not going very fast and we all got on.

A couple of hours later I looked to the back of the train and saw all the hobos standing up. They were doing the same at the front. The train was slowing and then three detectives were getting on the front of the train. The three started walking down the train with their rubber clubs. The hobos began hopping off.

Ralph said, "Come on, no use waiting until they get here."

We had no trouble getting off and the train went on without us. We could see the city. All of us started walking along the track until reaching the yards. Three more detectives were at the entrance so we walked around the city which wasn't very big. When we got on the other side, we were amazed to see about three hundred hobos standing and sitting on the ground. There were three detectives at this end of the yard. This wasn't a hobo jungle; there were no cook fires or shanties. This was just a bunch of hobos milling around. As we walked around the edge of the crowd, we asked an elderly hobo what all the people were doing there.

"We have a problem. We can't get close enough to the yards to catch the trains. If you move closer to the yards, they'll arrest you. I've been here for two days and some were here when I arrived. There are only two trains every twenty four hours. The one you came in on and another one leaving at eleven tonight. After it leaves the bulls leave but they'll come back when the trains leave."

We had never seen a situation like this that involved such a large amount of men. "Why are they doing this?" I asked him. "Just keeping them out here does them no good. It would seem they would want to get rid of the unemployed and possibly dangerous people when they get hungry."

"Everybody thinks a train came in here and a lot of valuable freight was stolen and they're taking it out on us."

"Does anybody ever catch a train?" He had seen three of four get on, but it was very dangerous and sooner or later someone trying it would be hurt really badly. We moved away and discussed the bad situation. The city police were probably patrolling the highway that we had crossed walking down there.

A cry went up from the crowd and we looked toward the yard. The train we came in on was moving. There was an overpass and the trains came through under it. We could get no closer than that to the yards. Twenty or so hobos crowded at the underpass to try and get on. The train had a long distance to get up speed to leave the yards. When the engine popped out of the underpass, two or three gave it a try. Only one got his hand on a ladder and climbed to the top and waved in derision at the police and detectives.

I turned to Ralph, "I don't think we've ever caught a train going that fast." He agreed.

As we walked around and listened to the groups talking, I could see trouble if these men were kept there much longer. There was talk of everybody going into the small city. If that happened it would give the police an excuse to use their weapons and people would get hurt. The hobos would be the ones to suffer. We were close to a river, and the men were drinking and bathing in it. We decided we might get cleaned up, but we had no intentions of drinking the water.

We were really hungry, but we decided to go down by the river to eat where no one could see us. If some of the men knew we had food, they would take it away from us. We found a place in a stand of trees, and we hurriedly ate, putting the small amount of food left in our bag. When the sun went down, we were invaded by swarms of mosquitoes from the river and swamp.

We were being eaten alive. What a feast they must have every night, feeding on all those hobos. Ralph suggested we move as far away from the river as we could. We walked through a wooden area and came out on an open field. The mosquitoes were not as bad there. We sat down with our back to a tree and talked about the alternative we had if we wouldn't get on the train. It was possible to walk down the railroad track to the next town, but it could be five miles or forty. We could try hitchhiking but if a lot of valuable goods had been stolen, the highway would be patrolled.

We decided to go back around ten o'clock and see if we could get the train. Catching a fast train at night was even more dangerous than in the daytime.

At ten o'clock we started back to the yards to wait for the night train. When we got to the viaduct there were about twenty hobos on each side of the track. They were huddled close to the entrance, but I didn't see how they would have a place to run without running into each other. The mosquitoes were really bad down there.

When we heard the train whistle and saw the headlight, everybody positioned themselves along the track. I told Ralph we would be foolish to try to get on the train with that crowd running down the track. When the train came through the underpass, it was going too fast. I saw nobody on this side of the train get on.

We went back through the small forest and out to the edge where we had eaten our evening meal. We decided to stop and sit with our back to the tree. Thankfully, the mosquitoes didn't bother us too much. We didn't get much sleep. In the morning we ate all the fruit and rolls and saved the sandwiches for our evening meal.

We walked to the river and decided we would take a bath. As we took our clothes off, Ralph said, "I wonder if there are any alligators in this river."

I hadn't thought of that, but the river wasn't deep and we stayed in the shallow part. After we were finished we stood around naked until the sun dried us off. We put on our clothes and walked down to the crowd which seemed to be bigger than yesterday. We wandered around in the crowd and we saw two women. Neither was the handsome one we had seen with a man. These two were on their own and seemed more self-confident than a lot of the men. Everybody was waiting for the train to come out, although nobody would be able to get on. As the time drew nearer, many of them went down along both sides of the track. There was no way to catch that train in that crowd.

While walking around I noticed a small bridge about three blocks away. It was about a hundred yards outside the yard fence. I showed it to Ralph and told him if we would get down there and hide under the bridge just as it got dark, we could stay there until we saw the night train getting ready to leave. The yard was not well lit. We could run to the fence and run down it until finding a hole and go into the yard and catch the train before it left the yard. We would be in behind the detectives and the police. By the time the train reached them, we would be in between the cars. One bad thing about this plan was that if we didn't get on the train, we might get caught inside the yards.

Ralph said we should give it a try, adding, "The damned mosquitoes are eating me even in the daytime. Not only that tonight, we'll be out of food and water. We have to get that train tonight."

We walked away from the crowd and ate our last sandwich. Then we started to try and find the little bridge in the dark. As we walked along, our eyes became night adjusted and we soon saw the bridge. We went under and found there was no water under it. There was nothing to do now but wait. We both wanted to smoke but were afraid to.

The city police car traveled twice down a lane about fifty feet from the yard fence. We were lucky. There was no moon. At ten o'clock we moved over to the fence, found a hole, and lay down in the grass where we could watch for the train. We saw three detectives walking down the tracks to the end of the yard. The train would be along shortly.

When we first saw the train about three city blocks away, we went through the fence and found only one string of cars to go over. We crouched in the shadows of the boxcars and watched the train approach. When it was about two hundred feet from us, we were along the track ready to run alongside it. When the engine went by, it always frightened me because it was huge and noisy with steam shooting out the sides. I grabbed the first car back of the engine and Ralph got the second. We got in between the cars and soon the train was picking up speed swiftly.

When the train went through the underpass, for a second I could see hobos running along the track. We quickly climbed on top of the cars and walked back away from the engine. About twenty minutes later we went through a small city and I saw four other people on top who had caught the train at the underpass. We were getting smoke from the engine so we walked back until we were three cars away from one of the hobos.

We were in good spirits; we had escaped from a very bad situation. We wondered how much longer the hobos could stay in that place. I thought they would probably go into the city late at night and see what they could steal. Some of them would probably be involved with the city police with bad consequences for the hobos.

We were waiting for the train to make a stop so we could find an empty car. We came to a city and the train slowed and stopped under the water tower. We got off the train and went to the fence. As dark as it was, we could have walked right into a detective's arms.

Ralph said one of the women was sitting three cars away from us. Up at the head of the train we saw two men we believed were detectives. When they started down along the train checking the cars, we were glad we had gotten off. Ralph asked me if I could still see the woman on top of the car. I looked and saw her still sitting in the same place. We started running down the fence and yelled for her to get off, that detectives were coming. She never moved or answered. When the detectives saw her they got up on the car.

After a few minutes, one got down on the ground and between the two helped her get off the car. She was having a hard time standing and both of the detectives almost carried her toward the passenger station. We concluded that she must have hurt herself badly when she got on the train. The thought went through my mind that this poor woman was living the rough hobo life, now evidently was hurt with nobody to care about her welfare. Would they take her to jail, would they get her a doctor at two a.m.? I didn't think so. When I put my thoughts in words to Ralph, he had been thinking the same thing. The officers left with the woman. We found an empty boxcar and soon the train pulled out on the mainline. It felt good to be back on the train and we were soon asleep.

When we awoke, the sun was shining in a clear blue sky with a warm breeze blowing. But we had a problem. We had nothing to eat. We sat in the car door and smoked a cigarette, watching the red clay surface go by.

"Remember the fellow and his wife picking us up in West Virginia and buying us the egg sandwiches?" I asked.

Ralph admitted we could use some of them now, but weren't likely to run into those folks again. We reminisced about an incident that had happened on another trip we had taken to the east coast.

Chapter Nineteen

One Sunday morning we were hitchhiking in the mountains of West Virginia. It was early morning and not much traffic was on the road. We sauntered along enjoying the mountain scenery dotted with an occasional oil well, even one that was pumping. We walked to it and noticed a grizzled mountaineer sitting on a stump.

We hailed him and he spoke to us. We asked him how many barrels of oil he pumped from the well a day. He informed us the well was twenty years old. He pumped it once a week, every Sunday morning. It gave about ten barrels a week. I wasn't aware that wells produced that long and he informed me there were wells that after forty years still produced about a barrel a day. He said they were called "stripper wells." We asked more questions but finally we told him goodby and went back to the highway.

It wasn't long before a man picked us up and we rode along talking to him, telling him all the places we had been. "You boys had anything to eat this morning?" he asked.

We said that we hadn't. A few miles down the road, we came to a small town and he left the highway and drove to a restaurant. "Come on in," he said. "I'm buying you something to eat."

The three of us sat down at the counter. He picked up the menu and said to the counter man, "Give these boys two egg sandwiches apiece and give me a cup of coffee. I've already had breakfast."

The egg sandwiches were large. Although I didn't relish egg sandwiches, we were glad to fill our stomachs. We thanked him and went back to the car. About twenty miles further on he said he had to turn off. We thanked him again for the food and waved goodby as he left.

The next ride was a couple who looked to be in their early twenties. We got in the back seat and thanked them for picking us up.

He asked us where we were going, where we had been, and then announced that they had gotten married the day before and this was their honeymoon. We congratulated both of them. As he talked we could see how proud he was of his new bride. When she looked at him we saw that she thought her new husband was the best man in the world.

It made me feel real good watching how much those two enjoyed each other. He turned to us in the back and said, "I'll bet you two haven't had anything to eat this morning." We had been told by hobos never to refuse food even if we had just had a meal an hour before, which was about where we were. We didn't answer and he said, "I'll buy you something to eat."

We protested but when we came to a small restaurant along the highway, he pulled in and stopped. Leaving his bride in the car, he took us in to sit at the counter. Without even looking at the menu he said, "Give these boys two egg sandwiches apiece."

I couldn't believe what I was hearing. When the waitress brought the sandwiches, they covered the whole plate and looked even bigger than the ones earlier. There was no way I could eat all of them. We started on one and the driver said he better go to the restroom. When he was gone, we both put our sandwiches in our pockets. When he came back he looked at our empty plates.

He said, "See, I knew you boys were hungry." We went back to the car and continued our ride with them. It was almost noon when they came to their turn off. I was glad because I could have seen that kind man turning to us at noon and saying, "I'll bet you boys could eat some more egg sandwiches for lunch." If he had, we would have had no more pockets to put them in.

Chapter Twenty

The train rolled along. We were so hungry our stomachs growled. The train slowed and then stopped on a siding in a small town. We got off and walked to the town and hoped the train would stay on the siding until we could get something to eat and return. It was a very small town and the only building which had once been a store was boarded up and closed.

We went up an alley, picked out a back door, and asked the man who answered if he had any work we could do for some food. He turned back around and called to his wife, "Do you want to feed these boys?"

She came into the kitchen and after looking at us, said, "I don't have much to feed you two on such short notice. Could you eat some scrambled eggs and grits?"

Yes we could and he said, "Come on in and sit down." He asked where we were going and where we had been while his wife cooked the eggs. I was so hungry just the smell of the food made my mouth fill with saliva. She must have known we were hungry for she cooked plenty of eggs to serve with several slices of corn bread, butter, and grits. When we finished we asked them again if they had work for us and that we would be glad to do it. They waved the suggestion away, so we thanked them and left.

The train was still on the siding and we got on the same car. An hour or so later a long freight train went by going the other direction and then our train moved out on the mainline. We were going almost north now so we were like the other hobos, not caring what city we ended up in.

Late in the afternoon we came to a large city. Not having any food with us slowed us down because we had to leave the train again. We got off at the yard entrance and on a street and started walking. We were going through a section of the city that looked somewhat prosperous. Why didn't we try hitting a back door again? It had worked earlier.

"Let's go," I said. We turned up the next alley and knocked on a door. A woman opened the door and before we uttered a word, she took one look and shut the door in our face. We heard the lock shut.

We walked back to the alley.

Ralph said, "Let's try another one."

That time the woman opened the door and we asked if she had any work for us to do for something to eat. She told us to sit down on the porch and she would see what she could find. In a few minutes she came out with a large serving platter and set it on the porch floor between us, saying she would be back with two plates. When she returned she told us we were eating leftovers and if the food agreed with us we were welcome to it. The platter contained five pieces of fried chicken, a small piece of beef roast, two wieners, a mound of potato salad, some sweet potatoes and the usual grits which she made hot, and bread and butter. It was a feast. She went back in the house and brought out a folding chair and sat down. She asked the usual questions while we were eating. When we were through, I asked her if this city was Atlanta. She informed us Atlanta was farther north, that we were in Macon.

I looked at Ralph. Macon was the city the huge dirigible was named after that we had seen in Akron, Ohio. We told the woman about it and that in our travels we had seen them making this large airship. She had never heard of it. When we described the airship to her, we could tell by the look on her face she had no idea what we were telling her. I said, "You never really heard of it?"

"I don't read the papers much," she said.

It dawned on me she probably couldn't read at all. With no other news avenue, she likely had never heard about it or knew what it looked like. We asked her if there was some work we could do for her, but she said she had none and we thanked her and left. We were full. If we could find a train before dark, we would be in good shape until tomorrow.

We followed the railroad yards, not going into the business section of Macon, but we could see the tall buildings. The yard had about a dozen tracks and seemed very busy. When we got to the end of the yard, we stopped and looked the trains over. We saw one train with two engines pulling, but all the cars looked like they were full and the doors locked. Probably it was a fruit train from Florida loaded with oranges. That would be a fast ride, but it would be cold at night riding on top of a car. We decided to look for another one. I watched one train coming slowly through the yard. I took another look. It was the one we came in on. The train had likely been loading and unloading freight all the time we were eating.

Ralph said, "Let's catch it on the run. I think I even see the car we were in."

We grabbed the ladder and climbed on top and looked over the other side. About twenty hobos were running to catch the train. They all got on as the train wasn't traveling very fast.

The train stopped to pick up freight in a small town and everybody got off to find an empty boxcar. All we had to do was go down the iron ladder and get in the car. We sat in the door and smoked a cigarette. Some hobos came by but when they saw us sitting in the door, they went on. The woman had told us Atlanta was north. It would be a big yard and we didn't want to be asleep when we got to it. Bigger yards usually had plenty of detectives.

I had eaten so much I wasn't even hungry. To keep from falling asleep, we talked about Angie and Mary and whether we could ever go back to Tampa. Our talk drifted to wondering if we would get a job when we got back home, and about what made the soil red in Georgia. The little cities we had passed through had very few public lights and hardly anybody in sight. They were poor and probably even worse than in Florida. We wondered what the people did for a living since we had seen hardly anybody trying to farm the land.

We stopped in another small town and two hobos came by. We asked if they knew where we were going. One replied that the engineer had said Atlanta, but after that it wasn't known since the engineer got off there.

We would have liked to get out of the car and walk a little ways but were afraid the train would start. It was very dangerous to try to get in a boxcar door when the train was moving. We could go on the roof, but it would be cold at night so we stayed in our side-door Pullman. We would have to get off the train at Atlanta no matter what time we got there. It was a large town with lots of railroads. I asked Ralph if he was hungry and, like me, he said he might not have to eat until he got home.

At a little after midnight by Ralph's watch, we could see the lights in the tall building and the train began to slow. We checked to see if we had everything and prepared to get off.

I had a strange, almost fearful feeling, as we watched out the door. Here we were hundreds of miles from home, in the middle of the night, waiting to leap from a moving train into a very dangerous area, with no money and no place to sleep. I was glad I wasn't alone. I had seen thousands of hobos who traveled by themselves. Tough times made tough men. I thought of myself traveling alone in a boxcar and I didn't like the thought. I was glad Ralph was with me.

The tracks began to multiply and the trains on them made us realize that we were already in a huge railroad yard. Our train was still going too fast for us to get off safely. We were going to have to go under or over several trains to get out to the yard fence. A brakeman threw a switch and we pulled off the mainline and stopped. We jumped down and ran as fast as we could, going under some trains and climbing over others. I heard someone yell at us, but we never looked back until we were on the other side of the fence. We walked down a street until we could see the passenger depot. There were several passenger trains stopped by it and a lot of people were getting off and going into the terminal.

I said, "Let's go by the station and see if we can get in and clean up and fill our water jars."

When we got there, Ralph said, "Let's wait until a passenger car unloads and we'll walk in with them."

In a few minutes we saw a colored porter with his wooden step move to a car. When he helped the passengers off, we fell in with them and walked into the station. We kept mingling with the passengers until we located the men's room. It was a busy place but we found a wash basin, stripped to our waists, and washed with plenty of water and soap. Ralph encouraged me to take my time so we might look good enough to be able to sit in the station until daylight.

"Let's try. With our bags, if there are police, they'll think we're on a train," I said.

We walked out and looked for two seats together. We found them by a large family of two adults and three children, the oldest a boy about fourteen. If we could start a conversation with them it would look as if we belonged there. Ticket stubs littered the floor. Ralph picked up a couple and handed one to me. They were of no value, but if challenged we could say we just came in on a train.

Several passengers were sleeping sitting up in seats. I slumped down in my seat but pushed myself back up; it would not do to sleep. Feeling something between the seats, I ran my fingers there and felt a coin. It was a nickel. I searched again and found a quarter. Further searching between the seats brought another nickel. I showed them to Ralph and told him where I had found them.

"Look on your side," I said. He searched but found nothing.

Whenever a passenger left his seat, we went over and looked for more coins, but found nothing more. Still, we were elated with the thirty-five cents we had. We dozed and woke and dozed again. At least it was better than sleeping on the ground. We were awakened by the increased noise of more passengers. We went to the restroom and washed up and walked from the station. I gave Ralph the thirty-five cents and told him, "Get as much food as you can."

We kept the yard in sight but were on the look out for a store. We found a grocery store, walked in, and asked a young man if he was the owner. He wasn't, but his father was. It seemed he was in charge, however, because his father was at home. He asked us what we wanted.

Ralph said, "We have thirty-five cents and we need enough food to last until we get home to Indiana."

"What do you have in mind?" the young fellow asked.

"Bologna or some kind of cold meat, second day bread, old rolls or donuts, anything that isn't selling well," Ralph answered.

He said he would see what he could do and got a large sack and went behind the meat counter. We looked around and found a barrel of pickles and a large bag of peanuts. When the clerk came back with the sack, Ralph asked if we could have some pickles and peanuts. The clerk filled a large sack with peanuts and found a cardboard meat tray and put four large pickles in it. We couldn't see what was in the bag; we would have to take a chance on him.

When we left the store I told Ralph, "We'll never be able to catch a moving freight with these two bags and the tray of pickles."

"We'll work something out," Ralph said. "Just be glad we have food to eat."

We walked almost to the end of the yard and saw a hobo jungle about a quarter mile away in a stand of pine trees. I could imagine what the red clay would look like in a heavy rain and was glad we didn't need to go to the jungle.

It was a busy yard, holding a lot of trains with steam up, but how were we to find a train going north? With the sacks and our bags we weren't going to be able to run very fast either.

We talked this over and decided that because I could run faster, Ralph would stay at the fence with the sacks and bags while I went to find a train north. Ralph told me if I were caught that he, too, would enter the yard, but I told him to use the spare dollar to call his brother to get the money to bail me out.

"But don't worry about it," I went on. "I've played basketball for three years and I know I can outrun any detective I've seen so far."

After looking around I started toward the first train. I went under the trains since I didn't want to spend much time climbing over them.

Of three engineers I asked, all were going to the east coast, a fourth to Chattanooga, Tennessee. I started back to Ralph at the fence. After looking around for the police, we made our way to the train, found an empty and climbed in. If the detectives came along, we would run and leave the food in the car. We watched out a door. In a while the train started and we saw the switchman throw the switch. We rolled out on the mainline.

We opened the sack to see what the man had given us for our thirty-five cents. We had sliced bologna, four ham ends, a large piece of cheese, a loaf of bread and some rolls, the four pickles and the sack of peanuts. "Not bad at all," I said to Ralph. We ate some of the rolls and shelled and ate some of the nuts. Finding the thirty-five cents meant that we could eat for a couple of days.

We were rolling along at a good speed; we would be in Chattanooga before dark. We sat in the car door and watched the towns and people as we passed. When we left the large cities, the countryside was very poor. Houses were shabby and the small towns were not much better. This was supposed to be peach country, but so far we had seen no peach orchards. All we saw was the reddish soil that didn't look like it would grow anything.

In the middle of the afternoon, the train stopped for coal and water near a small town. Two young hobos came along and climbed in our car. One asked where the train was going. "Chattanooga," I replied, asking if they were going anywhere in particular.

"We're going to Detroit. We think we have a job there. My uncle is a foreman at Ford and he thinks he can get us on." one said.

"Any chance he might get us a job there too?" Ralph asked.

"You're welcome to come with us, but I think we'll be lucky to get on. If my uncle wasn't the foreman there we wouldn't have a chance."

"Is this your first hobo trip?" I asked.

"Yes, this is the first and if we had any other way, we would have taken it. We spent what money we had eating in restaurants, but we spent the last cent yesterday morning."

"Where are you from?" I asked.

"Little Rock, Arkansas."

"If you don't get the job, do you think you'll go back to Little Rock?"

"I guess we would. We do have a place to stay there, but there's no work there."

We told them we had been in Florida and they asked about work down there. I said there was a lot of black labor that was very cheap. "That's the way it is in Little Rock," one informed us. The colored people worked long hours for food, clothing, and a place to sleep.

When it began to get dark, I knew we were going to have to share our food with them. We couldn't eat and them watch us, since they had no food for a day and a half. I opened the sack and asked them if they wanted a bologna sandwich. They admitted to being pretty hungry. We made four sandwiches and set the bag of peanuts between us and told them to eat all they wanted. When we were through, we rolled a cigarette and asked if they smoked. They did but had run out of cigarettes two days ago.

I offered the bag and the papers. "Where do you get this kind of tobacco?" one asked. I told them we picked up cigarette butts or "snipes" as the hobos called them, tore the paper off, and put the tobacco in the bag.

"You could buy two packages of one hundred papers for a nickel," I said.

"We don't have a nickel, not even a penny," he said.

"When we run out of papers, we roll them in pieces torn from a newspaper," I offered. He said he would remember that in case of need, informing me that if they didn't get the jobs, they were going back where it was warm. They knew they weren't going to like the cold climate in Detroit enough to stay for nothing.

We discussed what we were going to do when we got to the big city. I thought we should get off and walk through the city and Ralph agreed. The other two said that as long as the train was headed north they were going to stay in the boxcar. I asked if they weren't afraid of getting picked up by railroad detectives. They said they had heard of them, but so far hadn't been bothered by them. I wondered if they hadn't just been lucky getting as far as they had, especially riding the train through big cities. Perhaps they would learn like we did, but we hoped they would get out of the South before it happened. I was sure they knew about chain gangs in Arkansas.

When we arrived in Chattanooga, the train stopped on a siding as soon as we entered the yards. We bade them good luck in getting those jobs and jumped to the ground and ran across the tracks. We walked down a street that ran parallel to the railroad tracks. When we got to the center of the yard, everything was quiet and only two trains had steam up. There were a lot of trains to go under or over to reach the two engines, but we decided to go find out where they were going. The first engineer refused to answer our question or even look at us. The second one said he was ready to pull out and was going to Knoxville. Was Knoxville on our way home? We got out the map but the lighting was so poor we couldn't find it.

As we walked down the train, we came to an empty boxcar and Ralph thought we should go in, that he didn't feel like standing around there for the rest of the night. Before we could even get settled, the train pulled out. As it neared the yard, I saw several fires along the track. As we got closer, I could see men standing around the fire. When we were close they all started running for the train and climbed aboard. There seemed to be about forty of them. The next time we stopped we might get company when they got off the roof and started looking for an empty car.

We dozed off but were awakened by voices and people climbing into our car. They saw us and went to the other end. We thought there were three of them. Our sleeping was probably over for the night. We didn't sleep in the same car with hobos that we hadn't had a good look at. We could hear them still talking at the other end.

Ralph said, "Let's roll a cigarette." I handed him the tobacco bag.

I rolled one and we lit upon the same match. One of the hobos came to us and demanded a cigarette, not asking for one, but demanding it in a commanding tone. Neither of us answered him. We had no intention of giving him a cigarette. If he had asked for one, we would have given it to him. He stood looking at us, though uncertain what to do. I punched Ralph in the ribs and we both stood up. He backed off and returned to the other end and his companions.

Ralph was average size, about 5 feet 9 inches and weighing 165 pounds. I was 6 feet 3 inches and weighed 190 pounds. The three of them might have been able to take us, but we wouldn't have made it easy. If they made any more threatening actions toward us, we would get our knives out of our bags.

That was the first time we had been threatened in all our travels. We usually tried to stay away from the other hobos if we could, but lots of times we had to ride in the same car with them. We had enjoyed some hobos' company enormously because we learned so much through their telling of the places they had been and the things they had seen.

The three in the other end of the car were asleep but we were staying awake and would leave the car when we got to Knoxville. When dawn arrived we looked at the map and found Chattanooga was more east then north. We were also coming back into the mountains. They were different from Pennsylvania's and West

Virginia's mountains which were covered by trees and had a rounded look to them. These mountains were steeper with lots of up-ended rock, more bare of vegetation.

According to our map, we needed a train to Louisville or Lexington, Kentucky. By Ralph's dollar watch we arrived in Chattanooga after six o'clock. We got our first look at the three sleeping in the end of the car and didn't like what we saw. They were a rough looking bunch. When the train slowed in the yard, we jumped out and ran for the safety of the yard fence. We were glad to be rid of the three in our car.

We tried to keep the yards in sight, but the street took us toward the center of the city. It was either walk through fields or let the road take us away from the railroad. We decided to climb the fence and follow the yard. It was a very busy place with several trains having steam up, gathering cars, and putting a train together. We decided we would do what we had done the day before. Ralph stayed with the bags and sacks and I went into the yard and tried to find the train we needed. I looked closely at the trains. I saw lots of brakemen but no detectives. I climbed over a couple of trains and approached an engineer.

"Where are you heading?" I called up. He looked at me as if he didn't see me and turned back to watching down the track.

I climbed another string and called to the engineer. "Going north, Bristol and Roanoke," he answered. We didn't need to go further east.

The next engineer I asked answered, "Lexington and Louisville, Kentucky."

"How soon are you leaving?" I hollered.

He pulled out his big railroad watch and looked at it. "We'll be gone in about a half hour." While talking to him I had forgotten to watch for detectives. As I turned around I saw one about a block away running toward me and yelling for me to stop. I ran the other direction and he didn't stand a chance. I hadn't run two city blocks and when I looked back he had stopped running. I went under a couple of cars and ran for the fence, clambering over it into the field. I came up behind Ralph standing looking down into the yard.

When he saw me he said, "I thought you had been caught. I saw the detective chasing you, but you went between two trains and then I couldn't see you. If they're all like that fat slob, he couldn't catch his sister."

I told him about the train ready to pull out for Louisville. We took what was left of the food and put it in our pocket so we had to carry only our bags if we had to run. When we got to the train we found an open car with stacks of rock and granite in each end and decided it would do. We could go over either side if detectives appeared.

We had hardly gotten in the car when the engine gave a blast on the whistle and we pulled out of the siding. When the train came out of the yards, about forty or more hobos ran along the train and climbed on. We looked around at the car. We could sit with our backs to the slabs of stone and be out of the breeze and in the sun. It was a beautiful day, blue skies and sunshine. We stood every so often and looked over the side of the car to watch the rock formations, especially along rivers or large creeks.

We stopped in a small town to unload or load freight and the hobos on top came down looking for empty cars. A lot of them piled into our car until we had about twenty hobos sitting around. As usual, there was much talk and bragging about different places and trains they had ridden. One hobo, perhaps forty years old and well dressed for a hobo, held forth. Finally, almost all in the car were listening to him. According to his story, he had visited Canada and Mexico. He told of the fast trains he had ridden: passenger, cattle, fruit, and silk trains.

We had been in the bright sunlight when, suddenly, pitch darkness surrounded us. The hobo's voice ended in mid-sentence with a frightened shriek. We had entered a tunnel. A few seconds later we were back in sunlight. The talking hobo was slumped on the floor unconscious. We thought he had had a heart attack, but before anybody could get up to help him he regained consciousness and sat up. This hobo, who had been everywhere and ridden all kinds of trains, had never been through a tunnel and had fainted. Some of the hobos laughed at him. He talked no more. It might have been his first freight train, or first train, period.

Several of the hobos had pulled out sandwiches, fruit and even candy bars to eat, so we didn't feel badly about eating when noon came. Although the sun was shining brightly, I noticed a chill in the air. We were getting into the northern weather. I thought that at night we had better find a boxcar. When the train stopped for water we left the car and looked for a boxcar. We found no empties and returned to our original car. I knew now why all the hobos had gathered in the one car.

When we reached Lexington we would have completed a round trip from there of over three thousand miles. From Lexington, I thought the rest of the trip would prove very difficult.

The hobo who had fainted got off to wait for another train I guessed. We listened as one hobo talked about his twenty days on a chain gang in Florida. He said he worked twelve hours a day. The food was poor and not enough for the work being demanded. He lost a lot of weight; he thought about ten pounds. The biggest part of the sentence he worked cleaning out drainage ditches and repairing them. He said he would like to stop in the South where it was warm, but didn't want to take a chance ending up on another chain gang.

I asked how long he had been hoboing and he said ever since he had been laid off at the factory where he worked. I asked if he was married and he said yes, but after the little money they had ran out he had told his wife to go stay with her parents until things got better, maybe until after he got his job back.

For Ralph and me, riding freights was an adventure enabling us to go to different places and see different things. But for most of these men, riding freights was the result of a tragedy: the loss of their jobs and not being able to support their families. You would think that with millions of jobless men there would have been talk of insurrection of the overthrow of the government, but of all the men I talked to, not one ever mentioned or suggested that as a solution. I asked the hobo if he had been back to see his wife and he said not since he had left almost a year ago. He reached in his pocket and brought out a picture of his wife. I told him how nice she looked and handed back the picture. His eyes glistened as he carefully replaced it in his billfold. I thought that many of the men we met and talked to carried such pictures.

I had never been afraid of other hobos. Most rode the trains because they didn't want to stay in their home town; they had too much pride. Most of them were like our neighbors at home, except they had lost their jobs. But I had seen a few that I wouldn't want to ride with if I were by myself.

We came into Lexington and there was a discussion about getting off the train. With no empty cars, the detective would check cars to see if any had been entered. That train could take us right into Louisville. If we got off, we might not be able to get back on, but we certainly didn't want to be jailed a small distance from the Ohio or Indiana border. Most of the hobos decided to get off.

Ralph, me and about six others decided to ride through. I was uneasy. We weren't in a very good car if we had to get off and run. We all kept watch in every direction. The train slowed, but kept moving. We were half way through the yard and it was still rolling on the mainline. We saw the other end of the yards; the train was going on through without stopping. When we were out of the yards and picking up speed, we hollered and laughed. Even passenger trains had to stop in the yards at the station.

We were on our way to Louisville if the engineer had told the truth. It was getting colder and being in the open car was getting very chilly. We had enough food for that night but didn't think we would sleep much. When it began to get dark, we moved away from the other six men and ate out last sandwiches and the rest of the peanuts. I was sure those guys were hungry, but how would we share two sandwiches among eight people? They, like us, were used to missing meals.

By midnight we all huddled in the front end of the car. The full moon shone on us and Ralph predicted a frost before morning. When we stopped outside a small town for water and coal, the six hobos got off to find food and shelter. We decided to ride to Louisville and then hitchhike from there to home.

We didn't sleep. Sometimes we stood or ran in place to get warmed up. In fact, it seemed we ran half way to Louisville. When the sun came up, it had lost its warmth. We had endured a very uncomfortable night. We were traveling in rolling country, out of the mountains. When we arrived in Louisville we jumped off the car as it entered the yard and proceeded to a road on the other side of the fence. We walked along until we came to a log restaurant.

We stopped and Ralph said, "We're just across from the Indiana border. Let's get some hot cakes and coffee with part of the dollar."

We would still have enough money to make a phone call. "Sounds like a good idea," I said.

We went in and asked the woman what hot cakes and coffee cost. She said, "All-you-can-eat hot cakes and coffee will be fifteen cents each." We sat down at the counter. In a few minutes she brought the hot cakes and coffee. When we finished the first stack, she was there with another stack. It was warm inside and we lingered over the coffee and cigarettes until finally we knew we had better get started.

We walked through the city, crossed the bridge over the Ohio River, and we were back in the Hoosier state. It had taken us until one o'clock to walk through the city and across the bridge.

We got about a five-mile ride, glad to be getting warm when the car had a flat tire. We helped the driver get the tire off the rim, found the nail, pulled the tube out, and found the leak. We dug the nail out of the tire and got back in the car while he got his repair kit and patched the tube. It was three p.m. before we got the tube back in the tire. We took turns pumping on the hand pump until the tire was pumped up, then got back in the car. We had just gotten warm when he came to his turn off and he let us out on the road. We had spent over two hours going about ten miles.

We got a few small rides but at five o'clock, Ralph said we better stop in the next town and find something to eat and a place to stay. Even with a fire it would be a tough night. The next town we thought was big enough to have a police force so we walked on to its town square. Ralph saw a restaurant and suggested we get something to eat. That sounded good to me and we walked in and sat at the counter. For twenty-five cents we could have a full roast chicken dinner with dessert. We decided to get it because we hadn't eaten since morning. We would still have twenty cents.

We had asked the owner if they had a police force and he said they did, that the station was just off the square. We found it and walked in. An officer was sitting against the wall. The one at the desk looked at us like he knew what we were going to ask him. We told him it was a cold dark night and we had no place to get out of the cold.

"Would you lock us up for the night?" Ralph asked.

He turned to the other officer and said, "It's too late to feed you, but I guess we can put you in for the night. Take them back and give them a bed."

The other officer replied, "We only got four cells and prisoners are in three of them."

"I know. Let the Smith kid out. He's sobered up by now and his wife is wondering where he is."

We went back and he let a young man our age out of the cell and told him to go home. It was warm and we lay down and soon slept. We were awakened by a bell. When the officer came, he asked is we wanted breakfast. We told him we'd be glad to have breakfast. He said it wasn't much, just coffee, rolls or a donut. That sounded good to us, so he led all four of us to a large table with a pot of coffee and the rolls.

One prisoner asked what we were in for. We told him we weren't prisoners but just sleeping there. "You mean you asked to be put in jail?"

"Yes, we didn't have a place to stay," Ralph explained.

"When I get out of this lousy place, I wouldn't ask to sleep in here if I had to stand up all night."

He didn't know what he was talking about. Standing around an open fire makes for a very long and uncomfortable night. We stayed until the coffee was gone. It was after nine a.m. before we got out on the highway.

We had blue skies but it was cold. We got some short rides. It was one p.m. when we got to Indianapolis. By the time we walked through the city to the north edge, it was after three o'clock, but we thought we could still get home. We did poorly. At four o'clock when we got to the city of Anderson, it began to snow and we knew we wouldn't make it home.

We walked through the business section of the city until we found a police officer and asked him if he would lock us up for the night. He turned and pointed down a street and said, "Four blocks down that street is a mission. My name is Kelly. Tell them at the mission that I sent you."

We found the mission and told the man that Officer Kelly had sent us. "Kelly is a good man and will make chief one of these days. Come on in. You've got to take a shower you know."

"That's great," I said.

"Hurry, services start in twenty minutes."

When we had showered, we followed everybody into a chapel with a lot of benches in it. After everybody was seated, a middle-aged man came out with a Bible and began the sermon. He was a pleasant man with a soft voice and friendly manners, but after an hour, with our empty stomachs growling, he was still trying to save our souls. A few minutes later we stood for prayer and then lined up to eat meat loaf, potatoes, gravy and coffee. They filled our metal pie pans and told us to go back in the room where we had been and sit down and eat. We were in good shape. We were clean, not hungry, and had a warm place to stay. We washed the pan and utensils and followed the other men down to the room where we would sleep.

It was a large room with bunks three high on three walls and the floor was filled with wooden army cots. All the cots were taken. I asked a fellow how they got down there so quickly to grab the cots. He said they had had two feedings and these guys went to the first meal and claimed the cots. We found two bunks together. They were smaller than the cots and I could see I wasn't going to stretch out much.

As I lay thinking about home only forty miles away, it didn't really bother me too much that we hadn't made it yet. Was I getting to think like a hobo? No. Ralph and I were not truly hobos, for we had a sure place to stay tomorrow night. The lights went out except for one red light over the only door in the room.

After awhile I saw smoke from a cigarette clouding up around the red light. There was no smoking allowed in that crowded room. I guessed over a hundred men were sleeping there and if some hobo set the place on fire with a cigarette, a lot of us wouldn't get through the narrow door. I heard someone shout, "Put the damn cigarette out! What are you trying to do? Set this place on fire?" There was no answer and I saw no more smoke. The light cast a dim, reddish glow over the room that made me think that what was happening wasn't real. I went to sleep.

The next day we walked to the north side of town to the highway where we stood for almost an hour before we got a ride. But that ride would take us to our home town. He left Ralph out at the railroad track and he had to walk only one block until he was home. I got out at the courthouse and walked by the hotel where we had started on the trip.

When I walked in the house, my brother and sister were at school and my father was at work. So I kissed my mother and sat with her at the kitchen table and had a cup of coffee. She asked me what it was like in Florida. I laughed and said, "This is going to take some time."

"The kids don't get home from school until four o'clock, so start talking."

I told her all about Florida and knew I would have to repeat it again that night for the rest of the family.

A couple of days later I saw Ralph and while we talked I said, "We should go over to the hotel lobby and tell Ott that we're back." He thought so too and we agreed to meet there at nine o'clock that night.

It was cold when I left for home. I was glad when I got to the hotel. Ralph and Ott were there with four other men and the night managers. I shook hands with Ott and asked him how he had made out selling the oranges. "I got them all sold but it took me a long time so I don't intend to go back until times get better."

I sat down and Ralph said, "All right, we're both here so if you have any questions just speak up and we'll try to answer them."

One of the other men said, "Ott has told us about the trip down so why don't you start when you left him?"

As we told about our adventure, we were interrupted many times while one of them had a question. The courthouse clock struck midnight and the last question had been asked and answered. We walked out of the hotel at the same time as when starting the trip to Florida.

We started looking for work but the Depression hung over the United States and the world like an ugly black cloud. Rumors of jobs sent hundreds of men to stand at a closed factory for several days until they left in disgust. I went back to the glass factory and hung around with the other unemployed men hoping for a job, but I was kidding myself. There was nothing. I started going to the factory at eleven p.m. at change of shift. There weren't as many waiting at the gate at that time, and as the night passed, until three or four a.m. sometimes only three of four. All the rest had given up and gone home to sleep, to come back again.

Chapter Twenty-One

A local family owned the glass factory and I heard that they were large investors in the Auburn Motor Company located in Auburn, Indiana. They had a total of five automobiles, three large Auburn 115 with spare tires in the front fender wells. Those were very beautiful cars. The two sons drove Cord automobiles, also manufactured by Auburn. I saw them drive three of those cars to the glass factory every day except Sunday.

I had been there all night and as the sun came up I was struck with an idea. I knew these people didn't wash their cars. Maybe I could get a job washing all five cars. The office was about a hundred yards from the factory gate where we waited. We had been warned not to go any closer to the office than the factory gate. How could I talk to them except when they came to work? What could they do to me, tell me they would never give me a job? They weren't going to anyway.

At seven a.m. I walked to the office and sat down on the front steps. They usually came in about eight o'clock. As I sat there I hoped one of the two sons would be the first to arrive, but I knew the old man always came to work first. He was tough and bad-tempered, letting everyone know he was the head man at that outfit.

He drove in, parked, and walked toward the office. I stood up and he said, "What the hell are you doing here? Don't you know you're not supposed to ever be down in this area?"

"I need a job and I wondered if I could wash the five cars that you have," I spoke up. "I have had a lot of experience washing cars."

"We have a colored fellow we brought up from Florida and he washes all the cars and takes care of the gardening."

I turned to walk away when he said, "Come in here." I followed him up the steps and he unlocked the door and we walked in. "Don't think that I'm giving you a job," he said.

I said nothing. As he walked ahead of me, he stopped at a desk, picked up a notepad, wrote on it, tore the page from the tablet and handed it to me. "Now get out of here and don't ever come back around the office."

I looked at the paper. It was a note allowing me to enter the factory. I thanked him but he never answered and I left. He had not given me a job, but I could show that piece of paper to the watchman and walk into the factory anytime.

I showed the foreman the pass and I thought they got the idea that the old man wanted me to go to work for him. Soon I was put to work cleaning the molds. They were cast iron and very heavy. A stone was used to polish the inside of them. I didn't know it at the time, but it was a preferred job as it was warmed in the winter, and far enough away from the large glass tanks to be fairly cool in the summer. But I wanted to be in a shop around the tanks where molten glass was gathered and pressed and blown in the molds I was cleaning. There was noise and excitement there. They had to shout to make themselves heard. They had to wear gloves all the time because everything they touched was hot.

The mold job lasted until they needed someone in one of the shops. Later, I learned that in the summer it was so hot the 180 degree sprinkling system lead plugs would melt and drench us with water. They were then replaced with two hundred degree lead plugs. Even they melted on a 100 degree day and when that happened everybody went home.

Turning the glass from the molds, I acquired a red burn spot on my nose and cheekbones. I learned to coat my face with petroleum jelly before I went to work which protected me enough that my red burn spots went away. If I drank too much water when it was very hot I would become sick. Most of us drank water with ground oatmeal. We could drink gallons and not have it bother us.

After work my work clothes were crusted with salt from the perspiration. I dumped them in a pail of water to release the salt. I didn't work full time. If my shop wasn't marked to work that day, all members lost a day of that week. I averaged about three days a week. Any long lay off and I would be the first to be laid off.

The factory had two glass tanks that had to be repaired every nine months. When that happened, all last hired were laid off first. The next tank to be repaired was scheduled for June. For the work I did I received $1.76 a day, or twenty-two cents an hour and we had no lunch period. There were four jobs on the machine. We rotated every fifteen minutes. One of the jobs was carrying the hot glass to a lehr or oven. While on that particular job, we could eat our lunch. It wasn't much of a job, but I was thankful to be working at all.

Ralph was hired at a paper mill and under the same conditions. If the paper mill didn't work, he didn't work. On any lay off he would be laid off first. At least now we had a little money every week. On an average three day week, I received $5.28. After giving my parents two dollars of it, I had $3.28. My share was not all for fun and folic. I had to buy my clothes and everything else but food and lodging. I had enough left over to have a good time on Saturday night. Ralph and I both saved a little money each week so that we could get along when we were laid off for a long period.

The bottom of the Depression would be 1932. Ralph said if they didn't get more orders by May that he was going to be laid off for a long time if things didn't get better. I was looking at a tank going down for a possible three months. Ralph was laid off May first and the tank shut down June first. I was going to be laid off for at least three months until it was repaired.

We both got a job helping to repair roofs on large flat top buildings but it lasted only six days. When we were paid for the work, we stopped at the restaurant to see if his brother had heard of any jobs. He was the one who had told us about the roofing job, but he had heard of no others.

After a few minutes of conversation, Ralph said, "We got some money, why don't we go back to Atlantic City? This time we can take our bathing suits and swim, lay around on the beach, go on the boardwalk and the steel pier at night."

We were getting bored with our little city. "That sounds good to me. When do you want to go?" I asked.

"How about day after tomorrow? That'll give us plenty of time to get ready."

"I can be ready. Let's take enough food to last until we get to Atlantic City." Ralph thought that was a good idea.

When I packed my satchel I put in a new pair of trousers and a new shirt. With these clothes we might go in one of the luxury hotels and have a cup of coffee without fear of being shown the door.

The next night we walked down the railroad to the coal docks. The same train rolled in and stopped near midnight, just as it had three years before. Ralph had checked with his boss to see if there was any chance he would be called for the next two weeks. The answer was no. After Ralph told him what we planned to do, his boss said to go and have a good time.

Ralph and I bought the meat, bread and apples. My mother and I made the sandwiches and packed them in a strong bag. I talked to my father and mother until it was time for me to go. "Don't forget to send the cards," was the last thing my mother called.

I went by the hotel and saw Ott Pethel sitting in the lobby reading a newspaper. I went through the door and Ott looked up and said, "Did you come in to tell me you're going back to Florida?"

"No," I said. "Ralph and I are leaving tonight for Atlantic City for a vacation."

"I wish I was going with you. We had a lot of fun on that Florida run."

"We sure did and I wish you were going with us tonight."

"Well, I'm a little old for that. Maybe we'll take a trip again next winter to the South." I told him goodby and he wished us a good trip.

I left and walked to Ralph's house. He was ready and we began walking down the railroad track. Ralph pointed out that every trip we had taken had started at night.

"I know," I said, "and it was about this time three years ago we were walking down the same tracks to make our first freight trip."

When we got to the coal docks, we walked right on by not caring if the men saw us or not. We were veteran hobos now, knowing these workers didn't give a damn who got on the train.

When the train came thundering by breathing steam and smoke, I felt my heartbeat pick up a beat and the old feeling of adventure still pulled at me. We walked along the cars until we found an empty one and climbed in. We looked around the car; it was clean and uninhabited. The engine whistled and with a rattling of couplings we started moving. It took us awhile to get accustomed to the swaying, shaking, and the click-clack of the wheels on the rail joints, but soon we went to sleep.

When I awoke, the train was stopped on a siding in a small town. It was just getting light and everything was still except the far away snuffling sound of the train engine. Ralph came to the door and we thought we should be close to Columbus, Ohio. A passenger train called "Varnish Streaks" by the hobos came from behind us, possibly from Chicago, and flashed by. We talked of someday "riding the cushions" as hobos put it, to far away places when we became rich. Our engine whistled and we moved back on the mainline. We decided to eat our breakfast so we wouldn't have to stop on our walk through Columbus. Soon after we had eaten, the train began to slow. Looking out over the flat land, we could dimly see the tall buildings of the city.

We entered the yards. As the train slowed further we leaped from the car and then climbed over and under trains until reaching the yard fence. We weren't as impressed by the city as we had been the first time. After seeing New York, Miami, Memphis, and New Orleans, it didn't seem very big. It took us an hour to walk to the east side of the city. We didn't stop to look in all the windows as we did on our first trip.

When we arrived at the end of the yards, we saw a large group of hobos catching the different trains leaving. We walked back along the fence toward the part of the yard that was making up trains. We would do like we had before: go into the yards and ask about a train to Pittsburgh. We figured I could run faster than most detectives we had seen. If I got caught Ralph would bail me out. I gave him my money and walked into the yard. I crawled under some deadhead trains and went to the nearest one. "Charleston, West Virginia," the engineer said.

I went deeper in the yard. The next one was going to Cleveland, the next to Weirton. I thought that was close to Pittsburgh. When I asked the engineer he said it was close but he wasn't going on into Pittsburgh. I hadn't spotted a detective so far and decided to go and tell Ralph what I had found. We decided to take the train. Because I had seen no detectives, we would go and get on the train right then.

When we got there, we walked along until we found a clean boxcar and climbed in. We didn't try to hide from the bulls; they would always find you. We opened both doors and each of us stood in a door and looked up and down the track and in the area in front of us.

We had been there an hour when Ralph yelled, "Here they come!"

At the same time I saw a bull coming up on my side. We jumped out of the car and ran out of the yard. One yelled at us but we kept going; they were too far away to ever catch us. We were really upset after all the trouble we had taken to locate a train going in our direction.

We watched them look in the car we were in to see if anyone else was in there. They disappeared into the maze of the tracks. Our train was still setting there and we went back to it. We climbed back in the same car and took up our position at the doors. In a few minutes we heard the clatter of the couplings and the train moved forward. The train traveled slowly when we emerged from the yard and several hobos ran and climbed on top of the train. We could have done it that way too, but it was better not riding on top of a car. The train picked up speed. At that rate, we would be in Weirton by late afternoon.

We never tired of sitting in the car door and watching the scenery fly by. Going through the small cities we saw factories and mills closed. Only the ones with men waiting and hoping for a job were operating. If there were no men waiting at the gate, we knew the factory or mill was completely closed.

We ate our lunch and thought it we were careful we might have enough food to last us to Atlantic City. It was a beautiful day and we lay on our stomachs and looked out the car door. We had been making good time but then the train pulled onto a siding. We hoped it was just to let another train pass. In a few minutes the train left with eight or ten cars and disappeared in the distance. Some of the hobos got off and looked for empty cars. We had had that happen before but we never knew when the train would be back, or if it was coming back a week later to pick up the cars. One thing we learned hoboing around the country was patience. We were very comfortable lying there in the cool boxcar.

According to Ralph's watch we had been there three hours. We started worrying. A hobo came by and we asked him if he thought the engine would come back. "Well, I don't know," he answered, "but when they don't take the caboose they usually come back."

Before it got dark we ate our evening meal. We got off and walked up and down the track to get a little exercise and then got back in the car. We talked about the fun we were going to have when we arrived in fantastic Atlantic City. We planned to find the same house we stayed in three years ago if they were still in business. We were going to eat three meals a day and planned on staying two weeks or longer if we didn't run out of money. We had more money on this trip than any of the others. By ten o'clock we lay down to go to sleep.

When we woke in the morning we were still on the siding. We stayed away from the door while we ate breakfast. Some hobos might have seen us and attempted to take away our food. Most of them were sure to be very hungry. Several trains had passed by. We waved at the people on the passenger trains but we seldom got a returning wave. The train engine came back by itself and backed into the siding. We saw the brakeman drop off at the switch and the engine banged onto the string of cars. We rolled slowly out on the mainline and waved at the brakeman. We watched him catch the caboose.

It was almost noon so we ate another sandwich and took an inventory of the food left. It might not last until our destination. We had finished our sandwich when we neared Weirton, Pennsylvania. As we watched from the door, we passed steel mills and coke ovens, all shut down. Factories closed and large groups of unemployed lingered outside of the businesses that were still operating.

When the train entered the yard, it soon slowed and then stopped. We and the other hobos jumped off. I asked one hobo how far it was to Pittsburgh. "It's not far," he said, "about fifty miles."

We decided to find the highway to Pittsburgh and hitchhike there. We walked quite awhile and then got a ride all the way to Pittsburgh. The driver let us out on the west side of town and we walked up and down that hilly city.

We crossed some big rivers on high iron bridges and inquired where the freight yards were. When we got there, we had walked a long way and it was late afternoon. A large crowd of hobos were waiting for the trains.

I asked one hobo if he knew a train going east. He said, "I don't know but I would think a lot of them would be going east." I asked him what train he was waiting for. "I'm not waiting for any particular train. When a slow one comes out of the yard, I'll grab it."

"Maybe that's what we ought to do," said Ralph. "At least we'll have some place to sleep."

The hobo pointed out a slow oncoming train so I said to Ralph, "Let's get this one too. It's going to be dark soon."

We caught the train and climbed on top. We had to keep a watch out for tunnels and get down between the cars when we saw one. After a few miles heading east, the train seemed to be veering off to the south. In about an hour the train stopped at a small town on a siding. We got off and found an empty boxcar. Some local freight was unloaded and we pulled back on the mainline. It began to get dark so we ate another sandwich and an apple. After we had finished, Ralph, who had been complaining about his feet hurting because they were hot, said he was going to cool them off.

He took his shoes and stockings off and sat in the door with his feet thrust out in the cool breeze caused by the motion of the train. In the dark he didn't see the iron fence that lacerated both of his feet. He screamed in pain and rolled on the floor of the car. I didn't know what had happened and hurried to him.

"My feet! My feet!" he kept crying.

It was almost dark and I couldn't see well. I struck a match and saw the blood all over his feet. I got a couple of handkerchiefs and the water bottle from my bag and dampened the handkerchiefs. I told him I was going to wipe off the blood so I could see how badly his feet were cut.

He flinched when I wiped his feet. They seemed badly cut. Fear froze me for a second. How was I going to get him off the train? We weren't on a passenger train where I could pull the emergency cord and stop the train. We would have to ride the train until is came to a stop under somebody else's direction. One good thing was that he didn't seem to be bleeding very much from the severity of the wounds. I got his handkerchiefs out of his bag and, with mine, bandaged his feet the best I could. I struck another match and saw the blood was only coming through the bandages in spots.

"Are you hurting very badly?" I asked.

"No," he said. "My feet just feel like they're numb."

I rolled both of us a cigarette and we talked about what we would do when the train stopped. Since we hadn't stopped for some time, we thought it would be soon. I planned to take the bags and get off on the ground. He would sit in the car and I would back up to him so he could get on my back. Then I would carry him to a safe place and go for help. We planned for me to get the police and we would go from there.

Every ten minutes, I lit a match and checked to see how badly he was bleeding. The cloths had stuck to the wounds and I thought the bleeding was under control. I told him not to worry about it. It was almost an hour before the train started to slow and I looked out and saw the lights of a city.

The train pulled into a siding. When it stopped I helped Ralph to sit in the door. I took the bags and hid them by a pile of railroad ties. I could see a street a short distance away. I went back and got Ralph on my back and carried him to the street and set him down on the lawn of a house. I went to the door and knocked. A man's voice boomed from inside, "Who's there?"

"We need a doctor," I called back. "We've had an accident."

He opened the door a little and looked out. I pointed to Ralph and said, "He's hurt pretty bad." The man told me to wait a minute and then returned with a lantern. Light shone on his feet.

I asked, "Would you call the police to come here and I'll explain what happened?" He went back in the house and when he returned he said that the police were on the way.

I then told him that we were hobos, riding trains, and how Ralph had hurt his feet. When the police arrived, I went to the car and told them what had happened. They came and asked both of us where were from. They said they'd take Ralph to a doctor and get his feet sewn up. One of them said something about taking him to the hospital where there was always a doctor around at that time of night.

When we got to the hospital, one of the officers and I carried Ralph in. They found a young doctor who looked at Ralph's feet. He said to me, "How'd this happen?" After I told him the story, he asked, "Who bandaged his feet?" For a second I thought I had done something wrong. Finally I said, "I did. Did I do it wrong?"

"No," he assured me, "I think it was done very well." I felt better.

He took off the bandages, then got his instruments. The police asked me to come out and give them some information. I asked Ralph if he wanted me to stay with him, but he told me to go with the police. They took me into a visitor area and one officer got his clipboard and asked our names, where we lived, how old we were, and where we were going.

"When the doctor gets your friend sewed and bandaged up, what are your plans?" he asked.

"We have no place to stay," I said. "Would it be possible for you to put us in jail until Ralph's feet heal and we can go back home?"

The officer turned to the other and said, "We're about all filled up at the city jail. Why don't we call over to the county? They got a lot more rooms over there."

The other officer said he would go and call. When he came back, he said they would take us to the county jail for the night and talk about the next move tomorrow.

I was relieved for the time being. It gave us some time to plan further. I told them I'd like to be with Ralph and the officer with the clipboard said, "Go ahead. We'll be out here when he gets fixed up."

When I walked in the room, the doctor said, "I'm just finishing. Your buddy is lucky there are no broken bones."

I looked at Ralph's feet. They weren't bleeding but they were badly swollen. The doctor asked where we were staying and I told him at the county jail. "I'll stop in and look at his feet in the morning," he promised.

"Can he walk?" I asked.

"After I get his feet bandaged, I have a heavy pair of socks I'll put on him. It'll be some time before he can get shoes on." He turned to Ralph and said, "It will hurt when you walk. You'll not want to walk very far for awhile."

He went to another room and I told Ralph where we were going to stay for the night. I told him to give me his money and that I was going to hide it. He handed it to me.

When the doctor came in he said to Ralph, "I'm going to give you some codeine tablets so you can sleep tonight. When I see you in the morning, I'll bring you some again."

I asked the doctor if there was a restroom nearby. He pointed down the hall. I found it and went in the stall, sat down on the toilet and took off a shoe. I stuffed the bills in the shoe and put it back on. When I returned, the officers and Ralph were waiting for me. We carried Ralph to the car. I asked an officer what city it was. "Uniontown, Pennsylvania," he answered.

We would both remember that a long time. When we got to the jail, Ralph said he was going to try and walk in. I told him I didn't think that was a very good idea because he might tear some of the stitches loose. The officer insisted that he and I carry Ralph to the cell. Then I could come back and get us both signed in.

We got him out of the car and carried him to the jail, the other officer going ahead and opening the doors. The turnkey went with us and we put Ralph on a bunk in a cell. I told him I would be back as soon as I could.

We went back in the offices and up to a sergeant at a large desk. I had to tell the story again.

"Turn out your pockets," he said.

I took out my comb and seventy-six cents in coins.

He looked at it and said, "No identification."

"Neither of us has any," I explained.

"You can keep that," he said, indicating the comb and change. "We'll have to make a decision about you tomorrow. What have you got in the bags?"

I opened both bags, took out our knives and handed them to him, telling what we used them for. He looked through the bags and took our water bottles and said, "I'll keep these, too." He spoke to the turnkey, "Take him down. He can probably use some sleep."

I thanked him and followed the turnkey to the cells. He opened the barred door and I walked in. Ralph was already asleep. The codeine had knocked him out. I found an empty cell, took off my clothes and went to bed. What about tomorrow? If they wouldn't keep us, we had enough money to last about two weeks if we had a room. But where would we get a doctor to look after Ralph?

I decided not to tell them we had any money. I didn't think they would throw us out, and if we got to stay the young doctor acted like he was going to look after Ralph. From the looks of Ralph's swollen feet, I knew we weren't going back home for some time.

All our plans of living it up in Atlantic City were gone. All I wanted was to get us both back home quickly. The turnkey came back and looked in to see if everything was all right. I finally went to sleep.

Chapter Twenty-Two

When I awoke, for a minute I didn't know where I was. The jail looked different than it had last night. Some of the prisoners were walking around. The cell doors weren't locked and opened into a large barred area. There were large tables and chairs in the corner. I supposed it was an eating area.

I got up, put on my clothes, and walked to Ralph's cell. I asked him how his feet felt. "Pretty sore," he admitted.

I pulled the blanket off his feet. There were no blood spots on the heavy socks so the bleeding was in check. He stood and put his clothes on and I asked if he could walk. "I can, but not too far."

He had only one bad cut on the soles of his feet, most of the damage was on one side and on top of his ankles.

A couple of prisoners went with the turnkey to bring back breakfast. Breakfast was scrambled eggs, bread toasted on one side, oatmeal, and coffee. I told Ralph to stay in the cell and I would bring ours over so he wouldn't have to walk to the table. He was surprised at the good food.

Several prisoners came by and looked in while we were still eating. I called them in to tell them we weren't unfriendly but that my friend had an accident and couldn't walk very well. They wanted to know how it happened. For the fifth or sixth time in the last twenty-four hours, I told the story again.

"They put you in jail for that?" one asked incredulously. "What did they charge you with?"

I said that we had asked to be put in jail because it was the only place, and we were glad to get it. I took the plates back and asked the turnkey if there was a place to wash up.

After breakfast was shower time, just three prisoners at a time. I told the turnkey that Ralph, with his feet bandaged, wouldn't be able to shower. "Is there a washroom that he can use?"

He told me there were two sinks in the toilet that the deputies used, but he would have to ask the sheriff about Ralph using one. I went back and told Ralph what I had found out. "What do you think they'll do with us?" Ralph asked anxiously.

"Don't worry," I said. "They're not going to throw you out in the street. If you can't stay here, they'll take you to a hospital. Let's just sit tight and see what they come up with."

About ten-thirty I heard somebody calling Ralph's name. I slipped out of the cell to see the young doctor who had sewn Ralph's feet. I told him where Ralph was and he followed me to his cell.

"How are you doing?" he asked.

"They're pretty sore this morning," Ralph replied.

'Don't let me forget to give you some aspirin that I brought for you. I'm going to take the bandage off and see if you have any infection showing up. I'll dress your feet every day for a couple of days. If there's no sign of infection, we'll dress them every three days."

When he removed the bandages, he examined Ralph's feet very carefully. I looked up at the cell door. We had an audience. Five or six prisoners watched the doctor as he painted Ralph's feet with iodine and rebandaged them, pulling on the heavy socks.

"They look pretty good," he told Ralph. "Here's the aspirin and I'll see you tomorrow."

"They haven't told me I'll be here tomorrow," said Ralph.

"You're going to be here. I told the sheriff it's either here or the county hospital. After talking it over, they preferred you here as long as your feet don't worsen. This is a money choice. It's a lot cheaper to keep you here than over at the hospital."

"Will I be able to stay with him?" I asked.

"I brought it up and the sheriff said he would ask the council about it and let you know," he answered.

After he left I told Ralph that if they wouldn't let me stay I would offer to pay for my meals. Ralph thought I should wait and see what the sheriff decided. While we were talking, other prisoners went to the shower. I decided to get in line and ask about the wash basin for Ralph. I got my shower and asked the turnkey if he had asked about using the deputy's restroom. He said he hadn't seen the sheriff yet, but hadn't forgotten.

When the turnkey came to get two prisoners to help bring meals, Ralph decided he would try to walk to the table because he didn't want the other prisoners to think we didn't want to eat with them. He walked over and sat down and I told him I would stand in line and get both of our plates. Before we started our meal, we told the men at our table our names and they told us theirs. I had a chance to see all of the prisoners and I counted twenty-four including us.

It was a large jail. I noticed some cells had two bunks, while two large ones had four bunks apiece. After the meal the men got into groups of four or five to play poker. The stakes were wooden matches, which weren't furnished to inmates, so their value was much more inside the jail than outside.

The turnkey came with a deputy sheriff to take Ralph to get washed up at the deputy restroom. I asked Ralph if he wanted me to go and help him walk but he said he could do it.

I walked around and watched the card games and talked to some of the prisoners. Most of them seemed very friendly. I asked one if he knew where we could get some writing paper, envelopes and stamps. "The turnkey will get them things or cigarettes or soap or stuff like that if you have any money. He'll charge you a nickel to go across the street and get it for you."

When Ralph returned, we discussed if we should write a letter to our families or wait and see how fast Ralph's feet healed. We decided to wait for a few days.

Ralph said the deputy told him the sheriff would allow him to use the wash basin until he was able to shower. Two of the prisoners were released that afternoon. They had occupied one of the two bunk cells. I asked Ralph if he wanted to move in and he said, "Let's do it if they'll allow us." So I asked one fellow about it, and he said we could move in any cell that was empty.

When it came time for the evening meal, nobody had come to talk about whether I could stay. I decided to keep a low profile. When the food came, I took both of our plates to the table, sat down and looked at the food. I said to the man next to me, "This is the same stew we had at noon."

"Sure is. If you stay here very long, you'll get real acquainted with this stew." He explained, "The sheriff owns a store and a butcher shop. This stew's made out of everything that don't sell well at his two places of business. Most of the time the meat is from cold meat ends." I said I thought it was pretty good for jail food. "You been in other jails?" he asked. I told him about the black-eyed peas, corn bread, and molasses we had had every meal in Mississippi.

"I guess this would taste good after that," he agreed. "Even for breakfast they gave you that?"

"Even for breakfast," I replied.

After the meal was over, out came the cards and the poker games started. I watched one game. A player looked up and said, "Want to try a hand?" I said I had no matches to play and he told me the turnkey would get me a box for a nickel; the box itself would cost three cents. I told him I would get some tomorrow and Ralph and I both would play.

We went back to our cell and lay down on our bunks. Talking it over, we decided the jail wasn't so bad. It was clean, had showers, and the food was pretty good. We were eating better than we had on the freights and had three meals a day. We hoped that the next day the doctor would be able to give us a better idea when Ralph's feet would be healed enough to travel. The poker players got up from the tables, so it was time for the lights to go out.

The next morning we had the same thing for breakfast, scrambled eggs, oatmeal, and coffee. They brought in three new prisoners. Two left and three came in. The place was almost full. We liked seeing people go out, not come in.

If every bunk filled up, I knew I'd be asked to leave. The doctor came about ten thirty and took off the bandages. He again looked closely at the wound. To me, Ralph's feet looked bad: blue and purple bruises and so swollen the stitches looked like they were cutting into the flesh. I was surprised when he said, "Looks pretty good, just don't walk on them any more than you have to."

"How long do you think it'll be before I can get my shoes on and be able to travel?" Ralph asked.

"Even if everything goes all right, you're going to be here for quite a while," the doctor answered.

I would have to agree with the doctor. His feet looked awful to me.

"I'll be back in two days. Take the aspirin I gave you. Everything looks good."

When we had lunch, I asked the turnkey to get a box of wooden matches and gave him the eight cents. Playing poker helped pass the time away. For lunch we had chili with a hot dog on the side, bread and coffee. I told Ralph, "We might gain weight with this food and no exercise."

"I think this sheriff does pretty good for his prisoners," Ralph said.

When the poker games started the three new prisoners, Ralph and I could play, but we had no cards. One of the other prisoners told us to ask the turnkey for a deck. The decks were used ones donated by a bridge club and some gamblers who ran a poker game in a hotel.

We watched the games and when the turnkey came, I asked for a deck. He returned in a few minutes and handed them to me.

The three new prisoners had no matches so we sold half the box to them for eight cents and played until almost time for the evening meal. If our luck didn't change, we would have to buy another box of matches.

We played cards again after the evening meal. By lights out we were about even. We had learned the names of most of the prisoners and most were friendly. We were the youngest of all the prisoners, but were treated with respect. Most of them were in for assault, intoxication, or petty larceny. Two bank robbers waited for a trial date. Those two claimed they were innocent, but everybody thought they were guilty.

The doctor visited a third time. When the bandages came off, I could see no difference in Ralph's feet. He examined the cuts very carefully, then leaned over and smelled the cuts. The doctor said he didn't see or smell any infection so far. I saw that the swelling hadn't gone down and the bruises were even more colorful. We tried to be cheerful and took the doctor's word that everything was healing.

We had been in the jail for six days and nobody had said anything about me leaving. I wondered how long they would feed me when they weren't obligated to.

We still played poker but my mind often wandered. I had to admit that I was tired of playing poker for wooden matches. I didn't notice anybody reading and asked one prisoner if there was anything to read around there. He told me there were some books on a shelf in the back of one of the cells.

I walked down and found the shelf in the shadow of the cell block. I wouldn't have found it if I hadn't known where to look. There were about thirty books. I checked the titles. They were high brow stuff: two books of poetry, *Les Miserables*, *The Prince* by Machiavellia, *Trilogy* by Rabelais, *War and Peace*, and The Bible.

They must have been donated by a professor. I had heard that Rabelais was funny and our library didn't have it so I took the big book and went back to my cell. I told Ralph about the books and he said he might go down and look at them sometime. When the poker games started that night, I told Ralph I was going to stay and read the book.

After the games broke up, Ralph hobbled back to the cell. "Are you still reading that book?" he asked. "It must be pretty good. What's the name of it?"

I told him. He'd never heard of it. I told him it was supposed to be a classic but was a little raw in some parts. "Maybe you'll read it when I'm through," I said. I thought from its size that I would have to be there a long time to finish it. When the lights went out, I had hardly made a dent in the book although I had been reading over three hours.

We had been in there eight days and the doctor came once again. The feet looked better, but I figured it would be a long time before Ralph got his shoes on. A deputy sheriff called me over and said that I was going to have to leave because the city jail was sending over four prisoners which would leave only one extra bunk.

"Today's Saturday and I'm sure we'll be filled up by midnight," he said.

"How soon do you want me out of here?" I asked.

"They'll be here in an hour or so," he said. "Just holler for the turnkey. I've already told him to let you out."

I went back to our cell. Ralph and the doctor were watching. "Do you have to leave?" Ralph asked.

"Yeah, I have to be out of here in an hour."

"Why don't you go on back home? When I get so I can stand, I'll come home."

"I can't leave you here all beat up. I'll get a room and stay until you can get your shoes on."

"No way," he replied. "Where will you eat? Paying for a room and eating in restaurants, you'll be broke in a week. There's no use your staying around here, is there, Doc?"

The doctor said he'd leave the decision for us, but added, "I'll say that you're getting along very well, but I won't say when you'll be able to put your shoes on."

"What am I going to tell your family?" I protested. "That I ran back home and left you in the Uniontown jail? Even my family will probably give me hell for that."

"Come on, Doc. How can I convince him it's no use him staying here?"

The doctor said, "Why don't you write a letter to your family telling them the circumstances and that you don't want your friend Harry to stay here. You could say that I'll be looking in on you to see that you're all right."

Ralph asked him where he could get paper and he would write the letter. The doctor gave him a pen and called the turnkey to let him out, saying he'd be back in a few minutes. When he returned, he had a sheet of the sheriff's official paper. Ralph started writing and when he finished, the doctor wrote saying he was taking care of Ralph, and would continue until he was able to return to his home.

He shook hands with me and wished me a safe journey.

I took my shoe off. We had two fives and two one dollar bills. I said I was going to give Ralph the two fives and take the ones, but he protested, wanting me to keep half. I told him I didn't need it, and if he ran into trouble, he would have enough to come home on the train or bus.

"We do it this way or I'm not going," I said. "And another thing, I want you to buy some paper and stamps and write to me every couple of days, and if you need me I can be back here in two days."

I got my bag packed and was ready to go. I shook hands with Ralph and gave him a hug and walked to the gate. The turnkey let me out. I never looked back, for if I saw him standing there alone I wouldn't have left.

The sergeant gave me back my knife and water jar, which I filled at the water fountain. I walked out of the jail, not looking forward to my reception when I got home.

Ralph and I had both taken trips alone. He went to Washington, D.C., and I went to Detroit, Michigan by myself. But it wasn't as much fun without a companion.

I did feel better that he had the money to get back home "on the cushions" as the hobos said. I asked where the highway was and while walking there I came to a grocery store and bought some ham and buns. Outside of town, I started giving cars the thumb. Very shortly, I got a ride with a man who asked me where I was headed.

"Anywhere west," I said, "closer to Indiana."

"I'll take you to Wheeling, that will help you a little bit," he said.

He drove a really nice car. I hadn't noticed what make it was. "Would you like to hear the radio?" he asked.

"Yes, I'd like that." It was only the third car I had ridden in with a radio.

"One of these days I think all cars will have radios in them," he said.

I was getting hungry but thought I would wait to eat when I got to Wheeling. I didn't think he would like me eating in his luxurious car, and if I had a car like that I wouldn't want anyone eating in it either.

He let me out downtown in Wheeling and I started walking, soon coming to a large building that was closed. I sat on its steps and ate a sandwich, then proceeded to walk across the bridge over the Ohio River into Ohio. It was slow going, just short rides of ten or fifteen miles, but then I got a ride all the way to Zanesville, Ohio. When I got there it was about four o'clock, but I decided to try and get one more ride. As I waited for a ride I ate another sandwich.

It was almost dark when I was picked up by a trucker. Usually when we were picked up by truckers we got a pretty long ride, and this was no exception. He was going all the way to Columbus. I told him I was headed for Indiana and he wanted to know where I had come from. I told him Uniontown but didn't disclose that I had had breakfast in the county jail.

After about an hour of talking he said he was getting hungry and asked if I could eat something. He pulled into a roadside diner and we went in and sat down at the counter. The waitress brought the menu and I looked at it and waited for him to order.

"What are you going to have?" he asked. I hesitated and he said, "I'm going to have that T-bone steak." I still paused. He said, "I think I'll order for you," and turning to the waitress added, "He'll have the steak also."

I wouldn't have ordered that myself because the menu said it was sixty-five cents, or three hours' work at a glass factory.

Soon the waitress brought the steak, still sizzling on the pewter plate, with french fries, salad, and coffee. After we finished I thought that I could make it all the way home on that one meal if I had to. When we got back in the truck, I thanked him and told him that was the best meal I had ever had.

According to a jewelry store window clock, it was ten p.m. when he let me out in Columbus. I had to look for a place to sleep. It was warm and I didn't care if I was wakened early by the dew. The best place I found was also an odd place to sleep. In front of a monument shop, a large selection of tombstones rested on a beautifully tended green lawn. I walked to the largest tombstone and sat down. All the lights were out in the shop. I could lie down behind the stone and nobody would see me from the street. I would be awake and gone before the owner opened the shop. I lay down behind the tombstone, only waking when something pulled on my arm. My heart pounded and I yelled. A dog fell backward, then ran full speed away. I didn't know who was more frightened, me or that dog.

I was wide awake and sensed it was close to daybreak. I got up and started walking out to the highway. No people were on the street, so when I met an early riser I asked him he if had the time. He pulled out a large watch and held it up for me to see. It was almost five o'clock. I thanked him and he made some motions with his hands. It came to me immediately that he wasn't able to speak.

He smiled and waved goodby to me. It was cool and I was

making good time through the city, walking right through the business area. I came to a restaurant where a cook was frying hot cakes in the window. I stopped to watch and then thought they would make a good breakfast, one that would stay with me. I walked in and sat at the counter.

"How much for the hot cakes?" I asked the counter man.

"Twenty cents for a stack of four, and all the coffee you can drink."

I had noticed that the cakes were large, so I ordered them. I really filled up. After a couple of coffees, I left and continued walking through the city.

I reached Highway 40, a cross country National Highway running from the Atlantic Ocean to the Pacific. Most of the traffic was going into the city, but it wasn't long until I was picked up by a man and woman. I asked where they were going and they said Springfield. I told them I was going to Indiana. It was a good ride. I had hopes of getting all the way home later that day.

They wanted to know what I was doing over in Ohio so far from my home. I told them of the two-week trip we had planned to Atlantic City and what had happened to shatter our plans. When they let me out in the middle of the city, it was past noon so I ate another one of my sandwiches and hurried through the city and back out to Highway 40.

It was almost and hour and a half before I got a ten mile ride. Any thoughts I had of getting home that day were gone. A couple of short rides finally got me into Dayton, but it was getting late. By the time I walked through the city, it was getting dark. I asked a man if he knew a mission where I could eat and a place to sleep. He said there was one but far away. I got directions and started walking.

I found the mission at nine o'clock. The manager said, "You're too late to eat but there's a couple of bunks left if you want one."

The mission was an old gymnasium filled with maybe two hundred men. I walked around looking for an empty cot as I smelled the stink of the place. I decided I would rather sleep outside than stand the smell. I left and headed back to the highway, looking for a place to sleep as I walked through the city. The best I found was a doorway entrance of an abandoned building that once housed a market. The sign was still there, better looking than the building.

As I slumped down in a corner, I wondered what I was going to say to Ralph's brother and sister. I wasn't looking forward to it. I was glad I had made him take the money because he could go home on the passenger train or a bus any time he wished.

The night was really warm with a full moon making everything visible. I was on the outskirts of the city and the section looked really poor. Small businesses were closed, leaving the buildings with broken windows and sagging doors. When would this Depression end or would it go on forever? With that thought, I went to sleep.

When I awoke in the morning the sun was high. I was getting a late start. As I walked down Highway 40, I came to a small restaurant and remembering the hot cakes of the day before, decided to have some more. I went in, sat at the counter and looked at the blackboard with the menu chalked on it:

Hot cakes .... 15 Cents. Coffee .... 5 Cents.

I would do without the coffee and ordered the hot cakes. I ate the four which were smaller than the earlier ones. The waitress said, "A couple more cakes?" I asked how much and she told me there'd be no charge since she was going to throw the rest of the mix away. I ate the other two, thanked her, and walked out on the highway.

I got a short ride and asked the driver what time it was. "Ten o'clock," he answered. I was still a long way from home with the short rides of ten or twelve miles. But I finally got to Richmond, Indiana. I left Highway 40 and took the highway north to Muncie.

A large car approached. As it came closer, I saw it was a huge Dusenberg automobile. I usually didn't thumb expensive cars, having found that people who could afford them seldom picked up hitchhikers. But I wanted to get home and gave him the thumb. I was surprised when he stopped about fifty feet down the road. I ran and opened the front door. The middle-aged driver smiled and asked, "Where are you going?"

"Muncie," I said.

"Hop in," he replied.

I had never ridden in a Dusenberg and looked around. "This is really a great car," I said.

He smiled and admitted it was a very satisfactory car. He was a tall man, slender, and expensively dressed. I could smell whiskey on his breath as we rolled along at about twenty-five miles an hour. He drove very carefully but at that speed it would take a while to get home. I asked what kind of business he was in, surprised at his answer.

"I'm a musician on my way to play in a famous orchestra."

"Oh," I answered. "What instrument do you play?"

"Drums," he answered. "I have them in the back seat."

I looked over the seat at the most expensive and complete set of drums I had ever seen. When I turned back from inspecting them, he said very solemnly, "Young man, have you ever heard a waltz played on the drums?"

For a second I thought he was kidding me, but realized he was serious and didn't break into laughter. I also realized why he drove so slowly. He not only had been drinking, he was really loaded. He just didn't look or act drunk.

"No," I answered. "I've never heard a waltz played on the drums," without adding that nobody else had either.

"Would you like for me to play a waltz on my drums for you?"

When hitchhiking, I usually agreed to just about anything the drivers wanted or said, so I answered, "Sure, that would be nice."

There were very few cars on the road and he carefully pulled off onto the side. "Have you had any musical training or instruction?" he asked.

I admitted that I had not. He got out of the car and moved to the back seat where the drums were. The Dusenbergs were so large that there was plenty of room in the back seat for the drums *and* the drummer. I watched from the front seat. He got everything ready and then started. He began very intensely, slowly beating the drums with a lazy Ding! on the cymbal every so often. It didn't sound like anything to me, but when he finished with a little flourish, he looked at me and said, "How'd you like it?"

"Oh," I said, "I think it was real fine."

"Do you recognize the song?" he asked.

I tried to remember waltzes from my one semester in music. I got it. "Was it the Blue Danube Waltz?" I asked.

"Ah, my friend. You know more music than you say," he said. "Perhaps you can recognize this waltz."

They were, as far as I could tell, the same drum beats and cadence as the first waltz. When he finished he looked at me intently and waited for my answer. I knew we had listened to other waltzes in that music class, but I couldn't remember another one. To gain a little time to think of another waltz, I said, "It's such a beautiful song, can you play if again for me?"

He looked satisfied and slowly played the drums for the third time in the same way. It came to me in a flash. When he finished I said, "The Viennese Waltz."

"You knew it the first time. You just wanted to hear me play it again," he said.

"You're right. I did know it," I said.

I thought nobody, not even Ralph, would believe that I had sat in one of America's most beautiful and expensive cars while a very nice drunk played waltzes, which all sounded the same, on his drum set.

I asked what time it was, thinking I could get him back in the front seat and get me into Muncie. I had been in the car with him for over two hours. In that time he had not taken a drink of liquor, yet he acted the same as when I got in the car with him. I began to believe that he wasn't intoxicated, but a little crazy. He spoke softly but with a slurring of his talk, and he didn't stagger when he got out of the car. But I could smell the whiskey when I first got in the car. Maybe he was crazy and also a little drunk. I asked a second time what the hour was, and told him I would like to get home before dark. He immediately got out of the back seat and climbed behind the wheel.

We took off. When we got to the outskirts of Muncie, I thanked him for the ride and told him how much I admired his music. He quickly asked me if I wanted to come and hear him play in the orchestra. I thought he must own an orchestra, for that would be the only orchestra he would be allowed to play the drums in. And he could own one. He dressed well and drove a car that said "big money." If I hadn't been so anxious to get home, I would have gone with him to see what happened. But I turned him down and he let me out in the heart of Muncie.

When I got out of the car, people looked at the car and at me. I just waved to him as if he were my father. Let them think I have a rich parent, I thought, until they see me start hitchhiking.

It didn't take long to get a ride all the way home. I walked in the house just as they were sitting down to eat.

"Hey, have you got enough for me?" I asked.

"For goodness sake's, look who came in at meal time," my mother said.

"Did you have a good time in Atlantic City?" asked my father.

"I'm hungry," I said. "Let's talk about it after we eat." I wasn't sure how good my story was going to go anyway.

Chapter Twenty-Three

After the dishes were washed and put away, we all moved to the living room. Everybody sat down and looked at me. I might as well get this over with I thought and told them everything from the time Ralph and I had left until the time we ended up in the Uniontown, Pennsylvania jail. I told them how I had stayed about ten days with Ralph until I was told to leave because the jail was full. I stressed that Ralph had wanted me to go back home. We had argued about it but he had insisted I go back home.

"So here I am," I said. I spread my arms.

For a minute nobody spoke. Then my father said, as if in disbelief, "Ralph is still in the jail?"

I had known that was coming. "Yes, he's still in the jail." I went to my jacket and got the letter Ralph had written and the doctor signed. My father read it aloud and when he was through he asked, "You couldn't stay somewhere in the town until he was able to travel?"

"Yes, I could have," I answered. "We had enough money for me to stay for about ten days. Then we would have spent all our money. If he still wasn't able to leave, I would've had to sleep on the streets and beg food in town." Defensively, I added, "I gave Ralph all the money we had except for two dollars I used to get home. That left him with more than enough money to get home on the train or the bus. He doesn't want to spend the money to get home. He said when he could get his shoes on he'll come home." I also pointed out that both of us had been on hitchhiking trips by ourselves.

"How long do you think he'll have to stay in the jail?" my mother asked.

"Probably ten more days or longer. He said everybody treats him very well there. Even the deputy sheriffs like Ralph. They know he isn't a criminal. The fellow he plays poker with told me they would take care of him."

I sighed. "I know my leaving him there looks bad, and it leaves a bad taste in my mouth, but I think in the long run we made the best decision we could under the circumstances."

We talked a while longer before I excused myself. Even after a good meal, a bath and a soft bed to lie down on, I couldn't sleep. I knew my explanation didn't entirely satisfy my family, but I knew that was the way it was going to be until Ralph returned home. Tomorrow I might even get a hostile reception from his brother and sister. They both worked so it would be the next night before I could tell them.

The next morning while eating breakfast I asked everybody not to talk about what I had told them last night. I went to the factory, and as I was only temporarily laid off, I was allowed in. I talked to the manager and asked how long he thought it would be before the glass tank would be repaired. He told me about a month, but if they didn't receive more orders than they had at that point, it wouldn't be fired up right away.

The year 1932 was to be the bottom of the terrible Depression; everywhere there was despair and hopelessness. Rumors were everywhere about suicides, about people evicted from their homes. Pictures in the paper showed furniture moved out on the sidewalk.

Families lived in tents and shacks in larger cities called Hoovervilles, named after the President, Herbert Hoover. The Hoovervilles had no water facilities, very little heat, and kids were covered with newspapers called Hoover blankets. The President and the Congress didn't seem to know what to do to end the tragedy. Everybody knew we would have a new President and Congress in the fall.

I went to the paper mill where Ralph worked and hunted up his foreman, asking if there was any chance he would be called back to work in the next two weeks. I received the same answer. If more orders weren't received it might be a long time before he would be called back. "Where's Ralph?" he asked. I told him Ralph was staying with some relatives in Hershey, Pennsylvania, figuring that Ralph could tell him differently when he returned if he wanted to.

I went back home. I didn't want any of our friends asking where Ralph was. When I got home I wrote Ralph a letter. I told him I had gotten home safely but that I was getting a cold reception by my family because I had left instead of staying with him. I wrote that I thought I would do even worse when I went to his house and tried to explain it to his family.

My mother came in the kitchen and sat down at the table. "Are you writing to Ralph?" she asked and I nodded yes. "Let me see what you've written."

I handed her the paper. She read it and laid it back on the table. "From what you said last night, I gather that the decision for you to return home was made so that Ralph would have the money to come home any time he wanted to," she said.

"That's right," I answered. "But I didn't think you and the others saw it that way."

She shook her head and said, "After thinking it over, I think you done the right thing. I'm sure your father thinks the same. If you hadn't been made to leave, I think you would still be there in the Uniontown jail."

And of course I would have. If Ralph hadn't told me to go home, I would have stayed in the town until he was able to travel. But we decided that not spending money for a room and food just to hang around and see him only at visiting hours was wiser than wasting the money that way. It would be better for me to go home. He would then have the money to come home any time he wanted.

She patted my hand and said, "Tell Ralph to get well and get home."

After supper I walked to Ralph's house and knocked on the door. His brother answered. He looked at me in surprise.

"Where's Ralph?" he asked.

"Could I come in and tell you about Ralph?"

"He's not hurt, is he?" he asked.

"Yes, he's hurt," I said. "But he's all right."

I followed him into the house and his sister came in the room. I said, "If you'll sit down, I'll tell you the complete story."

After I was through, they asked when I thought he would be able to come home. I told them the doctor said it might be two weeks before he would be able to get his shoes on. I stressed the fact that Ralph had enough money to come home any time on the bus or train. If he came by train, their house was only two blocks from the train station. I was surprised. They seemed to take the situation more calmly than my family had. I showed them the letter he had written signed by the doctor. They said they understood the situation and would be glad when Ralph arrived home.

I felt a little better when I left, because I had stressed the fact that Ralph had more than enough money to come home, but he didn't want to spend it on a bus or a train ticket.

My mother and father were still up when I got home. My mother asked me how it went.

"All right," I said. "I think I presented the story in a different way than when I told all of you. Of course, like us they're concerned about Ralph and anxious to see him back here."

My parents went to bed, but I went out on the porch and sat in the swing. In a few minutes I heard the distant wail of a steam engine and knew the engineer was blowing the whistle for every country road crossing. In a minute and a half, the whistle would be closer as he crossed another country road. I heard the train pull into town and stop at the paper mill. I wondered if there were two teenagers waiting in the dark, watching the huge engine go by, then running down the train looking for an empty boxcar, climbing in and with their hearts pounding, waiting to start their first trip as hobos. Somewhere that's happening I thought, but not here.

The next day I went up town and walked by the commerce office. The man who ran the office called to me. When I went back he asked if I wanted to wash two cars. I said yes, that I'd be glad to.

"Where's your buddy Ralph?" he asked.

"He's out of town right now, but I can wash the cars." I wasn't going to tell anybody about Ralph. They might find out, but it wasn't going to be from me.

He gave me the keys and pointed out the two cars. We had washed for him before and he always gave us fifty cents a car. It took me all afternoon to wash and clean the interior, and when I took the last one back he gave me a dollar.

When I walked through town I went by the restaurant where Ralph's brother worked. I was past it when I heard a sharp whistle. I turned around and Ralph's brother was standing in the door motioning me to come back. He went back in and when I walked in he drew a cup of coffee and set it on the counter. "Sit down and have a coffee," he said. He went up to the counter and when he came back he slid a letter across the counter to me. I picked it up and saw it was addressed to him and postmarked "Uniontown."

"Read it," he said. I opened the letter and when I started reading I began to laugh and his brother smiled at me.

In the letter, Ralph in profane and no uncertain terms told his brother not to "scold" or "chew me out" for going home, and that he was the one who suggested I leave.

"Well," Ralph's brother said, "we didn't chew you out, did we?"

"No, I thought you treated me very well."

"I know what good friends you and Ralph are," he said. "It had to be a decision that you both made."

"Hey, this makes me feel a lot better, because I really didn't care except for your family and mine."

"Well, Ralph can tell whoever he wants to when he gets home, or he doesn't need to tell anybody."

"I've told my family not to tell anybody, and if you've told nobody, no one will ever know," I said.

"I haven't told anybody," he said. "We'll leave it up to Ralph."

When I left I felt pretty good. I felt a lot better and I had made a dollar. I felt good enough to contemplate going to the beer garden to see my friends and having a couple of nickel beers.

The next week passed slowly as I waited to hear from Ralph. I had received only one letter and he reported that the doctor would not set a date for him to leave.

There were two places in town where my friends and I hung out: a pool room and a Shell filling station on the highway running through town. The station was operated by a very good athlete when he was in high school who was only about four years older than we were. There were always three or four teenagers sitting around outside the filling station.

I walked down one afternoon to sit and talk with friends. It was hot and we sat on the grass in the shade of the buildings. One of the fellows said, "What's that walking down the highway? That's the worst case of road puffs I've ever seen in my life."

I stood up and looked at the figure. The heat waves from the road distorted whoever it was. It looked like it had huge shoes about two feet long. I knew who it was, the friend I had been waiting for.

"It's Ralph!" I shouted and ran down the highway toward him. Getting closer, I saw that what we thought were shoes were gunny sacks wrapped around his feet and tied with rope.

When I got to him, I gave him a big hug and told him how glad I was to see him. "You came all the way from Pennsylvania with those sacks around your feet?" I asked.

"It was *easy*," he said. "I started early yesterday and made it here in less than two days."

"You must have got a lot of good rides," I said.

"When I got out of a car, usually the next car along would pick me up. I had my shoe strings tied together and slung my shoes around my neck. Everybody wanted to know what happened to my feet. They even bought all my meals except today's noon meal."

"Where did you stay last night?" I asked.

"I got a ride on an empty furniture hauling truck. The driver was stopping at a small town west of Dayton, Ohio, and was going to be loading early the next day. When he found I had no place to sleep he said I could sleep in the back of the truck. He already had a place to sleep with a friend in town.

"We got there about ten o'clock and he backed into a loading dock and opened the back doors. There was piles of blankets to cover furniture and five or six on the floor to make a bed. The driver told me they would start loading at seven o'clock, so I didn't have to worry, they would wake me up with the noise they made. He even said he'd leave the truck door unlocked so I could open them to let a breeze in. I woke up before the men got there and shut and locked the doors for him. I was on my way. The first man who picked me up bought me breakfast, and it was clear sailing all the way."

"What made you decide to come home? Did they throw you out like they did me?"

"Not at all. They never mentioned anything about forcing me to leave. The doctor would have threatened them of taking me to the hospital. I just got tired of staying there. You know that good stew made out of the cold meat ends? Well, I got tired of it too."

When we arrived at the filling station, there were a lot of wise cracks and jokes about his feet. But there was also admiration for a teenager to travel five hundred miles without shoes.

After everybody had gone to bed that night, I sat on the porch swing until I heard the freight whistle. We had seen a lot of unusual cities and exotic people and had enjoyed our adventures greatly. I knew that trip would be the last, that we would no longer ride with the hobos.

We would miss the excitement but we knew riding the steam monster was dangerous. Perhaps it was telling us: "You don't have to ride, give it up."

*To order copies of **TEENAGE HOBOS** complete the information below.*

Ship to: (please print)

*Name:*____

*Address:*______________________________________

*City, State, Zip:*________________________________

*Phone:*____

______*copies of **TEENAGE HOBOS** @*	*$9.99 ea.*	______
Postage and handling @ $1.50	*$1.50*	______
Indiana Residents add 5% tax		______
	Total enclosed	______

Make checks payable to:
Talisman
P.O. Box 103
Hartford City, IN 47348